God, Christ, the Church

Questions and Answers

Edited by Arturo Cattaneo,
with the collaboration of thirty experts

Foreword by Msgr. Rino Fisichella

En Route Books and Media, LLC
Saint Louis, MO

⊕ *ENROUTE*
Make the time

En Route Books and Media, LLC

5705 Rhodes Avenue

St. Louis, MO 63109

Contact us at

contactus@enroutebooksandmedia.com

Cover Credit: Sebastian Mahfood using DALL-E

Copyright 2025 Arturo Cattaneo

ISBN-13: 979-8-88870-461-5

Library of Congress Control Number:

Available online at https://catalog.loc.gov

Table of Contents

i

Foreword

This volume edited by Arturo Cattaneo seeks to be like this Cross that leans toward the faithful, to support, encourage and hearten them, strengthening their faith, which is the foundation of hope. Perhaps, precisely for the men and women of today, there is a need to reawaken hope without falling into illusions, because we are often helpless witnesses to facts and events that unsettle certainties acquired over the years. Illusions, on the other hand, lead inevitably to disillusionment. Both remind us of the importance of centering everything on true hope.

We are pilgrims who hope because we are sustained and encouraged by the faith that assures us of God's Love revealed to us in Christ. A love that continually reaches out to us in the Holy Spirit, who never ceases to "radiate in believers the light of hope: He keeps it lit like a flame that never goes out, to give support and vigor to our lives. Indeed, Christian hope neither deludes nor disappoints, for it is founded on the certainty that nothing and no one can ever separate us from the love of God" (*Spes non confundit*, no. 3). As Benedict XVI wrote, "the strength of hope comes from faith" (Encyclical *Spe Salvi* – 2007 –, no. 37).

This book offers clear answers to frequently asked questions about faith. Questions and answers about God: his existence and the existence of evil, his connection with our daily lives, that he is simultaneously both one and three, the possibility of eternal damnation... Then, questions regarding Christ: proofs of his divinity and his Resurrection, on why he did not prevent being betrayed by one of his own apostles, why he presented to the people a model of the Messiah they do not accept, why he did not choose a less gory way to save us, on how non-Christians can be saved, on Christ being the only mediator...

Lastly, the book addresses several questions about the Church, which is often poorly understood or even rejected today, are. First, how to ascertain its foundation by Christ, how to explain so many errors, scandals, crimes and so many divisions among Christians. Questions are then asked about moral issues, such as the possibility of change in its teaching and, in particular, in sexual ethics, the outright condemnation of gender ideology is explained, the need to be in a "state of grace" to receive the Eucharist, the necessity of confession to a priest and not directly to God, the reasons for priestly celibacy. In short, these pages offer a practical summary of the Catechism of the Catholic Church.

This is a book full of those questions and answers needed not only to revive the hope of believers, but also to help them be sowers of hope always ready to make a defense to anyone who asks them to account for the hope that is in them (cf. 1 Pet 3:15-17). Sowers of a hope that "does not disappoint, because the love of God has been poured into our hearts through the Holy Spirit who has been given to us" (Rom 5:5).

It is my hope that this book will meet with the response it deserves, helping to strengthen the faith and, as a result, reviving the hope of many pilgrims.

Most Rev. Rino Fisichella
Pro-Prefect for the New Evangelization section
of the Dicastery for Evangelization

Presentation

For a long time, I have cherished the idea of publishing a book with the most frequently asked questions and answers concerning our faith in God, in Christ and in the Church.

Evidently, we have the *Catechism of the Catholic Church* and many catechetical works in which our faith is explained. In this book, with its relatively short questions and answers, we are especially looking for a more engaging way of conveying the main truths of our faith. As early as 1973, St. Paul VI urged us "to seek by every means to study how to bring to modern man the Christian message, in which, alone, he can find the answer to his questions and the strength for his commitment to human solidarity" (Address to the Sacred College of Cardinals, June 22, 1973).

We have here 33 questions, not sidestepping the more difficult ones, answered by 30 experts, theologians, philosophers, pastors and catechists, who accepted the not easy challenge of answering with solid and reasoned arguments, while expressing themselves in simple language, accessible even to the uninitiated. Pope Francis has pointed out, however, that faith always retains "a certain obscurity which does not detract from the firmness of its assent. Some things are understood and appreciated only from the standpoint of this assent, which is a sister to love, beyond the range of clear reasons and arguments. We need to remember that all religious teaching ultimately has to be reflected in the teacher's way of life, which awakens the assent of the heart by its nearness, love and witness" (Apostolic exhortation *Evangelii Gaudium*, no. 42).

In addition to this, the Pope also notes that "all revealed truths proceed from the same divine source and are believed with the same faith, but some of them are more important in expressing more directly the heart of the Gospel. In this fundamental core what shines out is *the beauty of God's saving love manifested in Jesus Christ who died and rose again*" (no. 36). There may seem to be, and there is, a wide diversity in the questions collected here, but this is because of the diversity in the aspects of our faith that are being addressed. However, in the answers one can detect a kind of golden thread guiding the reader to the discovery of that beauty to which the Pope refers: "the saving love of God manifested in Jesus Christ who died and rose again," that love that awakens the assent of the heart, decisive if there is to be the assent of the mind.

Who is this book for?

For all who in some way are searching for meaning in their lives, especially the young, but not only them. In a special way, it can be useful to catechists who are often faced with questions that are not easy to answer but who then, in their teaching, can ask young people questions with vital repercussions on which to reflect and leading to fruitful conversations.

My hope is that reading these pages may help many young people in their journey of faith and hope, offering them insights and stimuli for reflection and opening up new and attractive horizons. Indeed, as Antoine de Saint-Exupéry well wrote, "If you want to build a boat, do not gather men to cut wood, divide tasks and give orders, but teach them nostalgia for the vast and infinite sea." In this sense, Pope Francis exhorted young people, "We Christians are not chosen by the Lord for little things, always go beyond, toward great things. Play life for great ideals!" (*Homily at the Mass for those receiving confirmation,* April 28, 2013).

Arturo Cattaneo

January 2025

Questions about God

Can the existence of God be proved?

(Valeria Ascheri)

The question of God's existence is the most important and most radical question man can ask himself, because the answer, whether positive or negative, orients and determines our entire life, at every age and in the different spheres in which we find ourselves: as individual persons and in our family, in our professional role and in our civic and social engagement, whether in terms of the attitude we adopt and the choices to be made, or in the decisions to be taken and the commitments we undertake both daily or on a *one-off* basis. As Plato already wrote "gravest of all is the question of holding a right view about the gods and so living well, or the opposite." (*Laws*, X, 888 b). For those who choose not to answer this question, claiming to be in doubt, and thus declaring themselves skeptical, or claiming to "not know" (thus assuming an agnostic position), it almost always amounts to living as if God did not exist (*etsi Deus non daretur*) because, as Benedict XVI stated, God "seems so far removed from life today" – but, as we will try to explain in the next pages, at the same time – "[...] God has a thousand ways, for each his own, of making himself present in the soul, of showing that he exists and knows me and loves me," if "we are attentive to the signs of his presence" (*General Audience*, October 13, 2010).

1.   Is it possible to demonstrate the existence of God?

God's existence as a person and as Father – in the way we immediately think of him – that is, as God creator of the universe, by a free act of love, and benevolent, taking care of all his creatures, cannot be demonstrated by reason because a personal being, in the deepest sense, cannot be the object of logical demonstration or empirical proof, but can only come before us through a free revelation of himself.

God is not an object of sense experience, and therefore there can never be proofs – such as the proofs of the mathematical and natural sciences – that prove his existence beyond all doubt and with absolute certainty.

Nevertheless, in the history of cultural thought, especially in philosophical and religious thought (not exclusively Christian), it is true that a number of so-called proofs – some of them well very known and widely discussed – have been put forward and developed that conclude on the basis of rational arguments that one can be convinced by reason that a God, with specific characteristics, exists. Such arguments can therefore justify belief in something sacred, supernatural and divine, and this has always characterized civilizations, long before the Christian Revelation – belief which is also found in some manifestations of ancient pagan religions (such as those developed, for example, in Egyptian civilization, ancient Greece, Etruscan civilization and ancient Rome) – and which can also be a spur to those who are skeptical or atheistic to begin a journey of conversion and openness to revealed faith.

2. What kind of proofs are they? Are they understandable and acceptable to all or only to those who are already believers? What are they?

We are talking of proofs, indicators, or ways that lead to the recognition that God exists and do so in a way that everyone can understand and accept as a result of rational reflection. Of course, understanding will depend on each person's level of formation, their intellectual openness to delve deep and their willingness to accept the possibility of the transcendent (from "trans-ascendere": to rise beyond, that is, to go beyond the material dimension of the senses). The most immediate and most widely used starting point are what we know as "a posteriori" proofs: these are proofs that take their starting point from the observation of experienced realities, such as:

(a) observation of physical nature and what happens in the real world that we can all see and ascertain in different ways through sense knowledge and by questioning ourselves about some recurring dynamics;

(b) recognizing some particular and distinctive characteristics of the human person in comparison with other living beings.

We have here two routes that each one of us can take in order to try to reach back to God as the first cause that is non-material (otherwise we would have to ask where his matter comes from), but a pure spirit and transcendent (an entity external to us and to our thinking).

Regarding the proofs starting from creation, the best known are the five philosophical ways of St. Thomas Aquinas (13th century) in his *Summa theologiae* and his *Summa contra gentiles*, which in turn follow up arguments of Aristotle and other scholars after him: "Starting from movement, becoming, contingency, and the world's order and beauty, one can come to a knowledge of God as the origin and the end of the universe" (*Catechism of the Catholic Church*, no. 32).

Each way focuses on a particular aspect that belongs to God in order to attribute it to him as a conclusion of the analysis carried out, and all of them conclude with the statement, "and this everyone calls God." In fact, due to the richness and impossibility on the part of man to comprehensively define the notion of God as an absolute reality, none of these ways succeeds in giving us a complete and personal picture of God, but only of some aspect of him: his existence, his intelligence, his providence, etc... The first three ways are of Aristotelian origin and start from the observation that all natural entities are in motion (constantly becoming), are caused by other entities and are contingent (can be different and change due to different factors), and it can be deduced that their cause must be a stable Being (that does not and cannot change), a first cause, uncaused (totally unconditioned) and necessary (always identical to itself). The idea is that chains of causes cannot go back ad infinitum, but must stop at some point, arriving at an immovable first mover, a first cause, a Being that is necessary (which cannot and must not become anything else) and stable: this need to find a single stable source is evident in the continuous movement from potency to act and in the transition from efficient cause to effect which we see when observing nature.

The fourth way, by analyzing the different degrees of perfection found in all creatures, deduces the existence of a being that possesses all perfections and is therefore their source; this way is the most metaphysical one and originates from the medieval doctrine of the transcendentals of being, according to which there are certain properties (to be a being, a thing, something, one, true, good and beautiful) that are common to all beings, because the origin is one. Finally, the fifth way, of Aristotelian origin, starting from recognizing how order and finality are present in the physical world (laws, constants and regularities of natural cycles) and in every creature, comes to affirm the existence of an ordering intelligence as the final cause of all things; finality cannot be the result of chance or merely the outcome of mechanical natural processes, given their extraordinary complexity and efficiency at all levels.

These proofs have been worked on by many scholars in the following centuries and are still relevant and especially apt to be applied to reflections that may arise in the field of scientific research. For example, we can cite the story of U.S. geneticist Francis Collins, who from being an atheist and agnostic became a believer while working on decoding the human genome. Sometimes, these "a posteriori" proofs are called "cosmological proofs" (which start from the observation of nature, of the cosmos-universe understood as a single ordered whole) or, in the case of the fifth way, as a "teleological proof" (starting from the finality present in nature; *telos* in Greek means "end" or "purpose"). Naturally, there is an underlying conviction that reality is not limited to the empirical-experimental plane, and that human knowledge can pass from the plane of the senses (i.e. what is perceivable through the senses) to the intellectual and meta-physical plane (i.e. going beyond the material dimension), thus enabling one to trace back from effects to the ultimate transcendent cause. In this regard in several places in Sacred Scripture (Wis 13:1-9; Rom 1:18-20; Acts 17:22-27) and in some documents of the Church's Magisterium (e.g. Vatican Council I, Constitution *Dei Filius*, April 24, 1870; Congregation for the Doctrine of the Faith, Instruction *Donum veritatis*, May 24,1990, no. 10; John Paul II, Encyclical *Fides et ratio*, September 14, 1998, no. 67) the affirmation is made that the human intellect, starting from creatures, can come to know the existence of God the Creator.

3. **Is it possible for man to come to recognize the existence of God without studying philosophy and theology or studying nature scientifically, but based only on his personal experience of daily life?**

The desire for happiness, the mystery of life, the extraordinary power of love, the search for goodness and truth which we find in every person of every age and culture, can be recognized as signals and become stimuli that spontaneously lead to the perception of God's existence: these are existential experiences that provoke deep inner reflections to those who pause to think about them. That is, man asks himself about the meaning and significance of human life, which is so different from animal and plant life, and develops a spiritual life that leads him toward a perspective of transcendence that places him far beyond his horizontal biological dimension. Such a path may lead him to recognize that, above everything, there is a God, as was the case over the millennia in so many ancient civilizations that developed a sense of the sacred and gave rise to various forms of religiosity. Thus, in this regard, it can be said that there are "anthropological paths" that lead to God, always "a posteriori," that is, paths that start from the existential experience of man himself. In fact, in every human being there is a natural desire for happiness, goodness and truth that stimulate one to think that there must be someone outside of us from whom these aspirations derive and who is able to satisfy these desires, which are never truly satisfied on a purely human and earthly level.

Unlike the "cosmological ways," which, as mentioned above, cannot lead us to recognize the existence of a personal God, but at most of a first cause, an immobile engine or an ordering intelligence, the "anthropological ways" suggest to us that the entity whose existence they show must have personal characteristics, like us. For example, the presence in man of a moral conscience that enables us to distinguish between good and evil prompts us to think of some "Supreme Good" of which our conscience is a reflection. Significantly, starting from the experience of human conscience, without knowledge of biblical Revelation, not a few ancient thinkers initiated a reflection on the ethical dimension of human action. This fact may be an indication that every man is in some way an image of God.

Again, human beings, in addition to being able to distinguish between good and evil, also have an innate desire to be free, and recognize this condition as a prerequisite for moral action. In recognizing that they are free, they also sense responsibility for their actions, but for this they require the existence of Someone to whom to be responsible. The existence of human freedom and responsibility lead to the existence of God as lawgiver and rewarder. In some materialist and reductionist conceptions, the human being is placed on the same level as the animal, whose actions are the result only of drives and instincts that provoke almost mechanical actions and re-actions, or the seat of spiritual life (mind, consciousness, soul) is made to coincide with the corporeality of the cerebral and nervous organs, thus denying the existence of freedom and all moral life. This can be answered on various levels: on that of reason and the phe-nomenology of man it is possible to show that the human person is self-transcendent, as well as that there is a free will that operates even in choices conditioned by nature; while in a more scientific context it is possible to argue that the human mind is not reducible to the brain.

Many see the presence of evil and injustice in the world as a se-rious obstacle, if not a real impossibility to accept the existence of God: if God existed, they argue, he would not allow all this. Para-doxically, however, this question, in its dramatic nature, can itself become a "way" to God's existence. Man perceives evil and suffering as a grave injustice, as something undeserved, requiring the possi-bility of reparation and the restoration of justice. In order to be able to see the evil that is in the world as something wrong and unjust, which should be corrected, it is necessary for man to have in his depths a kind of "natural moral law," a tendency toward goodness that impels him to seek a higher truth to be set as a reference for all, to which each person can freely strive (cf. JOHN PAUL II, Encyclical *Veritatis splendor*, 1993, nos. 54-64).

4. So can we conclude that it is reasonable to affirm that God exists?

At the conclusion of our enquiry, we can consider the various arguments of reason as sufficient to admit that the existence of God is reasonable. None of the individual proofs is a guarantee that God exists, but if we bring them together as a whole, we have convincing and convergent motives for affirming that God exists. This conclusion comes not just as the best explanation based on one single phenomenon of our experience, but of many. It will never be a mathematical certainty, but the limits of the certainty of one proof are compensated in some way by having several proofs to rely on (for example, a judge may be convinced "beyond reasonable doubt" that a suspect is guilty of a crime, because, even if none of the several pieces of evidence on their own is sufficient, all of them together may justify that verdict). Furthermore, each proof can tell us something about God, such as a defining attribute (or the exclusion of other contrary attributes) and therefore the cumulative force of the proofs on the one hand gives a greater certainty of God's existence and, on the other, provides a better understanding of his nature in its various aspects.

In any case, if upon reaching this stage we were still skeptical about whether or not to believe in the existence of God, we could consider taking up the well-known "wager" of French mathematician and philosopher Blaise Pascal (1623-1662) in point 233 of his famous *Pensées* (published posthumously in 1670). Pascal asks the question, "Does the God of Christians exist or not?" The question is like the toss of a coin: the odds of God existing or not are even. "So," he says to himself, "if reason cannot give a definitive answer, we need to wager." Taking a look at the stakes, Pascal notes that on the side of the "God exists" option are the infinite and the eternal, while on the side of the "God does not exist" are the finite and the transitory. Therefore, if we bet "God exists" and have guessed right we win "an eternity of life and bliss"; if, instead, we guessed wrong, we lose nothing important. If on the other hand we bet "God does not exist," then if we win we gain something finite, but if we lose we run the risk of losing the infinite and the eternal. Given the disproportion between the two stakes (the infinite and the finite), Pascal says we cannot afford the risk of choosing "God does not exist", and therefore it is always better to opt for the infinite and eternal happiness, believing that God exists and living according to this belief.

If God loves us and is all-powerful, how do we explain the existence of evil and suffering?

(Giulio Maspero)

A very common and very specific question is this: how is it possible that God is all-powerful and loves us, if we experience pain, evil, death? We are faced, apparently, with a contradiction: either (*aut*) God is all-powerful, so he has power over evil, but does not love us, and so allows our suffering, or (*aut*) God loves us, but he is not all-powerful. If we accept this opposition, it is perfectly understandable to become atheists, because if God were all-powerful and did not love us, it would be better to flee and deny him rather than have dealings with him; or, alternatively, if this God loves us but is not all-powerful, we may as well turn to idols for some sort of protection. No, the question of the origin of evil cannot be answered lightly. On the contrary, the starting point must necessarily be the affirmation that evil, from the biblical perspective, is a mysterious aspect, because it has to do with the freedom of the human creature.

Let's look at one possible answer from a conversation I had with a bartender in Rome, when I was having coffee with a colleague. When I went to pay the bartender told me that he wasn't happy with the fact that God did not want man to know good and evil, as we read in Genesis, because for him to be able to choose between the two was a good thing. I told him gently that he was not a very good theologian, because evil in itself does harm. So why should we desire to know it?

Afterwards, this exchange prompted me to wonder what the bartender meant by "evil." Deep down, for him it was moral or legal evil, that is, what an internal or external law declares wrong or forbidden Instead, evil, as the Bible primarily understands it, is the absence of good. That is why I had told him in that conversation that I saw nothing good in knowing sickness, which is the absence of health, or in loneliness, which is the absence of companionship, or in hatred, which is the absence of love. We call evil evil because it does harm. Evil and good are not on the same plane, they are not contraries. Rather, the former is the absence of the latter.

This is very important because we are living in a culture that exalts freedom of choice. Man is conceived as an isolated individual who can only be happy if he chooses what he wants. Obviously such a perspective captures a fundamental element of our identity, namely the ability to self-determine, to choose in favour of a meaning of our existence. According to the Bible, this is related to the fact that we were created precisely in the image of God, with the gift of freedom. Therefore, no one can exempt himself from the religious option: even those who say they are atheists, agnostics or relativists, through the concrete choices that shape their lives decide for a meaning, choose their "god," which can be money, sex, fame, *likes*, consensus or many other things.

But to reduce freedom to the possibility of choice which modernity does is also generating a widespread sense of being inadequate, of not doing well, of never being enough, of not being able to meet expectations, to the point of generating crises of anxiety and panic. All this is explained by the fact that freedom reduced to freedom of choice is contradictory. Indeed, if I am free only when I can choose, then once I have chosen I am no longer free. Moreover, given that when I choose I can choose only one thing among many options, in the end I always lose out, because the options I give up are many more than the one I have taken. For example, if I choose to be a lawyer when I grow up, I am giving up becoming an economist, an engineer, a physicist, and many other possibilities. Thus freedom understood only as freedom of choice leads, paradoxically, to giving up freedom itself.

In such a setting, even love becomes impractical, because it means choosing one person while renouncing all the others. And this, unfortunately, we see with the spread of loneliness in our lives. But this also suggests a positive response. In fact, we also have the experience that we feel free when we are in relationship. The possibility of deciding for a meaning in our life, which we possess insofar as we have been created in the image and likeness of God, can express itself in choosing not only between different possibilities, thus as in a closed question, between already predetermined options, but also in creating personal relationships.

For example, in *The Little Prince*, a beautiful great little book by Antoine de Saint-Exupéry, the pilot in the desert seems free, because he can go wherever he wants, but he is not really so, because he has nowhere to go and, above all, no one to go with. But, when the little prince appears to him, he begins to be free. In fact, as the episode of the meeting with the fox also explains, we are free only when we are in relationship with someone, only when we love and are loved, only when we have friends. Then the world acquires meaning. That is why the little prince returns to his rose, which in the metaphor of the tale represents the author's wife. His freedom is fulfilled in choosing as the meaning of everything the concrete relationship with the loved one, despite difficulties and limitations.

So, going back to the dialogue with the bartender which we started with: choosing between good and evil does not liberate, but rather takes away peace and makes us feel wrong. And this is exactly what happens to Adam and Eve at the beginning of the Bible, as we read in Genesis chapter 3. They were created by God together and were placed in a beautiful garden that was made for them. The Creator himself drew them out of nothing, creating them in his own image and likeness, that is, capable of recognizing goodness and following it. So he entrusted to them the whole garden, which means the world, inviting them to multiply, that is, to beget, to enjoy and make others enjoy all its beauty.

But into this wonderful picture comes the devil, that is, the tempter, who twists God's words and gives Adam and Eve to understand that God did not want them to eat of the tree of the knowledge of good and evil because then they would become like Him. Here the lie is obvious, because God has already created them like Him, in his own image and likeness. And the fact that they do not know evil is related precisely to that, because God is the Good and everything he does is good. Thus, as soon as the two make room in their hearts for this false thought, proposed to them by the devil, they sense they have gone wrong, they become ashamed of their own bodies and try to hide, and the same can happen to us.

This is how evil has entered the world. Evil, therefore, is not an evil principle that opposes God, the good principle, like what we see in the movies. The ancient myths were all like that: they are narratives where in the end the good one defeats the bad one, which however existed from the beginning. So the question arises: but where does the bad one come from?

St. Augustine of Hippo was a brilliant young man born in the second half of the fourth century AD in Tagaste in northern Africa. His mother was a Christian; his father was not. He from an early age was nagged by the question of what evil was. He wondered where it came from. And the first answer he got was the one given by Manichaeism, which traces the world back to a struggle between a good and an evil principle. But in the end the very question of the origin of the latter made him discard that option. Instead, when he arrived in Milan, he began to follow the sermons of St. Ambrose, who had been a prominent Roman politician until the people called for him to be a bishop, practically forcing him to take up a career in the church. From him Augustine learned that evil is not opposed to the good, but is simply the lack of it.

The examples to explain this are beautiful: darkness is not the opposite of light, but it is the absence of light. That is why even when it is sunny, if we close the shutters, darkness is produced in the room where we are. We say it has become dark, but in truth we have prevented light from entering, so that the room is devoid of it. Another example is that of cold, which is not the opposite of heat, but is the deprivation of it. In fact, it is studied in physics that absolute zero cannot be reached, because temperature is related to heat energy, thus to the movement of molecules, which never completely cancels out.

So if evil is not the opposite of good, but its absence, how can it exist? If it is the opposite of being, it cannot be. Then why does it exist? This question requires the introduction of the distinction between being and existing, that is, "being there". Let's take the example of Emmental cheese, the one with holes in it. What are the holes? They are absence of cheese, so much so that you don't pay for them, because they don't weigh. However, these holes are there, that is, they exist, because they are surrounded by cheese. So darkness is not, but exists, because the absence of light is surrounded by light, and so cold exists because it is surrounded by heat, that is, it is a space where molecules move slower than in a context where they are faster.

But then, if evil is not but exists, because it is the absence of good, how come it was produced? Why did God will it? Is he not omnipotent? How did he let it escape? Why does he not eliminate it? Here Augustine offers us a beautiful answer based on the difference between three verbs: will, allow and dispose. God does not will evil because he is the Good and cannot will except what is good, just as sugar or honey cannot produce a feeling of bitterness because they are sweet.

But God allows evil, which, as we read at the beginning of Genesis, is the result of man's choice. Throughout history there are those who have argued that evil is produced by society; others have traced it to matter. The Bible, however, connects it precisely to a wrong use of freedom, because both society and matter are the work of God, who is Good and, therefore, does things well. Evil, on the other hand, arises from the rational creature, whose freedom is willed and respected by God to the fullest, and which therefore can be misused by us, directing it toward nothingness.

But why does God allow this? Why does he not prevent us from doing wrong and causing ourselves pain? Augustine touches a pinnacle of his thought here, asserting that God does not will evil, but allows it because he can make use of it. That is, God is so great that he can take those holes that man has created in reality and use them to produce a greater good. We can make a comparison with a musician: the pauses he makes are not the opposite of sound, but are the absence of sound, and he allows them because he knows how to arrange them in such a way that they contribute to form a wonderful melody. Another image Augustine uses is that of the shadows inserted by a painter into his painting: they are not light, but they exist because they are absence of light and are surrounded by it, and the artist knows how to arrange them to make the subject of his painting stand out (Augustine, Literal Meaning of Genesis, 5:25).

In conclusion, although the relativism in which we are immersed suggests that all choices are equivalent, so it would be a mistake to talk about evil and good, our lives tell us that there are events and circumstances that make us to suffer. Following the biblical reading of evil as the absence of good allows us to realize that the choice between good and evil does not liberate, because loneliness is not something, but is the absence of love, just as illness is not a desirable reality but the absence of health, and so on. Today, unfortunately, the loss of this conception of evil and good condemns us to a society where guilt has been replaced by shame. Instead of being able to say: I did this thing that is bad, because it is devoid of good, we feel we are mistaken, thinking that it is we who are not good, instead of the relationship between our actions and what is or is not, with what is good or is devoid of goodness. Thus we risk falling into despair, because by denying evil, we end up enslaved to what others think is wrong, and we feel ashamed even of actions or situations that are not bad. A person may feel wrong because he or she is not as beautiful as the characters on the screen, or does not perform as well as others would expect of him or her. But that does not mean that person is bad. In fact, the Bible tells us that we were created by God who is the Good and therefore does everything well, so we are beautiful, we are good, we are true. When we are told that there is only one way to be good, or beautiful, or good, we are being deceived. In fact, our Creator is infinite and always pours out life and good even on those who really do something wrong or harmful. Thus, the biblical doctrine on evil is profoundly liberating, for it tells us that evil consists in turning away from the unconditional love of the Father who thought us and created us, sending his Son and his Love, that is, the Holy Spirit, to bring us back that goodness that grounds our being. So it is always possible to return and become good again, if we embrace the distinction between good and evil, understood as the absence of the former, and recognize the wonderful value of our freedom as children of God.

This comes through our relationships, that is, through meeting people who already have the experience of the fact that evil is only the absence of good and, therefore, are able to free us from the illusion of the idol, bringing us back to that primacy of reality over the idea that Pope Francis speaks of. This is possible thanks to the Cross, which God allowed because from it would come the ultimate victory over death and all evil. The encounter with the risen Christ after he had been nailed to the wood and laid in the tomb is the foundation of any possibility of recognizing that evil is mere deprivation of good, which, however, is always stronger. The path back to goodness is, thus, always possible and passes through friendship, fraternity, and the Church.

Assuming God exists, what does that have to do with my everyday life?

(Antonio Petagine)

Imagine that some scientists have just discovered a new galaxy millions of light-years away from Earth. However much such a discovery might excite our scientific interest and curiosity, we are entitled to think that it has little to do with our daily lives. The question of whether or not God exists is quite different, for it arises primarily from our search for the meaning of life. Ludwig Wittgenstein, one of the greatest philosophers of the 20th century, said that "to believe in God is to see that life has meaning" (L. Wittgenstein, *Notebooks, 1914–1916*, Harper Torchbooks, New York 1969, 8.VII.16).

The question about the meaning of our lives arises in us due to the fact that living does not mean for us only surviving. Our daily life is made up of feelings and actions, of relationships with others and the no less demanding ones with ourselves. Living for us means building projects in work, affections, culture and social life; it also means measuring ourselves against pain, injustice and violence (done to us, of course, but also done by us to others), love that we have not reciprocated and disappointment in what we would have liked to receive. Every day we have to live with the mediocrity and wickedness of those who govern peoples and nations and with the endemic injustice of a society that is happy to exalt those who should be ashamed of what they do but makes life difficult for those who really do good. If we learn to look at our lives in a deeper way, we will be able to discern in ourselves an infinite desire for good, for love, for happiness, which is matched by the inescapable awareness that no good, being finite, can completely satisfy such a desire. Do we not care, then, to understand how this disproportion is possible? What is the point of such a thing? Questions about life become even more challenging when we reflect on our origin and our end. Our very beginning seems to have come from an unlikely combination of a series of unrepeatable factors, while our end, though unknown, is nevertheless certain, since no one can escape death. It is as if we are on a train we do not choose to get on and on which we are not allowed to choose to stay. Man's great challenge, even before achieving goals, satisfactions and results, is to give himself and the people he loves a credible answer to *all this*.

To seek the meaning of life is to seek an answer that illuminates this complexity in such a way as to point us to a valid purpose, that is, a good that does not wear out and a happiness that is not illusory. God's existence has to do with precisely this. Indeed, St. Augustine in his *Confessions* stated, "How then do I seek you, Lord? In seeking you, my God, I am seeking the happiness of life" (*Confessions*, X.20.29). If God exists, then everything we listed earlier can be given meaning: not only that which is beautiful, rewarding and pleasant, but also that which may seem painful, difficult or hard. In fact, if God exists, then good, truth and love are not just nice words, because there is for all intents and purposes an infinite good that corresponds to the infinite desire for truth, happiness and love that animates our hearts. The existence of God gives substance to the idea that there is an intimate logic that links together the events of nature, the happenings of daily life and the deep aspirations that animate our consciences. The very heart of man does not appear in fact as an empty abyss, but as a place inhabited by an intimate law, which directs man to a good that is his, but not for that reason arbitrary. What indeed is that "law of the heart," represented so well by Sophocles' *Antigone*, if not that universal admonition to respect human dignity, which the twentieth century sought to express in the Universal Declaration of Human Rights? Does not the thirst for justice and the existence of rights and duties in people's lives appear more consistent if there is a God who rules and judges history than only men with their precarious judgments?

In seeing God as the one who gives the answer to life's question of meaning, biblical Revelation, particularly the Gospel Revelation, marks a decisive juncture. Before the spread of Christianity, the gods were predominantly seen as mysterious wills endowed with an uncanny power to interfere with our lives. For this reason, pagan gods appeared to be beings primarily to be feared, and the job of religion was to point out to men ways of ingratiating themselves to the gods with propitiatory rites and sacrifices. This idea of the divine is totally overturned with Christian Revelation: rather than wanting us to make some sacrifice for him, it is God himself who sacrifices himself for us, asking us rather to accept this sacrifice to the full, by imitating him in our daily lives. Through the sacrifice of Christ, and the Resurrection of the one who was crucified, God reveals himself as Love capable of saving man from the fear of death and the devastating effects of sin on his life.

Paradoxically, the idea that God is profoundly involved in our everyday lives comes not only from those who believe that God exists, but also from those who have wanted to reject this idea.

Friedrich Nietzsche, in *The Gay Science*, 1882, imagines a mad man, who, announcing that "God is dead," invites those present to take the significance of such an event seriously, asking them, "Is there still a high and a low?" (*The Gay Science*, aphorism 125). By speaking this way, Nietzsche means to say that to live without God is to convince oneself that life is without order, without meaning, without points of reference (the high and low of the aphorism). Without God, moral values or duties lose consistency. At that point, however, would not Dostoevsky be dramatically right when he states that "if God does not exist, everything is permitted"? Jean-Paul Sartre was well aware of this when he wrote that without God, "all possibility of finding values in an intelligible heaven vanishes; there can no longer be an *a priori* good, because there is no infinite consciousness to think it; nowhere is it written that good exists, that one must be honest, that one must not lie, and for this precise reason: we are on a plane on which there are only men" (J.-P. Sartre, *Existentialism is a humanism*, 1946, p. 48). This last passage of Sartre's is important, because really to think that God exists is to think that there is an infinite consciousness that scrutinizes our hearts, looking at us as who we really are, while every other view of us, including our own, is always imperfect, since it is based only on limited aspects and is subject to error, ignorance, and evil. If God is in himself Good and Love, as Christianity teaches, then an authentic purification of our daily lives is possible. In the infinity of divine consciousness, in fact, everything we have experienced can be saved from oblivion, including the smallest gestures of love, the most hidden forms of self-denial, the beautiful moments forgotten. Even the evil we have done can be looked at in its truth, placed in a horizon in which justice will not be without mercy (which is tremendously difficult to do for us, who struggle to be both just and capable of forgiving, even toward ourselves). If God exists and is Love, our history and memory will finally have a chance to be redeemed and cherished in a purified way.

To think that such a God exists is also to think that evil, however much it dominates the scene of this world, generating destruction, pain and death, does not have the last word in human history. Evil can be redeemed, sin can be forgiven, justice can be repaired. If God is Good and establishes an order of good, then everything that happens within our lives can be placed within a horizon of the good. This is not to say that misfortune, sickness or injustice cease to be such, but that they can stop fueling evil if they are credibly orientated towards a further direction, which it is up to us to explore. The existence of God then allows us to hope for true liberation from death, because there is someone who has the power to give eternal life and to make all lives precious: not only those made famous by history, but also those that are hidden and anonymous, as well as those that are very short or very painful.

We can consider a further aspect, convincingly illustrated by St. Augustine. He asserted that each of us is faced with a problem of love, which places us at a crossroads: to love God, to the point of forgetting self, or to love self, to the point of forgetting God (cf. *De civitate Dei*, XIV.28). Augustine is telling us that there are no atheists, only idolaters: the man who does not trust in God is not someone who simply lives as if God was absent, but someone who puts something else in God's place: success, money, pleasure, his own intelligence, power. In short, Augustine warns us that positing that

God exists is essential if we wish to put everything in its proper place. Only by placing God at the summit of human goods will we avoid absolutizing any of them, creating disharmony in our lives and in the lives of others. We have been created to live among the plurality of goods that mark our daily lives, but in order then to truly live properly we need to convince ourselves that our happiness is not satisfied by any particular good, no matter how ardently we may desire it or possess it permanently. For if we put human love first in our lives, we would easily find ourselves subjugated to the need for consent, making our relationships toxic; if we put work, we would destroy affection; if sex, power or money, we would simply become their slaves.

When we exalt our *ego*, we produce the paradoxical effect of debasing our dignity and losing our esteem for ourselves and who we are, and also our taste for the things of the world. This is the verdict of Gilles Lipovetsky, when he observes that contemporary individualism has generated a widespread and slow-witted indifference: "God is dead, great purposes are extinguished, but no one cares one bit" (*The Age Of Emptiness*, 2019, pp. 40-41). These words are ideally echoed by Fabio Rosini, who observes that in our world, which celebrates the religion of the ego, we do not love each other at all; in order not to suffer even more "we make use of refined instruments of narcosis. Not feeling pain seems like a solution, but escaping the real only makes the magma of the unresolved grow" (*The Age Of Emptiness*, 2019, pp. 58-59). We need to live our daily lives admiring the beauty of the things we can do in work and other life activities and becoming aware of the value of the people we meet and the relationships we enter into, but without any of these things becoming our "secret god." Thinking that God exists allows us to acquire a different view of things, one that frees us from the burden of having to make everything turn around us and depend on us: if God exists, as Lessing said, it is up to men to write the figures, but up to Him alone to draw the sums.

Let us also add this: if God exists, then none of the authorities of this world will be "God"; if God alone is the holder of truth, none of us taken in isolation will be, nor will any of the bearers of the ideologies that claim to have the last word on good and evil for all humanity. The thought that God exists may appear to be something uncertain, since God is not an object of direct experience, yet posing his existence prevents us from falling into a definite error: that of an idolatrous view of ourselves and the things of the world. Such a view exposes us dangerously to various forms of slavery and foolishness, which threaten daily our true freedom, which is that of thinking and loving.

Considering what we have said so far, we can answer some particular questions:

1. **Do those who think that God exists seek consolation for their lives?**

The answer to this question depends on what we mean by "seeking consolation." If by this we mean what those who look down on religious faith mean, we have to admit that belief in God does not provide easy consolations. It is not a comforting "it will be all right," helping us to face any difficulty. Those who claim that religion offers "opium to the people," inventing fanciful doctrines to cope with the harshness of living, perhaps do not understand what religion is. In fact, in no authentically lived religion does consolation take on this character. God's existence does console in the sense that it offers a reason for living and for dying, freeing us from a life without meaning and giving a credible hope of redemption from evil and death (cf. 2 Cor 1:3-11). This means that genuine faith in God is always something demanding, prompting a response of commitment and self-sacrifice.

2. Aren't those who believe in God in danger of despising earthly life, placing all value in the hereafter?

Following on from what we have just seen, we can say that taking seriously the idea that there is God in no way means despising the world. On the contrary, it means loving it more and better. Rather, it could be said that those who think that God exists will be willing to put the values of the spirit before all others. But what are the values of the spirit? They are precisely those that enable us to recognize what really matters, making us able to appreciate to the fullest what is good, beautiful, and worthwhile in daily life. Paradoxically, it is precisely those who idolize particular goods who end up debasing them, generating conflict, dissatisfaction, pettiness. Therefore, those who love God are ready to "love the world passionately," as St. Josemaría Escrivá wrote, because they are ready to discover and experience a new dimension of meaning, beauty, and joy in the different places and circumstances in which ordinary life unfolds. In this perspective, he could affirm that "the Christian vocation consists of making heroic verse out of the prose of each day. Heaven and earth seem to merge, my sons and daughters, on the horizon. But where they really meet is in your hearts, when you sanctify your everyday lives." (*Passionately Loving the World,* in *Conversations of Josemaría Escrivá,* no. 116, 1968. Link: https://escriva.org/en/conversaciones/passionately-loving-the-world/).

Why do we say that God is one if there is God the Father, God the Son, and God the Holy Spirit?

(Bruno Forte)

If someone asked me to help them to get to know the Trinity, the God whom Christians believe in, and to intuit at least a little bit how there can be three Persons in one divine nature, I would gladly undertake to answer their request, simply because it would involve talking about the God to whom I have given my whole heart and life. There is a New Testament text, in the first letter of John, that shows us how to speak of this God when it states that "God is love" and that "he who does not love has not known God" (1 John 4:8 and 16). The story of this love is told to us in the Bible: the story from the very start of human beings and its sole purpose is to make us partakers of that infinite love. Out of love God created the world, out of love he called each of us to exist just as we are, out of love he sustains us and accompanies us on the journey of life and history! When man used freedom – given to him as a gift – to turn against God, the God who is Love suffered, but he respected his creature's choice. One of Jesus' most beautiful parables tells us about this: "A man had two sons. The younger one said to his father, Father, give me my share of the inheritance. And the father divided the wealth between them. After not many days, the younger son, having collected his things, departed for a far country and there squandered his property in loose living..." (Luke 15:11-13).

The story, however, does not stop there: God loves men too much to abandon them to themselves. In the face of our rejection, God manifests the depth and boldness of his love by sending his Son, who became man like us and gave himself up to death out of love for us: "In this the love of God was made manifest among us, that God sent his only Son into the world, so that we might live through him. In this is love, not that we loved God but that he loved us and sent his Son to be the expiation for our sins. Beloved, if God so loved us, we also ought to love one another... God is love, and he who abides in love abides in God, and God abides in him." (1 John 4:9-11 and 16). To lay down one's life for another is to love him of the greatest love: "No one has greater love than this: to lay down one's life for one's friends" (Jn 15:13). This is how God loves us. The Cross is God's declaration of love for us, the revelation of the great heart, the divine heart that loves infinitely: the reason God loves us this way is that he is in himself love.

This is the center of the Christian message, the source, the womb and the goal of all that exists: God is love! It is the most important thing we are given to think about! The deepest truth is not "cogito, ergo sum" (Descartes), that is, "I think, therefore I am," but "amor, ergo sum," "I am loved, therefore I exist"! I try to say it as simply as I can, aware that I am barely stammering about the holy mystery from which we come, in which we move and exist and toward which we are going in the journey of time, because, as St. Thomas Aquinas says, when we have done all we can to know God, he will always remain beyond all our achievements: "In fine nostrae cognitionis Deum tamquam ignotum cognoscimus" (*Summa contra Gentiles*, I, 49, 5).

According to the statement quoted from the first letter of John, "God is love": inasmuch as loving implies a relationship at least between two, it is easy to see how the Eternal cannot be solitude in itself. To love only oneself is not love; it is selfishness. God who is love is then at least one who has always loved and one who has always been loved and reciprocates love: an eternal Lover and an eternal Beloved. The one who has always loved is the source of love: he is never tired of beginning to love and loves for the sole joy of loving. He is God the Father in love, infinitely free and generous in loving, motivated by nothing else to love than by love itself: "Sinners," Luther states in this sense, "are beautiful because they are loved, they are not loved because they are beautiful" ("peccatores sunt pulchri, quia diliguntur, non ideo diliguntur, quia sunt pulchri": *Disputatio Heidelbergae habita* – 1518 – in *Martin Luthers Werke. Kritische Gesamtausgabe*, Weimar 1883 ff. 1, 365).

The other in love, the eternal Beloved, is the One who has always received the love that begets Him: he is the eternal gratitude, the thanks without beginning and without end, the Son. When the Son becomes man, he is united with each of us: therefore the Father, loving him, also loves each of us united with him, loved in the Beloved, made capable of receiving love, which is the eternal life of God.

Perfect love, however, is not confined to the circle of the two: "To love is not to stand looking into each other's eyes, but to look together toward the same goal" (Antoine de Saint-Exupéry, *Terre des hommes*, Gallimard, Paris 1938). The Father and the Son experience a love so rich and fruitful that together they turn to a divine Third Person, the Holy Spirit. The Spirit is the One in whom their love is always open to give itself, to "go out of itself"; therefore the

Spirit is called the gift of God, the living source of love, the fire that kindles in us the capacity to reciprocate love. And therefore he breathes on creation in the first morning of the world and on the new creation, of which the Church is the sign and promise, in the proclamation to Mary (cf. Lk 1:35) and on the day of Pentecost (cf. Acts 2:1-13). Inasmuch then as it is Love received from the Son and given by the Father, the Spirit is also the bond of eternal love, the unity and peace of the Lover and the Beloved. In the Spirit we are all embraced by the love that unites, liberates and saves.

As Love, God is thus Trinity, the eternal event of love, uniting the Three who are One: the Father, the eternal origin of Love; the Son, the eternal advent of Love; and the Spirit, the future of eternal Love, the One in whom divine love, from ever being equal to himself, is ever new, eternally young and at the same time unchanging in his faithfulness. This eternal love story has been told to us in the supreme sign of Jesus' surrender on the Cross: the Cross is the story of the eternal Lover, the Father, who delivers his beloved Son for us; of the eternal Beloved, the Son, who gives Himself up to death out of love for us; and of the Holy Spirit, the eternal love that unites them with each other and is ecstasy ("ek-stasis": being out, coming out) of divine love, which opens them to the gift they make to us, making us sharers in divine life. These Three are one: not three loves, but one, eternal and infinite love, the one God who in his essence is love.

It can be said then that "you see the Trinity, if you see love" ("immo vero vides Trinitatem, si caritatem vides": St. Augustine, *De Trinitate*, 8, 8,12). And you see love if you look at the Cross where the Father offers his Son for us, while the Spirit stands between one and the other, as if to unite them and offer their love to us. The Cross is the story of God's Trinity, the revelation of infinite love: therefore, often in the Western tradition the divine Trinity has been depicted with the scene of God the Father holding in his arms the wood of the Cross, from which hangs the abandoned Son, while the dove of the Spirit unites and separates the Lover and the Beloved, the Abandoned One and the One who abandons him (for example, the Trinity depicted by Masaccio in Santa Maria Novella in Florence). The Christian East has sought to convey the same message to us with the scene of the three Angels who appeared to Abraham at the oaks of Mamre (cf. Gen 18) and who were one, chosen as a figure of the three divine Persons who welcome men into the circle of their love at the banquet of life (as does Andrei Rublëv in the famous icon of the Trinity, in Moscow).

Try then to stop before a Crucifix or the icon in which the three Angels call you to enter into the divine dialogue of love: be willing to listen to God's declaration of love and accept his gift. Seek to become united with the beloved Son, abandoned and risen to life for you, and feel the Father's love enveloping you and the Spirit uniting you to Jesus and in him to the Father. You will be able to live in faith the beautiful experience of knowing that you are loved by God: enveloped in the love of the Three, you will understand that God-Love is not an empty word, a distant story, but the story of the eternal Love, which has come to express itself in time, so that each of us, listening to it and believing in the divine love of the Three, who are One, may be reached and transformed by this eternal story of love. And this will fill your heart with joy: the joy of knowing that you are loved always, forever and in every instant of the infinite love of God,

One in the love of the Three, who give themselves to each other and envelop you in this love, ever new and faithful in eternity...

So, if God created us to then live with him for ever, why did he not manifest himself more clearly and convincingly?

(Arturo Cattaneo)

In his interview with St. John Paul II, in *Crossing the Threshold of Hope* (1994), Vittorio Messori phrased the question this way: "Why doesn't He give everyone more tangible and accessible proof of his existence? Why does his mysterious strategy seem to be that of playing hide-and-seek with his creatures?" I like to recall the core of the answer that St. John Paul II gave, now that we are celebrating the 2025th anniversary of the Incarnation of the Son of God. In fact, the Pope noted that "God's self-revelation comes about in a special way by his 'becoming man'." Precisely in his "birth, and then through the Passion, the Cross and the Resurrection that the self-revelation of God in the history of man reached its zenith" (pp. 42 f.).

At the same time, it is also true that Christ's life, from his birth in Bethlehem to his death on the Cross, is a great act of humility, of lowering himself. It could also be argued that these events occurred two thousand years ago and therefore we have little certainty about their historical reality. Why has God not found a way to manifest himself more clearly to man today as well?

On closer inspection, as to the historical reality of those facts and the divinity of Christ we have many certainties, as was illustrated by the answers to the previous questions, "Jesus is a historical character, but what proof is there that he is God?" (G. de la Morena). "What certainty do we have that Christ rose from the dead? Could not the apparitions narrated in the Gospels be hallucinations due to auto-suggestion?" (D. Arasa). "Couldn't the Resurrection of Christ be a myth similar to those found in other religions?" (M. Vanzini). "If Jesus is God, why was he unable to convince his people that he was the Messiah?" (G. de la Morena).

These are well-argued and convincing answers but, one can still insist, asking why God has not manifested himself unequivocally, irrefutably?

The answer is, after all, very simple and will be one of the shortest in this volume. He certainly could have done so, thus obliging every man to submit to him, but in so doing he would have taken away the freedom he himself has given us, as Scripture reiterates, "From the beginning God created man and left him in the hand of his own counsel. If you will, you can keep the commandments; being faithful depends on your good will. He has set before you fire and water: there where you will stretch out your hand. Before men stand life and death: to every one shall be given that which pleases him" (Sir 15:14-17). God has thus willed to leave man "in the hand of his own counsel," so that he may freely seek God and, through adherence to him, come to full and blessed perfection (cf. GS 17).

As the *Catechism of the Catholic Church* teaches, "God, who created man out of love, also called him to love, the fundamental and innate vocation of every human being" (no. 1604). It is a vocation to which man can respond only through freedom. God, in creating us by an act of infinite love, has bestowed on us a dignity that is in a sense infinite (cf. Declaration *Dignitas infinita*, 2024, no. 6). A dignity that would be denied if God, manifesting himself unequivo-cally, obliged us to acknowledge and submit to him. Man's freedom therefore requires that he act without coercion, either internal or ex-ternal. "For God willed to leave man 'in the hand of his own counsel' (Sir 15:14), so that he would spontaneously seek his Creator and freely arrive, by adherence to him, at full and blessed perfection" (GS 17). God is love and cannot impose his love. He would cease to be the God-Love. Love proceeds by attraction, finding the desire of God inscribed in man's heart (CCC, no. 27). It is God who pours himself into the heart of the one he loves. He knocks at the door of the heart, but we are free to open it.

The freedom that God has given to man is thus an essential part of our dignity as children of God, created in his image and likeness (cf. Gen 1:26-27). We can thus understand, because our freedom is so valuable, that God – as has been said – "has wanted to *run the risk of our freedom*" (St. J. Escrivá, Homily *Christ Present in Christians*, no. 113). There is an absolutely real risk of abuse that unfortunately has taken place and is taking place so many times in the lives of men, an abuse committed even by one of his apostles, chosen and trained by him, as Amedeo Cencini explains in this book, answering the question, "If Christ is God, why did he not avoid being betrayed and precisely by one of His apostles?"

All of this was admirably summarized by Blaise Pascal (1623-1662) – mathematician, physicist, philosopher and theologian – with the famous phrase from his *Pensées*, "God has put enough light in the world for those who want to believe, but he has also left enough shadows for those who do not want to believe."

The light that God has placed in the world should be understood first of all with respect to the work of creation. One only has to look at it in its immensity and wondrous harmony and beauty to recognize that it cannot be the result of chance. A person contemplating a beautiful painting will never think that it could have made itself... As we read in the Book of Wisdom, "From the greatness and beauty of creatures by analogy we contemplate their author" (Wis 13:5).

But in addition to the work of creation there is above all the work of redemption. The fact that God respects our freedom with extreme consideration does not mean that he has not done and continues to do his utmost in thousands of ways to win us to his love. Beginning with original sin, by which man freely separated himself from God, rejecting his plan of love – as Luis Cano explains in his response to the respective question – the entire history of salvation tells us of God's multiple initiatives to show his love and reestablish his covenant with man, initiatives that culminated in the Incarnation of Jesus Christ and then continue through the Church, through which he prolongs in space and time his saving work. "This first alienation generated many others. The history of mankind, starting from the origins, stands as a witness to the misfortunes and oppressions born from the heart of man, as a result of the misuse of freedom" (CCC 1739).

Certainly, the path man is called to take toward God is not without difficulties, his freedom being "really wounded by sin" (GS 17), and he cannot travel it to the full without the help of divine grace. But, as a recent document of the Dicastery for the Doctrine of the Faith has well pointed out, "even when he draws us with his grace, God does so in such a way that never is our freedom violated"

(Declaration *Dignitas infinita*, 2024, no. 30). More so, as the Catechism of the Catholic Church has pointed out, "by the action of grace, the Holy Spirit educates us in spiritual freedom in order to make us free collaborators in his work in the Church and in the world" (CCC 1742).

This "divine logic" was expressed by St. Augustine in his famous phrase, "God, who created you without you, cannot save you without you" (Sermon 169:13). A logic we also see in the way Jesus calls people to follow him, without impositions or threats, limiting himself to an invitation. A perfect example is the dialogue with the rich and well behaved young man who asks Jesus what he lacks. Jesus answers, "If you want to be perfect..." (Mt 19:21). His way of drawing us to himself, of winning our hearts, is with love, manifested with his whole life, to the extreme of self-giving with the sacrifice of the Cross.

How can it make sense that all men should suffer the effects of Adam and Eve's sin, that is, original sin? Is it not unfair to be penalized for a sin for which we are not in the least responsible?

(Luis Cano)

Judeo-Christian tradition holds that the so-called "original sin" was an actual event that really happened, although its historical explanation is not easy to understand. To this end, the Bible "uses a language of images" (CCC 390) to expound a "primordial event (...) that happened at the beginning of human history." Through this language, the Bible conveys to us that evil, pain, and suffering, which so often mark our lives, do not have their origin in God, for God is good and loves us. On the contrary, these negative realities appeared when man broke a covenant of love that united him to his Creator and made him deeply happy. This was the "original sin."

Today, in the light of discoveries about human evolution, it seems more difficult to understand how that original sin could have occurred, that is, how it is possible to reconcile the data of paleontology with what the Bible tells us. However, what is important about original sin is not so much understanding how it happened, but to find a reason and a meaning for the problem of evil, the presence of suffering and the chain of misfortunes that humans have unleashed throughout history on earth.

Christian doctrine holds that evil entered into human life because of that "primordial event" (cf. CCC 403). That transgression involved the rejection of a being who loved us as a Father. From then on, human beings have always felt fear: fear of God, whom they sometimes see as an implacable judge waiting for the moment to punish them for their transgressions; fear of the world around them and of other beings, who from that moment became competitors or enemies. Also, since then, we alternate between moments of satisfaction and disappointment with ourselves. The book of Genesis speaks of Adam and Eve's shame when they discovered their own nakedness after their sin (cf. Genesis 3:10), a feeling of vulnerability that showed itself openly when their own weakness and imperfections became obvious.

That pain and suffering entered history because of the estrangement from God, brought about by the first sin, is easy to understand when we consider that perhaps the worst evils that mankind has suffered have had a human cause.

It is true that nature can sometimes be hostile, can even kill or cause suffering. But in itself nature is not evil. Natural processes respond to biological, geological or cosmological needs: the world is constantly developing, it is dynamic, and this implies that some things are destroyed and others are built up; some beings live and others die; some eat and others are eaten; geography is formed through violent convulsions and so many other things. God has given mankind the ability to foresee and, to a great extent, mitigate these destructive effects, so that many of them can be controlled (cf. Genesis 1:26) or we can protect ourselves from them, even if we do not always succeed completely.

On the contrary, as we have said, it is human beings who have brought about constant wars and all manner of violence; injustices and mistreatment of other human beings, especially the weakest and most innocent; murders, slavery and so many other forms of behaviour that do harm to our neighbors or ourselves. Even the effects of some natural disasters could have been alleviated if there had not been so much selfishness and hardness of heart among humans. All these evils are the responsibility of people like us and arise from inside us, from our hearts, as we say.

Human beings, however, are not evil in themselves and it is fair to say that most people have good feelings. But we notice that evil is present in us and in some cases it can turn a normal person into a sadistic killer. However, it is not uncommon for us to feel an inclination to do evil when it is easy and convenient, interesting or pleasant. Especially, if we can do it with impunity, without anyone knowing, avoiding any unpleasant consequences and gaining advantages. We know we should not do it, but we end up falling into what we reject and later regret doing.

From days of old, thinkers have wondered why we act in such an illogical way. The pagan poet Ovid, in the first century AD, puts the following words into Medea's mouth: "If I could, I would be wiser: / but an unknown force drags me against my will, and passion advises one thing, / the mind another: I see better things and approve of them, / but I go after worse things" (Metamorphoses, Book VIII, vv. 20-21).

A few years after Ovid, St. Paul expressed it in another way: "I cannot understand what I do: for I do not what I want, but what I detest (...) for I do not do the good that I want, but the evil that I do not want" (Letter to the Romans 7:15, 19).

This paradoxical situation presupposes that human beings are able to grasp a universal moral law, regardless of their religion or culture, which could be formulated as follows: "do good and avoid evil" (cf. St. Thomas Aquinas, *Summa Theologiae*, I-II, q.94, a.2). Although this principle is clear, the fact is that "an unknown force" sometimes drags us "to the worst things," to the "evil I do not want."

This weakness in the face of evil is compounded when we are unclear about our destiny in this world, or simply ignorant of where our true good lies. Imagine that a four-year-old boy was given a credit card with the assignment to do the weekly shopping for his family, in a large supermarket. It is easy to imagine what the contents of the shopping cart would be: the child would buy all kinds of sweets and useless things, because he does not know what the requirements of a balanced diet are, nor does he know the value of money, nor is he able to navigate his way through the various possibilities, nor does he have willpower to resist his whims.

Somehow, even an adult human being manifests a certain weakness and disorientation in moral matters, which can be compared, making due differences, to the example of the child in the supermarket. Without proper moral education, a person can harm his own life and the lives of others. Religions and various philosophies have been very aware of this, providing wise ethical advice, helping people find balance and peace, fostering understanding in families, communities and nations. And they propose a path to happiness and personal fulfillment. In general, almost all religions and the thinking of philosophers have encouraged the practice of virtue and self-control, respect for one's conscience and objective moral principles. All of this is of great help in resisting evil and as guidance on how to do the best. But in spite of all that, we see how people as holy and experienced in virtue as St. Paul have not been able to behave as they really want to.

Religions have tried to explain this presence of bad tendencies in us in various ways. Some speak of a dual principle of good and evil, residing in our nature. Or they identify good with a good god and evil with another god who is bad, the two constantly in contrast, fighting in us, which would explain the alternation of good and bad things in our lives and history. Or, for those who believe in reincarnation, everything has a relation to previous lives.

As we have said, for the Judeo-Christian tradition and, to some extent, also for Islam, there has been an initial sin by our ancestors. That rupture was influenced and instigated by the deception of an evil being, whom we call Satan or the devil, who is not a god of evil – as some believe – but a powerful and intelligent creature, though of limited power, who had also previously fallen into sin and the rejection of God (CCC 391-395).

We have already talked about the consequences of this. Even if apparently it has not affected our physical DNA, it can be said that the fruits of sin are found present in our spiritual DNA, so to speak. This explains our inclination to evil and weakness in resisting temptation. This does not mean that we are prisoners of these bad inclinations, like an addiction that cannot be overcome. We are free, but the truth is that it costs us a lot to always behave well. Every day we have the opportunity to choose between good and evil, regardless of what our ancestors did. We are not paying for the faults of others; we are free to choose.

But every day we see that however much our mastery over our negative drives improves – and there are very expert techniques that seem to promise this – we will never succeed in always and at all times resisting the suggestions of evil. Christianity calls this concupiscence, which remains in us as a consequence of the first sin. In itself it is not sin. It is an attraction we can reject. If we do not give in to it, no evil is done

However much this legacy of original sin weighs, the good news is that our intelligence and will are powerful tools that God has given us to combat many evils and overcome their consequences. Thanks to the sciences, such as Medicine, many physical ills, such as disease or injury, can be solved. In the vast field of the experimental sciences and technology, advances have been made that have improved living conditions incredibly, eliminating or helping to forestall problems of all kinds. Law has been able to establish rules of peace and coexistence, pushing back evil and helping the re-education of delinquents. Politics, if oriented to the common good, can find intelligent and just solutions to a thousand daily problems. All this tells us that man is well equipped to resist evil, both physical and moral. Marriage and family life exist to support human beings at every moment of our lives, helping us and offering us the love we all need to develop in a balanced way as people. However, we also see that sin many times weakens or corrupts these awesome realities: family, politics, technology, etc.

What history shows is that sin ends up being very destructive to the person and society, even though often its consequences are not outwardly noticed. The very best human relationships and levels of happiness are get broken because of sin. First a breach is produced, the second time it is easier to give in and the third time even more so. Thus one gets into a negative habit, for example, such as addiction to a substance, a vice or a toxic relationship. Or great friendships, relationships or very important ties are broken.

According to the Bible, our first parents, Adam and Eve, were virtuous and felt no inclination to sin. They saw God, which made them immensely happy because they knew his immense love for them. As a fruit of that relationship they were at peace with nature, which they saw and appreciated as a beautiful gift from God. They were also at peace with themselves because they felt they were children of a wonderful God who loved them and endowed them with very precious qualities (cf. CCC 374, 377-379). What could distract them? Moreover, theologians think they enjoyed special supernatural help, which provided them with greater knowledge and strength to behave according to their own good and true to God's plans for them and the world (cf. CCC 375-376).

But the temptation of an evil being created an imbalance. Theology teaches that God allowed it so that people should love him freely, for who He is, with full trust in his love. Sin began when Satan succeeded in undermining that trust. Everything in life can be criticized, everything can be misunderstood, everything can be viewed negatively, and even we can go so far as to portray an earthly paradise as a little hell, where we are not allowed do what we want. This is what the devil succeeded in doing, twisting reality and showing it falsely in a negative light. "God the Creator is placed in a state of suspicion, indeed of accusation, in the mind of the creature" (St. John Paul II, Letter *Dominum et vivificantem*, no. 37).

When they disobeyed God and broke the covenant they had with him, they saw themselves deprived of his closeness and felt alone and abandoned in the world: naked, ashamed and full of fear. Sin multiplied: one of their sons, Cain, killed his own brother, for a futile reason (cf. Genesis 4:3-8).

To get out of this situation, some religions have proposed that men can achieve victory on their own, through self-control or purification. But the Christian religion maintains that no one can redeem himself. To restore the covenant with God, it was not enough to accumulate merit or to seek to attain perfection on his own. Christianity maintains that man was incapable of restoring that relationship with God, so it was necessary for God himself to rebuild it, which he did in a wonderful way. The second Person of the Holy Trinity became man, receiving the name Jesus, which designates his mission as Savior. Thanks to him and only in him could a new covenant be forged between God and man – for Jesus was and is true man – and one which was much stronger than the one that existed before. Sin lost its power and condemnation was also abolished for all who believe in Jesus and put their trust in his saving power. In Christ we have been reconciled to God and have become his true children, indeed temples of the Holy Spirit, who was given to us as a Gift.

This has meant that mankind has gained more than what had been lost. Any new guilt can be erased at any time by God, because Christ's infinite love has made up for all the sins which mankind is capable of committing. This brings us before a paradox: if original sin had not existed, such superabundant redemption would not have been possible. From an evil has come a much greater good. As St. Paul says, "where sin increased, grace abounded all the more" (Letter to the Romans, 5:20). We emerged victorious, which is why the Church calls original sin a "happy fault" (Hymn *Exsultet* in the Easter Vigil).

If it was undeserved to suffer the guilt of Adam and Eve, it was equally undeserved to benefit from the obedience and holiness of Jesus. If it is easy to fall, it is even easier to be forgiven and get up again. Without the coming of Christ to free us from original sin, we would not have had the possibility of being much happier, more complete and more united men and women to God than our first parents were. We can now say that the coming of our Redeemer was the greatest benefit that mankind has received in all its history.

The Christian faith affirms that God is Love, has revealed himself as Love and is infinitely merciful. How then do we explain those passages in the Bible that speak of the "wrath of God"?

(Giorgio Paximadi)

1. Introduction

The theme of the "wrath of God" is one of those typical topics that pose a problem for today's mentality and give rise to commonplaces, such as, for example, the contrast between an Old Testament God who is wrathful and violent and a New Testament God who is all merciful and good. The biblical pages, as one might expect, offer a far more nuanced view of this matter.

2. The theme in the Old Testament

2.1. The terminology of divine wrath

The Old Testament vocabulary in this regard is very rich, counting as many as five distinct terms: *harôn*, *qeṣep*, *'ebrāh*, *za'am* and *ka'as*. The first is the main word used for divine wrath, whether or not combined with *'ap*, literally "nostrils," and it turns out to be the generic word for anger, both human and divine. More precisely, the term indicates the feeling of wrath. The underlying metaphor for this terminology is that of fire and flame (root *Hrh*). The word is generally used to express God's wrath toward Israel or toward other deities (cf. Josh 7:1; 23:6; Jdg 2:20; Deut 6:14-15; 11:16-17; 31:16,17).

2.2. The ancient near eastern background

From this cursory analysis it can be seen that wrath is widely mentioned in the Bible to depict an attitude of the God of Israel. In many religious traditions of the Ancient Near East we find that the gods are subject to passions and attitudes that are definitely human, and it seems evident that this aspect must be understood as an anthropomorphism.

The idea that the deity can or should be represented in human forms and acting in ways typical of human beings is common in Ancient Near Eastern religious thought, although contrary examples are not lacking. In fact, gods are often depicted as animals or plants, one thinks of the well-known Egyptian zoolatry or the cult of the sacred tree in Semitic but also Indo-European traditions, or as inanimate objects with symbolic value, such as sacred stones, very common in the Syrian-Canaanite sphere, or cosmic elements (e.g., the Aton sun disk of the religious reform of Amenophis IV - Akhenaten). A consequence of this anthropomorphism is the fact that not only does the deity have a human appearance, as for example in the second chapter of Genesis, but also feelings, thoughts, and actions typical of men, such as anger or sexual arousal. Some of these feelings may then be independent of the human depiction, but they too are nonetheless anthropomorphisms. The representation of the wrath of the God of Israel, whose worship itself does not involve symbolic images or objects, may originate from an anthropomorphic mode of representing relationship with the divine.

It is possible, however, to see how the attitude of the gods of the Ancient Near East is radically different from that of the God of Israel. Often these deities fall prey to an irrepressible and unreasonable wrath, which other gods struggle to appease. Thus the god Ea rebukes the god Enlil for destroying mankind with the flood because he was in the grip of unreasonable anger. In Egyptian mythology, the wrath of the solar god Ra is even manifested in another deity, the terrible lioness goddess Sekhmet who, however, after getting drunk on beer dyed red to imitate blood, becomes the cat goddess of love Bastet. The Canaanite Anat is also depicted as the blood goddess par excellence. Worship is given to appease the fury of these deities with quasi magical acts: offerings of food or calming perfumes.

The wrath of the gods is sometimes unreasonable, but sometimes provoked by human behavior, such as cultic sacrilege (the desecration of a temple). In each case the deity's own "character" will be directly implicated. However, the wrath of the gods can also be triggered by other kinds of behavior, more related to moral, or legal matters, such as, for example, the breaking of treaties, of which the god is guarantor. This theme can also take on a function of political justification: thus in the poem of Tukulti-ninurta (13th cent. BC) Assyrian intervention against Babylon is justified by the fact that the Babylonian gods are outraged because the Babylonian kings have repeatedly violated border treaties with the Assyrian kings. The parallels with the wrath of YHWH over the breaking of the covenant are obvious, but the theme is presented in the opposite way: the prophet lashes out at Assyria because it has failed to recognize that it is merely an instrument of YHWH's outrage against his people (cf. Is 10:5-19). The wartime defeat is thus attributed to the outrage of one's God but is not a justification of the enemy. Within the biblical framework, then, these ancient traditions, indebted to an anthropomorphic conception of the relationship between the divine and the human, are reinterpreted from a salvific-historical perspective, based on covenant theology. In the case then of the ancient neareastern gods, the outraged intervention of the deity is certainly often – though not always – attributable to the god's wounded sense of justice, but the idea always remains that, somehow, his violent character is involved.

3.   Characteristics of divine wrath in the OT

Certainly, some texts present God angry for inexplicable reasons: as, for example, of Jacob's night struggle (Gen 32:23-33) or the mysterious episode of Moses' circumcision in Ex 4:24-26, or even the text of 2 Sam 6:6-11, in which God is angry at Uzzah taking hold of the Ark of the Covenant and strikes the unfortunate man down. However, all these episodes are reinterpreted from a theological perspective: particularly to introduce the idea of God's transcendence and the ineluctability of certain commandments, such as circumcision. We are far from mythological language here.

Nevertheless, what triggers God's wrath in most cases is man's sin. In this sense, an unexpected misfortune can be interpreted as revealing sin and wrath. Consider, for example, the account in 2 Sam 12:15-18 in which the death of the son of guilt is attributed to GOD's condemnation of David's sin with Bathsheba. Again in Ex 9:14 God punishes the Egyptians for their treatment of the Israelites, and in 2 Sam 24:21 the whole people are struck because of the king's sin: we have here a corporate conception of responsibility far from our own attitude but absolutely unquestioned at that time. Unlike the normal perception in other cultures of the Ancient Near East, when it is not possible to attribute the misfortune to a specific fault, in the Bible the cause is not identified with the capriciousness of the divinity, but we are being clearly told that man is sinful before God.

However, this conception will later be criticized, and it will give rise to the problem discussed in Job: faced with his friends who try to induce him to confess a guilt that he does not recognize as his, Job protests his innocence in a kind of defiance of God. What is important to note is that, in this case, God does not thunder at Job's presumption, but declares him righteous and satisfies his innermost desire by revealing himself to him in his powerfulness. As can be seen, the depth of Israel's theological thinking is far removed from mythological conceptions, and the theme of God's wrath and its relation to human sin ends up becoming a stimulus for delving deeper into important questions of theodicy. Even GOD's attitude described in the first pages of Genesis is not one of wrath in the face of human sin. The first time wrath is mentioned is when Moses attempts to evade his calling (Ex 4:13-14). So God's wrath is unleashed against man's unwillingness to fulfil God's plans, and in a special way against the breaking of the covenant, with particular reference to the mistreatment of the orphan and the widow; cf. Ex 22:21-24. Another of the triggers of God's wrath is the "murmuring of the wilderness," that is, Israel's stubborn refusal to get in tune with GOD's plan by relying on his providence. Consider in this regard the episodes we read in Nm 11; 14; 16.

Israel's rebellion against God's sovereignty is the main cause of divine wrath in the OT; and it does not matter whether the rebellion is due to murmuring against God (Deut. 1:26-36; Ps 78:21-22), flagrant disobedience to divine command (Josh. 7:1), more generally to disregard for God's word (2 Chr. 36:15-16) or idolatry (Ex 32:1-10; Num 25:1-5; Deut. 13:2ff.). Failure to ensure social justice also makes Israel subject to divine wrath, insofar as it is an implicit break of the covenant (Ps 50:21-22; Is 1.23-24; 42.24-25; Am 8:4-10; Mic 6). Much of Deuteronomistic history is built on the theme of Israel transgressing the covenant (Josh 23:16; Jdg 2:20): Israel violates the laws because it wants to irritate God (cf. Jer 7:18). However, the arrogance of the pagan peoples also triggers God's wrath (Isa 10:12). The references to divine anger that appear especially, but not only, in exilic and postexilic times change the object from Israel to the nations that oppress her: the same nations that at one time are instruments of the wrath directed against Israel (Jdg 2:11-15; 2 Kgs 13:3; 2 Chr 36;15-17; Zech 7:11-14; Lam 2), at another time are themselves the objects of God's wrath (Jer 50:25; Eze 36:1-7; Mal 1:2-5). This divine wrath directed against the nations has basically two motives: the first is vengeance directed against those who have done harm to his people (Jer 10:25; Ez 25; Nah 1). These texts seem to have a nationalistic perspective, but nevertheless one should not forget the theme of election, which makes Israel to be God's people and that this particular election is also manifested by a particular protection. In other passages God's anger is directed against the nations not only because they oppressed Israel, but also because they failed to realize that in doing so they were not acting autonomously, but were merely pure instruments wielded by God (Is 10:5-19; Jer 25;7-14).

As time goes on, the theme of divine wrath changes and becomes more and more universal and tends to flare up in the face of the prevalence of injustice in history. The growth of malice among men will be countered by a final intervention of God, in which he breaks into human history his with his justice and salvation. This gives rise to the theme of the "time of the Lord's indignation" and the "day of the Lord's wrath." This is especially present in apocalyptic texts (Is 26:20; Ez 22:24, Dan 8:19; Ez 7:19; Zeph 1:15, 18; Prv 11:4; Job 21:30). Since the present world is God's enemy, its eschatological moment is regarded as the day when God defeats his enemies. In any case, after the manifestation of God's wrath, there is the possibility of a period when reconciliation is established and God's people flourish (Is 27:1-6). What seems to be ruled out in any case is the idea of God's wrath as a function of his character: the God of Israel is not angry because he is led to it by an anthropomorphic predisposition of his own, but rather because he is affected by human behavior.

However, the theme of God's wrath is inextricably linked with that of his kingship. In the sources of the Ancient Near East, it is possible to see how wrath is the characteristic feature of rulers: Sargon II acts in a sudden fit of rage, and Pharaoh is also represented, in a formulaic and stylized way, as Sekhmet rising up against those who do not bey his commands. In these texts, the anger of the ruler is not a character trait of the ruler, but an expression indicating the political will to dominate and extend territory. This language is used by the biblical texts as a way to speak of God's omnipotence, who acts as king in the face of the transgressions of his people, but also acts against the chaotic elements to assert his sovereignty over the world (Job 9:4-13; 26; Ps 89:5-13).

As mentioned above, a frequent image of divine wrath is that of the cup, which takes on the value of a symbol of this theological theme. It is used in the OT to indicate God's wrath in its consequences on the offender: it indicates the upheaval that seizes him in the face of punishment (Jer 25:15). The cup contains God's punitive wrath, which deprives the one who drinks of it of his wits (cf. Jer 13:13; 51:39; Obad 16; Nah 3:11; Ps 11:6; 60:5). The image speaks of the ambivalence of wine as a drink that can be a sign of joy and happiness but can also lead to drunkenness and loss of reason. Another possible origin of the image of the cup of wrath can be found in the oracular cup: the cup by which divine judgment takes place, distinguishing the guilty from the innocent. In this sense Jer 51:7 can say that Babylon was a golden cup in the hand of God, with which he intoxicated all the earth; of its wine the peoples drank, therefore they became mad.

4.   Divine wrath in the New Testament

In contrast with the Old Testament pages, in the New Testament the Greek lexicon on wrath is relatively poor: the words used are *thymos* and *orge*. This lexical difference undoubtedly corresponds to a downplaying of the theme's importance, not, however, to its disappearance, as is sometimes too hastily concluded. Per se *thymos* represents inner emotion, while *orge* expresses more outward expression. The LXX, however, uses the two words indifferently to indicate the wide lexical spectrum Hebrew possesses on the subject; the NT also conforms to this lack of precision.

In the Gospels the concept of *wrath* appears mostly in an eschatological context; cf. the Baptist's lines in Lk 3:7; Mt 3:7. There is also the connection between wrath and the destruction of Jerusalem, in the eschatological discourse of Lk 21, with particular reference to the fall of Jerusalem (v. 23), therefore in a context that is not immediately eschatological but rather historical. The verb *orgizomai* is used in a metaphorical sense to refer to the king in the parables who represents God in Mt 18:34; 22:7; Lk 14:21. In Mk 3:5 Jesus is said to be angry at the hardness of heart of his opponents, but the verb *orgizomai* and the corresponding adjective are never used in the NT with God as the subject. An allusion to the subject of divine wrath can almost certainly be found in the cup of Mark 14:36, which recalls the "cup of wrath" of Is 51:17-23; Jer 25:15-29. The image serves to emphasize Jesus' identification with sinners and is used by Jesus on two occasions to indicate his impending passion: the dialogue with the sons of Zebedee (Mk 10:38f. and parallel texts) and the prayer at Gethsemane (Mk 14:36; Mt 26:39; Lk 22:42; cf. also Jn 18:11). Jesus thus represents his own passion as taking upon himself the judgment of God, thus resolving Job's contradiction. The only explicit reference to divine wrath occurs in Jn 3:36: "Whoever believes in the Son has eternal life; whoever does not obey the Son will not see life, but the wrath of God hangs over him." The sense used is clearly non-eschatological: the experience of divine wrath is the opposite of the eternal life that is experienced in the present hour by believers: note the present tense verbs in the text.

As far as the Pauline *corpus* is concerned, the theme of divine wrath has both a historical and an eschatological aspect. The association of the concept of wrath with the idea of final judgment is clearly present in Rom 2:5; 2:8; 5:9; 1 Thess 1:10; 5:9. But the wrath expected in the future is already experienced now by those who resist God's saving plan in Christ, just as the hope of eternal life is already now part of the experience of believers. The Jews who persecute Christ and believers are subject to the final wrath (1 Thess 2:16), which is particularly revealed when God delivers the people to the consequences of their choice (Rom 1:18, 32). Paul speaks explicitly of God's wrath only in Rom 1:18; Eph 5:6 and Col 3:6. God's wrath in Paul is never anthropomorphized, so as to be a consequence of his wrathful character, but it is always linked to his executing justice with regard to sin.

God's wrath is generally understood as the consequence of spiritual alienation from God (Rom 1:24,26,28; 1 Th 2:16). Condemnation at the final judgment is presented as the fulfillment of this alienation from God. Thus God's wrath contrasts with salvation (1 Thess 5:9), and with justification itself (Rom 1:17-18; 5:9).

God's wrath should also be linked back with his love: however, love and holiness are a permanent feature, while wrath is relative to human sin. If there is no sin, there is also no wrath. Moreover, God's opposition to sin exposes man to his wrath, but God's response is to offer in Christ the means of deliverance from wrath itself. Christ is the means of propitiation (Rom 3:25), but it should be noted that this means is given by God himself. In Christ, God himself absorbs the destructive consequences of sin. Thus, a division is created between those who are delivered from wrath through trust in his

merciful love (1 Thess 1:10; 5:9; Rom 5:9) and those who remain under the power of this wrath because they despise this mercy (Rom
2:4-5,8; 9:22-23; Eph 2:3; 5:6; Col 3:6).

In the Apocalypse we can see a similar perspective to that St Paul:
wrath is an eschatological phenomenon that already casts its shadow
on present time: the judgment on Babylon (Rome) heralds the coming of Christ at the end of the present age. Cf. the sixth seal (6:16-
17), the seventh trumpet (11:18) and all of ch. 16, which describes
the sequence of events leading to the destruction of Babylon as "the
seven vials of God's wrath." This cup corresponds to the cup of passion and lust that Babylon made the nations drink (14:8). This same
cup becomes the cup of God's wrath (14:10): God, then, uses human
passion to exercise his punishing wrath. Sin has a self-destructive
characteristic, and God's wrath is not irrational or vindictive, but
surrenders the worshippers of the beast to this process of self-destruction. The most characteristic image is that of the wrath of the
Lamb: The Lamb, in chapters 5-6, is presented as the one who is
slaughtered to redeem men for God (5:9), his wrath is thus the wrath
of the One who has gone through the experience of distance from
God through death; those who are faithful to him can be delivered
from this distance, because he has taken it upon himself: it is by his
death that the Lamb overcomes.

If God is infinitely merciful, how can we explain the existence of demons and hell and the possibility of eternal damnation even for humans?

(Andrea Villafiorita)

Hell is a serious problem.

If we stop a moment to contemplate the reality of hell, the horror of eternal, endless suffering, we are left speechless: days, years centuries of ... suffering? How is it possible that eternal suffering exists? And how is it possible that God, in his infinite mercy, allows such punishment to exist?

It is a difficult issue, to such an extent that there have always been Christians who have sought to deny that hell is an eternal, never-ending condition. From early on in the Church there have been voices proposing a limit to the eternity of hell, claiming that there will come a moment, at the end of time, when hell will be emptied and all the souls there will be redeemed and ushered into the bliss of Paradise. This alleged end of hell has been given the name of *apocatastasis*, and apparently was first advocated by a third-century author, a Greek-speaking theologian, Origen, whose positions on this point were later condemned. Over the centuries the proposal has been taken up by various theologians, but it has always been rejected by the Church.

An alternative hypothesis to deny the eternity of punishment in hell and which still enjoys some popularity today, especially in some Protestant communities, is that people who have turned permanently against God will not be condemned, but upon their death will simply cease to exist and be "annihilated." This is a bizarre theory that denies God's faithfulness to his work and forgets that God created us to last for ever, and even when our history should turn for the worst, he does not go back on his creation.

These and other hypotheses try to sidestep the problem of hell, the paradox of an eternity of suffering, but in reality they fall away from the faith of the Church. On these troubling questions, we are not allowed to take comfortable shortcuts, adopting simplistic positions, because, when we deal with realities that escape our direct experience we must stick to Christ's revelation and the way it has been interpreted in the Church. And on this point the Magisterium has solemnly committed itself and, authoritatively interpreting the biblical data, has affirmed that hell exists, and that it is possible for someone to end up there. Early pronouncements to this effect are found, for example, in the profession of faith called *Quicumque* or that of Pope Pelagius I in the sixth century. This is a constant teaching, held by the Church since time immemorial.

Even the hypothesis, which has recently been aired in Catholic circles, that while hell exists it may be empty, is in fact unconvincing: if hell were indeed empty, it would not exist *for us*, because ending up in it would become an entirely unreal hypothesis. In fact, if going to hell were so difficult that no one goes there, how can Christ in the Gospels have warned us of the possibility – which he seems to consider entirely real – that the ultimate outcome of life is failure? "If your hand causes you to sin, cut it off; it is better for you to enter life with one hand, rather than with both hands to go into hell, into the unquenchable fire" (Mk 9:42; and see many other texts, e.g. Mt 13:30, 41-43 or the Last Judgment in the grandiose depiction in Mt 25:31-46).

Hell exists, although the Church has always refused to affirm infallibly that any specific person after his or her death has ended up in hell (it is not affirmed even of Judas!). See, for example, Pope Francis' Morning Homily of April 8th, 2020). We know that someone is in hell: the devil and the other rebellious angels, and that – indeed – hell was created precisely for them. For example, in Mt 25:41 Jesus states that "eternal fire" was "prepared for the devil and his angels"). This helps us to understand a first important aspect of hell: since the angels do not have a body, not even rebellious angels, hell should be considered above all as a situation, a kind of kingdom (see e.g., Lk 11:18) composed of all those – angels and human beings – who have chosen to set themselves against God and are crystallized in this choice forever. Hell is not the prison, the torture chamber to which God confines the damned, but it is the condition of those who have *chosen* to turn away from God permanently. And so, the problem shifts: hell is eternal because turning permanently against God, whether for the devil or for damned souls, is a free and – indeed – definitive, and therefore eternal, choice.

But now we are back to square one: why is the choice final? Why does God allow man, or the devil, to choose definitively against him? Andagain: why does this choice against God result in a state of suffering, of punishment?

Keeping in mind that we are moving on the threshold of mystery, some observations can help us. First of all, we must consider that we cannot reach Heaven by our own creaturely strength, because salvation is a free, gratuitous gift from God, a gift that God offers to all men and angels, but a gift that he wants to be accepted and not imposed. For God wants to be loved, not forcibly served, and no one can be forced to love. "I no longer call you servants, for the servant does not know what his master does; but I have called you friends" (Jn 15:15). If God were to save us without our consent, we would be his servants, not friends. And so God, in order to be loved, accepts the *risk* of rejection, and for our choice to be serious, real, God has set a limit beyond which the choice for him or against him becomes final. This limit for man is death, and for angelic creatures some unspecified moment (some believe the beginning of time, but that is just a guess). After this moment, the choice cannot be changed.

We thus understand why it is not correct to think of a temporary hell, as Origen argued, that at the moment of the apocatastasis would be emptied: how can we say that the choice for God is free if in the end everyone, sooner or later, is as it were forced to choose *for* God? If we say that the choice *against* God is only provisional, honesty would lead us to affirm that in order to remain free even the choice *for* God can only be provisional, so that in the end neither man nor angel would be allowed to choose anything in a serious and final way.

Hell, seen from this perspective, appears less and less as a punishment and more and more as a choice, a choice that is certainly bewildering and somewhat surreal, but still a choice. Recent documents of the Magisterium point precisely in this direction; soberly, for example, the Catechism of the Catholic Church states:

"We cannot be united with God unless we freely choose to love him. But we cannot love God if we sin grievously against him, against our neighbor or against ourselves [...] To die in mortal sin without having repented and without accepting God's merciful love is to remain forever separated from him by our own free choice. And it is this state of ultimate self-exclusion from communion with God and the blessed that is designated by the word 'hell'" (no. 1033; and see also John Paul II's *Catechesis* of July 28, 1999).

Having specified the arguments why it is reasonable that the condition of rejection of God be eternal, it remains to be understood why such a choice entails any punishment, why, that is, hell is a place of suffering.

The most intense pain of the damned souls arises from the realization that they have radically failed in life. We – and the angels too – have been made for good, and, whether we like it or not, our highest good is God. To choose *against* God signifies cancelling the very possibility of adhering to our highest good, and thus of attaining the ultimate (and ultimately only) meaning of our existence.

To this can be added that he person who chooses *against* God also chooses to manage his relationship with creatures in a disordered way, that is, he chooses to live his relationship with his neighbor and with the goods (pleasures) of life in a negative way. As regards neighbors, it is rightly asserted that those who hate their own brothers go to hell: the Lord takes mutual relationships seriously, and those who choose hatred weave their relationships as a web of hatred, and will eventually find themselves trapped and responded to in this hatred for their brothers.

In this respect, both Heaven and Hell extend the lifestyle chosen before death: those who have chosen to hate will hate and be hated by their fellow sufferers, and those who have chosen to love will love and be loved for eternity.

As for created goods, theologians like to say that those who have misused material reality will suffer a kind of vengeance from material reality itself, meaning that those who use the goods of this world in a disordered way will be "consumed" by those very goods. This is a suffering that theology calls the "punishment of the senses" or "fire," and which has stirred the imagination of poets and artists, originating the idea of the *contrapasso*, or "counter-suffering". But on this point one must be very cautious, because fanciful representations, which appealed so much in the past, risk scandalizing today's mentality. A better way of understanding this is to think that when we misuse material goods, already in this life, beyond a momentary well-being, we remain crushed by these same goods. Thus, for example, those who use food in a disordered way become slaves to it (with the vice of gluttony) to the point that they can no longer care for their deepest good because they are burdened by an increasing addiction to food itself. The hellish state prolongs and absolutizes the relationship with the material goods we have chosen in earthly life, so that if we had used them in an orderly manner, material goods would have cooperated with our bliss, but having used them in a disordered manner, they will permanently crush us and distance us from our ultimate good. In this respect also: as in life, so after death.

So, hell is not primarily divine punishment, and the suffering of hell is not God's vengeful retribution. Hell, more simply, is the dramatic and necessary consequence of a definite choice of hatred against God and disordered adherence to the goods of this world. In this sense, it is not God who condemns to hell, but it is man who chooses Heaven or Hell, directing his life in one direction or another, as C.S Lewis well summarized, noting that "the gates of hell are locked from within" (C.S. Lewis: *The Problem of Pain*, ch. VIII. *Hell*, London 1940).

St. Catherine of Genoa, a great mystic of the 1400s, when speaking of Purgatory stated strikingly that "on God's side Paradise has no doors. Whoever wishes to enter it enters, because God is all mercy and to receive us into his glory he stands turned toward us with open arms" (*Treatise on Purgatory*, 14). This is a real consideration, and it applies inversely to the souls in Hell: the presence of God would, for those who chose to hate God, be an intolerable suffering, worse than Hell itself. The damned do not enter Heaven because *they do not want to* enter it, and Hell is simply the place where God, in his mercy, is hidden, where one lives *without* God and *against* God, and therefore, tragically, in a situation of suffering and despair.

What has been said so far holds true on an objective, somewhat generic level, but when we begin to think about these realities as concrete possibilities in our lives, we emerge from abstract reflection and some questions become urgent for us: how many souls are really in hell? Or, how difficult is it to go to hell? And, how difficult is it for *me* (or for this or that person dear to me) to go to hell?

Here our reasoning goes out the window and we are confronted with mystery, so much so that different historical epochs have argued, depending on the dominant sensibility, either that hell is almost full or that it is almost empty: many ancients, for example, who emphasized individual commitment and ethical responsibility, considered salvation almost an exception, while contemporaries, who have a very high and perhaps somewhat simplistic view of God's mercy, like to think of a sparsely populated hell. The idea of an empty hell, indeed, almost smiles at contemporary man, because it seems the only possibility reasonably composable with God's mercy.

But mercy should not be trivialized. *Mercy* means that God loves man, and his love is so intense that he, in order to save man, chose to become man and die on a cross. The Passion and the cross are not simply acts that automatically accomplish apocatastasis, but are rather the living testimony to the seriousness of our life and ultimate destiny, to how much God cares about our choice and pleads with us to choose *seriously* for him and for our salvation. As Jesus said to St. Angela of Foligno in 1301, "I did not love you as a joke." God's mercy is seen in the cross, and the cross does not mean that hell is empty because God is merciful, but, rather, it should help us understand the size and gravity of our sin, the tragic nature of choosing against God and the dramatic nature of its consequences. God dies to convince us to choose to live.

Thinking about hell, however, should not lead us to uncontrolled anxiety about our own or our loved ones' salvation, but rather should help us understand that God's love is a serious matter and not a *joke*. And that this life is the time of choice, the time when we are called to love God, and therefore it is a precious time and, again, not a *joke*. We cannot reduce God's love – mercy – to a kind of do-goodism that debases our ability to choose and for which everything is fine. God could have taken us all to heaven, attracting and bewitching us with his infinite beauty, but instead he chose to treat us somehow as his "equals"; he did not enslave us but wanted to make a "covenant" with us, as he did with Abraham, with the people of the Old Testament and as he does now with the Church (visible and invisible), that is, with the community of the saved. He placed great value on our freedom and regarded it as an indispensable condition of our love, of our choice for him, even accepting the risk that his blood would be shed in vain. Hell does not deny God's mercy, and God, in his mercy, has gone as far as death, and death on a cross, in order to convince us to love him.

"One thing is certain: God, who is love, does not hate even the devil. The cause of distance from God for eternity lies not in God, but in man" (Ziegenaus, *Die Zukunft der Schöpfung in Gott: Eschatologie*, MM-Verlag, 1996, p. 183).

Today, cosmology is virtually unanimous that the universe originated from the Big Bang some 14 billion years ago. What then is the point of the biblical account of creation in six days (cf. Gen 1:1-31)?

(Antonio Staglianò)

1. Galileo Galilei to justify himself against his accusers quotes Baronius' statement, "the intention of the Holy Spirit is to teach us how to go to heaven and not how the heaven goes." The biblical account of creation in six days is not a cosmology treatise on the beginning of the expanding universe. It does, however, tell the truth about man, "created in the image and likeness of God," and about his salvation, which is "to live like God," obeying in all freedom the Creator's commandments, to realize his humanity in fullness, loving all his brothers and sisters and, thus, living happily in the earthly paradise, until reaching the ultimate destiny of eternal joy in the heavenly Paradise, represented by the "heaven of heavens": Scripture therefore teaches "how to go to heaven." It is for science to explain "how the heaven goes," observing it with the scientific method which looks for "necessary demonstrations and sense experiences." Galileo built his spyglass to contemplate the planets, the moon, and the sun and had sufficient grounds to "prove" that *it is the earth that revolves around the sun and not vice versa.* He was tried and condemned by the Catholic Church as a result of a literalist and

fundamentalist interpretation of the Bible. Today it is taken for granted that the biblical account was written according to a particular "literary genre," and that it needs to be understood according to what the authors meant to communicate. Literalists, on the other hand, took some verses of Scripture to be literally true, such as Josh 10:12-13, where Joshua at the battle of Gibeon *commands the sun to stop*. And the sun stopped. Now, if Scripture speaks the truth, how could Galileo affirm the contrary? Who is telling the truth? What is the source of truth: the authority of God's Word in Scripture or Galileo's scientific observation? Already in modernity, the metaphor of the two books (that of Nature and that of Scripture) was elaborated – to avoid conflicts between science and faith – keeping the sphere of faith distinct from that of science, so as not to give in to the temptation of fundamentalism, a harbinger of serious harm, because it creates ostracism of all kinds.

2. Galileo's spyglass developed and, in the 20th century, became the Hubble astronomical telescope, and discovered new galaxies. Today, astrophysicists are able to make certain measurements and they believe they establish accurately that the universe began 13.8 billion years ago with a "big bang". All the energy in the universe was compressed in singularity in the cosmic vacuum and, by "inflation," began to expand rapidly. Only three hundred thousand years after the *Big Bang*, light – embedded in the cosmic plasma – broke away from it, producing an extraordinary acceleration, giving rise to stars, planets, galaxies, galaxy clusters, black holes: even "white holes" and "wormholes," tunnels that would allow one to pass from one dimension of reality to another? Of course! Of the latter, however, science has no information, although they are predicted by the

1915 equations of Einstein's *Theory of General Relativity*. The scientific imagination of the world has changed. Everything moves in the universe, even the sun, dragging the solar system with it, thanks to its enormous mass. And it is a wonder to consider *the stability* of certain ratios and measurements in the earth's spinning around the sun (as well as around its own axis). Life on planet earth depends on it. If the distances did not remain perfect in the "habitable zone," we would be scorched by solar winds or freeze to death from ultra cold temperatures.

3. This image of the world, if truly scientific, is destined to be transformed and is already changing. The new telescope of the 21st century – the *James Web Space* Telecope – equipped with (infrared) technology to penetrate into the depths of the universe is already posing many problems thanks to the objects it captures with its images. According to some scientists, the discovery of spiral galaxies, larger than those currently known, born just 250-400 million years after the *Big Bang*, raises important questions about the date of the first "big bang." These are galaxies that – by the Standard Model – need several billion years to form. If so it will be necessary to backdate the beginning of the *Big Bang* by a few billion years. That would be surprising, however, because it would melt – like snow in the sun – the (scientific) narrative produced so far. The other hypothesis is that the model describing the formation of galaxies must be revised. Even this, however, would be no small thing, because of the innovation of the picture of the world, with parameters, constants, and mathematical measurements used for the purpose of advancing the knowledge of our universe. On top of this, developments and successes in quantum physics – working in the infinitely small of

elementary particles – put scientists of the infinitely large in a position to hypothesize different images of the world: apart from the *multiverse* hypothesis – for which inflation affected not only the "bubble" of our universe, but billions of others "wallowing" in the cosmic void –, our universe would have arisen *not so much from a Big Bang, but rather from a Big Bounce*, a great upturn, that of an old universe, first expanded and then contracted (*Big Crunch*) becoming an "unstable singularity," as containing an infinity of energy in a space so small as to be as if nonexistent.

4. On the other hand, after Einstein's equations of *General Relativity*, phenomena of strange beauty can be imagined in the universe. The young physicist, Karl Schwarzschild, from a hospital bed, wrote to Einstein, interpreting his equations: he imagined a super massive star (20 times, 100 times, 1000 or a million times larger than the solar mass) which when it dies is attracted by the force of gravity toward its center and implodes into itself, becoming a black hole. Even today astrophysics studies the "Schwarzschild radius," or the radius below which a collapsed star becomes a black hole: nothing within this radius can escape the star's gravitational field, not even light! The star curls up into itself and "forces" all its mass into a singularity without space-time, obviously too dense not to bounce back and, therefore, "burst" (a *Big Bang from a Big Bounce*) starting new stars or constellations. *It really does not suit theology (and thus Christian preaching) to bind itself too closely to accounts from science about the beginning of the universe.* The approaches of theology and science are different and remain distinct. Although they cannot/should not remain "separate." Unfortunately, it was a quirk of Enlightenment modernity to interpret "distinction" as "separation." The

Enlightenment separated and opposed reason and faith, believing and knowing, with a bogus, critically unchecked dogma that has become a prejudice that is still persistent today: "faith believes and does not know, only reason knows and, because it knows, it must not believe." The vice lies in establishing that only reason (that is, scientific reason) is the source of true knowledge or the truth of reality, while Revelation (any revelation), accepted in faith, would be a mythology or fable, to which no rational credence should be given.

5. In this scheme of things, the creation account in the book of Genesis is considered mythological, and would not let us know anything about the beginning of the world. The first beginning, in fact, would not need a Creator. If anything, the world *originated from chaos by chance.* The Greeks were right, for whom "in the beginning was Chaos." Is there Chaos or Logos in the beginning? If science remains respectful of its method of seeking truth – and *does not turn into scientism, which is an ideology* – it cannot lead to either faith or unbelief. To believe or not to believe is a philosophical and existential option. There are many scientists (recognized as such) who are good believers. One must beware of the Enlightenment bias that inhabits even the most open minds. An example: the first person to discover "scientifically" (equations in hand) the *Big Bang*, was a priest, George Lemaître. Acording to this theory, the universe at first was as if nestled in a "primitive atom" that then exploded. Lemaître presented the equations to Einstein, who rejected them, because – here's the bias! – he believed that "the priest wanted to prove the existence of his Creator." Today even atheist scientists agree with Lemaître. For Pope Francis: "The Big-Bang, which today is considered the origin of the world, does not contradict divine creative

intervention but demands it. Evolution in nature does not contradict the notion of Creation, because evolution presupposes the creation of beings that evolve." He was speaking to the Pontifical Academy of Sciences (on Oct. 27, 2014). He went on, "when we read in Genesis the account of Creation, we risk imagining that God was a magician, complete with a magic wand capable of doing all things. But he was not. He created beings and let them develop according to the internal laws that he gave to each one, so that they would develop, so that they would reach their own fullness." With great intellectual honesty, the Pope introduces a distinction between "beginning" (scrutinized by science) and "origin" (about which science can say nothing): "Origin is a theological concept and presupposes a Creator. The beginning, on the other hand, does not presuppose one: it is a scientific concept according to which at "x" time what is called the Big Bang occurred." At the origin there is a Supreme Principle who creates out of love. *"To create out of love" means precisely "to generate."* Unlike man who "creates by producing his artifacts," even those that today amaze like Artificial Intelligence, *God is fruitful in his love,* so the whole creation is the result of his "bowels of love." It is Love that is the principle of everything: "the love that moves the sun and the other stars" or "the love that quenches this heaven" (Dante, *The Divine Comedy*).

6. Of course, beyond any trivializing anthropomorphism, God did not create with a "magic wand", as Pope Francis has also said. This means that "there is a reason why he created the world, freely and by an act of love. We are the fruit of this free and loving act of God. A magician does not create out of love, but uses magic; God creates out of love." Beyond all concordism (i.e., the search for

concord between the biblical text and the results of scientific re-search), the time immemorial admonition also applies today. When we speak of the Big Bang and Genesis: "we must be careful not to trigger dangerous short circuits." Genesis is a biblical account and is subject to exegesis, "Scripture is never literal. Let us not stop at Adam and Eve. Divine inspiration must be related to the culture of the time, these are symbolic (allegorical) accounts to express the Creation of the universe. God, on the other hand, is the ultimate cause of Creation, he does not fill in the gaps that science cannot explain (like 'Intelligent Design'), but he is on another level" (Pope Francis). This does not mean that *analogies* cannot and should not be *sought* today that help compare the two narratives (the scientific one and the biblical one) showing their not weak assonances. Scientific questions can inspire theological conceptions and vice versa, not to say that in the invoked *transdisciplinarity* of the plural sciences (cf. *Ad Theologiam promovendam*) there exists the possibility of a mutual "fermentation" of all knowledge, whereby the truths acquired in the different fields of human knowledge must be able to be translated into the categories and concepts proper to each individual knowledge, all drawing mutual benefit from it.

7. In this perspective, the biblical account in six days would pose no problem for the scientific account of the *Big Bang* placed at 13.8 billion years, thanks to what physicists are beginning to tell us about time "not existing" and the contraction of time into "timeless singularities" or even the different rearticulation of past-present-future. The language of myth can no longer be relegated to the "world of fairy tales": the ability of human wisdom to concentrate in a few words "meanings" that, in other fields, stretch over millions of years

must be recognized. The book of Genesis tells of the creation of the world from nothing and introduces into the creative act the image and likeness of God for man, who then has the task of "naming" all things, as "concretizing" them, that is, grafting them into his own being. God creates man at the end of the creative journey – which ends with his rest and not before – by endowing him with intelligence and freedom. From this comes a great provocation to the scientific account: if everything evolves so that man emerges as an event on earth (cf. *anthropic principle*, in its weak and strong formulation), what "kind of man" is destined to evolve? This is a question that science can never answer unless it enters into "synergy" with philosophy and all other critical knowledge. The knowledge of faith (i.e., the Revelation of God in Christ, found in the Gospels and throughout the New Testament), through theology (which develops it in its critical and culturally appreciable form) *posits the hypothesis of eucharistic man* as the final goal to which the evolution of the universe tends. Not man "in general" or even man defined by Aristotle as a "rational animal" or any other wisdom about the human, but Eucharistic man.

8. And the man who shows his original stuff, that is, the man endowed with sensitivity to human meaning, *open to honor the justice of love* and, therefore, to acknowledge as love not all the appearances of love, but *only the truth of love*, that for which to love is to push the gift of life to the point of dying for others. One can then better understand the meaning of the Genesis account, grasped in the light of Christian Revelation, which sees in Jesus the image in which God created man. In the love of the Trinity love there is an eternal begetting of the Son from the Father and it is in this "eternal

generation" that man is created, "created by generation" and not by production. This is a theological challenge presented by the biblical account, so that the scientific account, does not reduce the humanity of man, imagining a post-human condition, based on silicon: the android of Artificial Intelligence. No, the human being is not replaceable. For man was created in love, for love, by love.

The Bible was written by different human authors. Why then does the Church affirm that it is "God's Word"?

(Călin-Daniel Pațulea)

1. Introduction

The Bible, before being a religious, sacred book, a written word, has been a historical event lived out over centuries, whose protagonists were God and mankind, represented first and foremost by the people of Israel. Such history is witnessed in the Old Testament, but it has since involved all mankind, with the purpose of knowing, through Revelation, the mystery and vocation to the contemporaneity of Christ in the New Testament. In the pages of the Bible we are presented with the history of salvation, a living and dynamic history in which God manifested himself to man, entrusting him with God's message of salvation. This has been summarized as follows, "Salvation comes in stages, revealing the divine pedagogy [...]. With the coming of Jesus we have the fulfillment of the promises and the new covenant. Christ is the key to the Christian reading of the Bible [...] The more one scrutinizes the Scriptures, the closer one comes to the mystery of the 'unsearchable riches of Christ' (Eph 3:8)" (Orsatti, *Introduction to the New Testament*, Lugano-Reggiani -I- 2005, p. 17). Sacred Scripture is thus not a book of the past, but is the book of the present and will be the book of the future of the community of believers. The task of Christians and of the Church, our task, is to discover and welcome the truth contained in it, the bread of life, allowing ourselves to be led by the Holy Spirit, in Christ, to the encounter with the Father, because "Scripture is the book of God and the book of our life, of our history" (Mazzeo, *Come e perché leggere la Bibbia*, Milano 2008, p. 9).

2. How and why can we call the Bible the "Word of God"?

God made himself known to man gradually, in a pedagogical way. He went in search of man, manifested himself to him, initiating Revelation, that is, *He removed the veil*. He made himself known to a group of people deprived of freedom, freeing some Jews from Egyptian slavery, starting for this group the path of freedom. God spoke and the people responded, beginning a dialogical relationship that leads toward another important event, namely, the covenant, the willingness to live "as two": "I will be your God and you will be my people". This willingness for communion commits God to be the faithful guide of the people and the people to observe the "ten words" which are a visible sign of a love. Israel tells its history, a sacred history that it first hands down orally, and then fixes in a written text describing a religious experience that leads to the birth of the Bible. God guides this experience toward a "goal that only he knows, toward which he makes everything converge, in supreme and mysterious respect for human freedom" (Orsatti, 2005, p. 55). He will be the great director, as Vatican II teaches: "God chose men whom he used in the possession of their faculties and abilities, so that, acting in them and through them, they might write as true authors all and only those things which he willed" (*Dei Verbum*, 11).

God called for the cooperation of people with different talents, similar in everything to their contemporaries, with whom they shared the mentality and many conceptions about the world and life. The Bible thus bears the human marks of style, language, customs and mentality of the time in which it was written. Thus the Council again states, "Since God in Sacred Scripture spoke through men and in the human manner, the interpreter [...] must carefully seek what the hagiographers actually intended to mean and what it pleased God to manifest in their words. To derive the intention of the hagiographers, one must take into account among other things literary genres" (*Dei Verbum,* 12). All its content, with all literary genres, are "inspired" by God; the Bible is God's Word, that is, "inspired." Its consequent normative value is reflected in at least two classic NT passages: 2 Tim 3:16 and 2 Pet 1:20-21 (cf. 3:16).

The Word of God starts from God and became incarnate in the person of Jesus of Nazareth. It is a living word that descends from the transcendental world into our existential reality to guide the believer's free choices: "Scripture is in fact considered the record of divine Revelation, that is, the human documentation of the Word by which God made himself known, first through the prophets and then in fullness in the Son Jesus" (Doglio, *Introduction to the Bible,* Brescia 2010, p. 5). Sacred Scripture is a revelation written by believing men; it is the testimony in written form of what God wants to convey to us for our salvation.

3. The function of Scripture is to transmit to us the truths that introduce us into an understanding of the salvation that has Jesus Christ as its center (cf. 2 Tim 3:16)

St. Paul speaks of with precision, stating that "all Scripture is inspired by God, useful for teaching, persuading, correcting and training in righteousness, so that the man of God may be complete and well prepared for every good work" (2 Tim 3:16). We find there, uniquely, the adjective "inspired by God" (in Greek *theópneustos*, composed of *theo, Theos, God,* and *pneustos*, from *pneō*, to *blow*) to indicate its divine origin, that by which it is inspired, that is, written with the special assistance of the Holy Spirit. It is not the thought of men, even though written by men, since God remains the primary author of Scripture, even though he asks for active and intelligent cooperation from men. It is divinely inspired, *God-breathed*, that is, coming from the mouth of God. The Church professes that the books of the Bible contain God's truth, "for our salvation" (*Dei Verbum*, 11). God has made use of men as docile instruments, so that what was written by them is the true word of God and, as such, is free from even the slightest error. In itself, inspiration is a supernatural influence of God on the mind, will and executive faculties of the sacred writer, so that he conceives and judges rightly, and is willing to write faithfully, with infallible truth, all that God wills and only what God wills and in the way God wills, so that God is truly the principal author of the written book.

St. Paul indicates for what purposes Scripture is useful: teaching, persuading, correcting, and training in righteousness (holiness). The first usefulness is didactic in nature; for Scripture contains truth, and truth is the subject of teaching; the second usefulness lies in conviction, in the persuasion of spirits, aimed at leading them to the truth and refuting errors; the third is correction, to lead errant and sinful people to the truth and the moral life; finally, Scripture aids the formation to righteousness, that is, to the moral life according to which God wants one to live. In this way Scripture works to form the believing man and the apostle who with Scripture is able to fulfill his ministry, being provided with every tool to exercise it fruitfully. Knowledge and formation in the Scriptures become a common heritage through teaching, the means of salvation that must penetrate into the life of every man. Paul solemnly asks Timothy to carry out, without fail, the mission he conveys to him. He implores him, reminding him of Jesus Christ who will come to judge the living and the dead. Paul's warning concerns preaching. He admonishes and exhorts Timothy, calling God and Jesus Christ to witness: St Paul is aware that he is fulfilling his duty in commanding Timothy to preach. Timothy is to preach the word as a herald who has glad tidings to communicate; he is to insist, to seize every opportunity, even when to the hearers the voice of the preacher of truth seems inappropriate, he is to reprimand them, to exhort them; but the preaching in itself is always appropriate; all preaching, moreover, even when it rebukes and shows error is to be done with gentleness, waiting patiently for its fruit, and it is to have for its solid basis doctrine, the word of God, which is efficacious through its very self. Reading these theoretical and practical norms of pastoral pedagogy, the minister of the word will know how to combine prudence and boldness, strength in rebuking and convincing of error and the meekness of fatherly love; he will know how to instruct minds with the light of truth and instruct hearts with the warmth of apostolic zeal.

4. The sacred scriptures cannot be interpreted and explained according to each one's private feeling

Holy Scripture has God as its author, and therefore only God can explain its precise meaning. The Scripture passages contained in 2 Peter 1:20-21 and 2 Tim 3:16 contribute to the understanding of the inspiration of Holy Scripture, as has been noted, "If the prophets were able to be God's spokesmen through the action of the Spirit, it follows that no 'prophetic writing' (read: 'written prophecy') can be interpreted for personal and arbitrary ends. Prophetic writings and prophecy-word (oral) are both placed on the same plane and participate equally in the Spirit of God. Prophecy in its outward appearance is human speech, but in its inner nature it is God's word. Therefore, the word of the prophets which is the word of God does not permit arbitrary interpretation, but must be read within the framework of a tradition of meaning that leads to understanding in it the beloved Son" (Chiarazzo, *Prima lettera di Pietro*, in *La Bibbia*, Casale Monferrato (AL), 1996², p. 3029).

Now Jesus Christ himself explained several points of the sacred books, either directly or through his Apostles, and he gave his Church the power to authentically explain everything else (cf. Lk 24:45), and, consequently, no private person has the right to interpret Sacred Scripture according to his own lights. We read in the Constitution on Divine Revelation of the Second Vatican Council, "The divinely revealed truths, which are contained and expressed in the books of Sacred Scripture, were written by inspiration of the Holy Spirit. Holy Mother Church, by apostolic faith, considers sacred and canonical all the entire books of both the Old and New Testaments, with all their parts, because they were written by inspiration of the Holy Spirit (cf. Jn 20:31; 2 Tim 3:16); they have God as their author and as such have been delivered to the Church. In composing the Sacred Books, God chose men whom he used in the possession of their faculties and abilities, so that, with him acting in them and through them, they, as true authors, consigned to writing everything and only those things which he wanted. Since, therefore, everything that the inspired authors or hagiographers assert is to be held to be asserted by the Holy Spirit, it must be held, accordingly, that the books of Scripture teach with certainty, faithfully and without error the truth which God, for our salvation, willed to be delivered in the sacred Scriptures" (*Dei Verbum*, 11).

The expression "prophecy of Scripture" should be taken to mean the entire Old Testament, which as a whole is nothing but a continuous prophecy of Jesus Christ and his Kingdom. No prophecy of Scripture is the prophet's own explanation (Gr. *epílysis* - explanation, interpretation), that is, his own invention. The prophets did not write what they wanted, but what God wanted. This is the reason why it does not belong to a private individual to interpret the Scriptures. They are not a human invention, nor were they brought to men by *human will*, but have for their author God Himself; for the holy men of God, wrote them *inspired* (gr. *ferómenoi*, lett. *driven, carried*) by the Holy Spirit, that is, under the supernatural influence and motion of the Spirit of God. This is why God is the primary author of the Holy Scriptures and their words are truly God's words (cf. Vanni, 1991, p. 1339). God has spoken in Holy Scripture through humans and in a human manner (cf. *Dei Verbum*, 12). Therefore, it can be said that the nature of the Bible is both divine and human, since it contains God's message in human language, so that the two natures are indissolubly united in it in a way similar to the two natures of the Son of God made man (cf. Doglio, 2010, p. 7). Therefore, as Vatican II teaches, the Bible must "be read and interpreted with the help of the same Spirit by whom it was written The manner of interpreting Scripture is ultimately subject to the judgment of the Church, which fulfills the divine mandate and ministry of preserving and interpreting the Word of God" (*Dei Verbum*, 12).

5. Inspiration and truth in Sacred Scripture according to *Dei Verbum*, no. 11

Dei Verbum is the council document that deals expressly with the Bible, its value and meaning for ecclesial life; it deals with it in the context of Revelation, obviously. *Dei Verbum* throws light on many aspects of Scripture and Tradition, the proper understanding of which is the responsibility of the Church's Magisterium. An experienced biblical scholar has written regarding this coucil document, "It encourages a more comprehensive approach to Revelation: biblical inspiration exists to ensure the integral and perennial transmission of divine Revelation. The language has untied itself from scholastic terminology and it no longer speaks of efficient, principal, instrumental causes, although the concepts are preserved: the philosophical categories of other times have been replaced by biblical and more accessible concepts ("God acts with them and through them"). The expression 'true authors' is emphasized. This is the first time in a document of the Magisterium that the writers are recognized as being in full possession of their faculties. The studied conciseness with which *Dei Verbum* treats the mystery of inspiration is a model of teaching wisdom" (Orsatti, 2005, p. 59). God exercised upon the sacred writers – who are called hagiographers – a special action, which is also found in the unique quality of the books in the biblical canon because of their divine origin. Between Sacred Scripture and the Word of God there is an indissoluble and very close relationship, so much so that the Council states, "The Sacred Scriptures contain the Word of God and [...] are truly the Word of God" (*Dei Verbum*, 24).

We have seen that *Dei Verbum* specifies in no. 11 how the inspiration that led to the redaction of Sacred Scripture is to be understood: "In composing the Sacred Books, God chose men whom he used in the possession of their faculties and abilities, so that, with him acting in them and through them, they, as true authors, consigned to writing everything and only those things which he wanted."

The text goes on to specify the truth and inerrancy of all that is contained in the Holy Scriptures: "Since therefore everything that the inspired authors or hagiographers assert is to be held to be asserted by the Holy Spirit, it must be held, accordingly, that the books of Scripture firmly, faithfully and without error teach that truth which God wanted put into the sacred writings for the sake of salvation."

The constitution *Dei Verbum* has fostered and stimulated a return of the Word of God, by placing it once again at the center of
ecclesial life, so that every Christian has access to a new understanding of its message and can rediscover their own human and Christian dignity, their divine filiation as adoptive children of the heavenly Father. All this will be possible thanks to the new way of teaching inserted in *Dei Verbum*, which has placed the Bible at the center
of the Church's life so that the reader, moved in turn by the Holy
Spirit, can continuously participate in the Revelation present in Sacred Scripture, understand it and live it.

6. How do you explain the presence of the fourfold gospel?

The Latin *evangelium* comes from the Greek *euaggelion*, a word
meaning *"glad message, good news."* In ancient times it indicated
both the good news communicated and the reward given to the
bearer of the good news. The biblical world knows a secular and a
religious use of the term gospel. In the Old Testament the noun appears only six times, almost always with secular sense For example,
"He also brings *good news*" (2 Sam 18:25). The good news here is
news of a military victory and especially the safety of David's son
Absalom.

The religious sense of the verb "evangelize" appears from the
second Isaiah onward: "How beautiful on the mountains are the feet
of the messenger of glad *tidings* who proclaims peace, the messenger
of goodness who proclaims salvation, who says to Zion, 'Your God
reigns'" (52:7). The word becomes a technical term in salvation

theology, differing significantly from the Hellenistic concept of imperial worship.

The New Testament, whose central object is Jesus Christ, delivers to us the definitive truth of divine revelation. At its core are the four Gospels according to Matthew, Mark, Luke and John, as the main testimony about the life and teaching of Jesus (cf. *Catechism of the Catholic Church*, no. 22). In the New Testament context, "*gospel*" means the glad tidings par excellence, the announcement of salvation by Jesus, the Messiah. He was the eschatological messenger, as we find in his reply to the disciples of John the Baptist, "Go and tell John what you hear and see: 'The blind recover their sight, the lame walk, lepers are healed, the dead are raised, the *good news* is preached to the poor'" (Mt 11:4-5). With Jesus, the "gospel" has reached theological fullness; this is the Word of God and of Christ, filled with power, as St. Paul summarized well: "For this very reason we also thank God continually, because, having received from us the divine word of preaching, you have received it not as the word of men, but, as it truly is, as the word of God, working in you who believe" (1 Thess 2:13).

From the end of the first century, the gospel is also a written text, which allows us to know Jesus, the person *par excellence*, what he said and did. Knowing him through "the good news" we enter into communion with him. The expression "the four gospels" has become customary. However, it should be received with great reservation. More correctly one should speak of one gospel in four forms, that is, a "fourfold gospel," because the gospel is unique as a literary genre and also unique in terms of content, although it is presented from four different perspectives, that is the "gospel according to Matthew, Mark, Luke and John" (cf. *Dei Verbum*, 19).

The transmission of Jesus' words and the deeds concerning him first took place in oral form. "The apostles, after the Lord's ascension, transmitted to their hearers what he had said and done with that more complete intelligence which they, taught by the glorious events of Christ and enlightened by the light of the Spirit of truth, enjoyed" (*Dei Verbum*, 19). Two very important elements emerge here, namely, the Paschal event (faith in the dead and risen Christ) and the gift of the Spirit (cf. Jn 14:26; 15:26; 16:1).

The material of the oral preaching was then taken up and ordered through the work called "redaction," resulting in four writings, three very similar to each other that take the name of "synoptics" (Matthew, Mark and Luke) and the fourth, John, with its own different literary and theological itinerary. This process is described as follows by Vatican II: "Holy Mother Church has held and holds with utmost firmness and constancy, that the four aforementioned gospels, whose historicity she unhesitatingly affirms, faithfully convey what Jesus the son of God, during his life among men, actually worked and taught for their eternal salvation [...]. The sacred authors wrote the four gospels, selecting some things from the many which had been handed on by word of mouth or in writing, drawing up a summary of the others or explaining them with regard to the situation of the Churches, finally preserving the character of preaching, always, however, in such a way as to report about Jesus things that are true and sincere" (*Dei Verbum*, 19). M. Orsatti comments, "Historicity is not to be confused with mechanicity or as an aseptic recording of facts and words. The same document recognizes an activiy of the evangelists that certainly does not compromise but enhances historicity" (2005, p. 165).

The fourfold Gospel – the heart and culmination of the entire Word of God – was thus written in the early Church and was intended for the guidance of the Church, for the reading and study by the individual and by the community, ensuring access to the person and message of Jesus of Nazareth, so that it would continue to enlighten and sustain the lives of people.

Questions about Christ

Jesus is a historical character, but what proofs do we have that he is God?

(Gonzalo de la Morena)

In the proper sense, Jesus' divinity cannot be proved but is to be believed: it is an object of faith because it is beyond the capacity of reason on its own. St. Paul writes that "no one can say 'Jesus is Lord' (i.e., God) except under the working of the Holy Spirit" (1 Cor 12:3). In other words, we know it by revelation, not by demonstration. This does not mean that it is an absurd belief, because it is one thing to be above reason and another to contradict it. Consequently, even though we cannot demonstrate that Jesus is the Son of God, we can firmly state the reasons that make this belief a sensible proposition.

1. Why do we believe that Jesus is God?

The simplest answer would be "because he has said so, and it is reasonable to believe him." Jesus has in fact manifested his divine status in deeds and words, presenting himself not only as the expected Messiah, but also as the Son of God, understanding this sonship in a sense that exceeded all expectations. During his earthly life he performed deeds and uttered words that only God could do or say. After his death on the cross, his message was confirmed by the Resurrection and fully understood through the action of the Holy Spirit.

Let us see first that Jesus declared himself to be the son of God; then we will argue in favor of the historicity of this claim; and then we will see that, by his acts and words, he acted as only one who considers himself divine can act.

2. What proofs do we have that Jesus affirms that he is the Son of God?

The main proofs are the testimonies of the New Testament. The Gospels show that Jesus declared himself the Son of God in a new and unique sense. These documents also tell us that Jesus invited his disciples to relate to God as Father in a new way.

Jesus' divine sonship appears both explicitly in his words and implicitly, permeating many of his teachings and actions, particularly his prayer and preaching about the Father.

When Jesus prays, he invokes God calling him *Father* or *my Father*, with the sole exception of "*Eloi, Eloi, lemà sabacthàni*" (Mk 15:34 et par.). In this case, Jesus is reciting the opening words of Psalm 22. When instead the words come from within himself, his relationship with God is always expressed in filial terms. On one such occasion, moreover, the Aramaic term *Abba* is preserved (cf. Mk 14:36), a familiar term that could be translated as "daddy." This term denotes such confidence that its use to invoke God was previously unheard of.

When he preaches about relating to God and exhorts trust in Him, Jesus often refers to God as "my Father." It is important to note that no Old Testament character had ever referred to God as "my

Father" in the singular. By contrast, the Gospels show with amazing naturalness that for Jesus God is "his Father."

His filial trust shows in his life of poverty, his depending totally on the Father for his daily bread, and in his total dedication to the Kingdom, lived to the point of death. Jesus seeks to instill in his disciples this same attitude of filial faith by teaching them the Lord's Prayer, preaching trust in "your heavenly Father," and fostering in them a relationship with God that must be expressed in paternal-filial terms.

Jesus makes clear the uniqueness of his filial relationship with the Father. For example, in the parable of the murderous vinedressers (Mk 12:1ff and par.) Jesus presents himself as "the beloved Son" sent by the Father and rejected by the vinedressers, qualitatively superior to all previous envoys, the "servants." In another passage, Jesus expresses the uniqueness of his relationship with the Father in this way, "no one knows the Father except the Son, and no one knows the Son except the Father and the one to whom the Son wills to reveal him" (Mt 11:27ff and par.). In its context, this knowledge indicates a living personal relationship; it thus manifests a mutual and exclusive intimacy between the Father and the Son, inaccessible to anyone else except by revelation from within. There is a qualitative leap between them and any other subject. The superiority of the Son over any other creature is also implicit in some of Jesus' words (cf. Mk 13:32 and par.) and explicit in others, "I and the Father are one" (Jn 10:30). In short, the sonship Jesus ascribes to himself cannot be understood as a mere metaphor, but expresses such a claim as to be considered blasphemous by the Jewish authorities (cf. Mk 14:61-64 and par.).

3. The most reasonable explanation of a radical religious transformation

The New Testament witnesses a religious transformation whereby God is called Father in a new way that does not fit the previous Jewish faith, the matrix of nascent Christianity.

Certainly, the Old Testament already speaks of the fatherhood of God. However, the use of the term has changed radically, both in its religious centrality and in its meaning. The quantitative data are telling: of the 1213 times the word "father" appears in the Hebrew Bible, only 15 refer to God. In the New Testament, by contrast, the word "father" designates God 255 of the 413 times it appears. But the qualitative contrast is as striking as the quantitative one. In the Old Testament, God's fatherhood is one metaphor among many that describe God's benevolent disposition toward his people and toward creation. In the New Testament, God's fatherhood is not just another image, but constitutes the revelation of his personal identity, first with regard to the unique divine filiation of Jesus and, second, with regard to the adoption of believers as sons. According to St. Paul, the prayerful cry *Abba* expresses a new relationship with God: those who believe in Christ have moved from being "servants" to being considered "sons" (cf. Gal 4:4-7).

The religious innovation represented by this new conception of divine fatherhood cannot be explained simply as a natural evolution of Jewish religious thought at that time. Rather, it requires a historical explanation that accounts for its origin and impact. Considering the multiplicity of New Testament sources that coincide on this point, as well as the heterogeneity of their authors and locations, it is reasonable to attribute this innovation to a common source authorized to bring about a change in the image and relationship with God.

The most plausible explanation is that this transformation was initiated by Jesus himself. The Gospel account of Jesus, who regarded himself as the Son of God in a new way and introduced his disciples to this new relationship with God, is not only theologically credible but also supported by arguments that support its historical authenticity.

4. Is there any other evidence that Jesus claimed divine authority for himself?

In the Gospels, Jesus performs actions and speaks words that could only be performed or uttered by someone who considers himself to have supreme authority, placing himself on the level of God.

Jesus taught with surprising confidence superhuman truths – such as God's intentions in creation (Mk 10:5-9 et par.) or the reality of the afterlife (Mk 12:25) – by speaking in the first person and in his name. When prophets spoke on behalf of God, they repeated the formula "oracle of YHWH" or "thus says the Lord". In contrast, Jesus' characteristic formula is "truly I say to you." While other teachers based their authority on the Scriptures, Jesus goes further, relying on no other source but his own authority. He himself states, "Heaven and earth will pass away, but my words will not pass away" (Mark 13:31). The authority of his words was cause for astonishment for some (Mk 1:22 and par.) and scandal for others (Mk 11:28 and par.).

Moreover, his teaching was substantiated by portentous signs. Other Old Testament figures also performed miracles, but they did so by invoking the power and action of the Lord God, not their own (cf. 1 Kings 17:21). Jesus, on the other hand, performed them in his own name: "Maiden, I say to you, arise" (Mk 5:41; cf. Lk 5:24; 7:14). The contrast also extends to the signs performed by the apostles, who did them "in the name of Jesus Christ" (cf. Acts 3:6; 16:18).

Jesus presented himself as one who has divine authority. For example, he claimed to have the power to forgive sins and for exercising this divine prerogative he was considered blasphemous (cf. Mk 2:5 and par.). Jesus presented himself as the promised "bridegroom" of Israel (Mk 2:19 and par.), a role that in the biblical narrative properly belongs to God (e.g., cf. Is 54:5). He declared himself "Lord of the Sabbath" (Mk 2:28 and par.) and "greater than the temple" (Mt 12:6). When he called his disciples, Jesus did not hesitate to ask them to leave everything to follow him. In this way he put himself at the center of his followers' lives and asked them to love him above all else: "Whoever loves father or mother more than me is not worthy of me..." (Mt 10:37). He also considered himself able to bestow thrones on his followers to judge Israel in the eschatological judgment, where he himself will appear as a universal judge (cf. Mt 19:28; 25:31), a function the Hebrew Bible assigns to YHWH himself. In short, Jesus acted as one who believed himself to be invested with the same divine power.

This short list informs us of the lofty claims that Jesus claimed for himself. They are prerogatives that implicitly declare what his opponents understood: "We do not stone you for a good work, but for blasphemy: for you, who are man, make yourself God" (Jn 10:33).

His works and teachings converge in his declaration, "I am the way, the truth and the life. No one comes to the Father except through me" (Jn 14:6). This statement by Jesus places him in a unique position not only in Israel's history but in the history of all religions. Other charismatic or religious leaders *point the way* to God, or perhaps *open the door*. Jesus alone dares to claim for himself the status of the way and the only door to the Father.

5. C.S. Lewis's "trilemma"

This brings us to the well-known "trilemma" argument popularized by C.S. Lewis. Considering the claims Jesus made about himself, it is not possible to think that he was only a "wise man" or a "good teacher." So tall are his claims that they leave room for only three options for understanding his identity: either Jesus was a liar, or he was out of his mind, or he was who he said he was, the Lord. The first option would imply that Jesus knew he did not possess the authority he claimed, but deliberately deceived his followers. Lewis points out that Jesus' ethical teaching, as well as his life of humility and self-giving to the point of death, directly contradict the possibility of a life based on lies. The second alternative suggests that Jesus sincerely believed that he was the son of God and the Lord, without realizing that this was an illusion. Now, anyone who deludes himself into believing such lofty claims cannot be sane; he should suffer from some kind of delusion or mental disorder. However, Jesus did not teach as one who is out of his mental faculties; on the contrary, he showed a deep understanding of human nature, which suggests a healthy and balanced mind. Having ruled out the hypotheses of the liar and the lunatic, all that remains is to accept the claims that Jesus made about himself, believing in his divinity. According to Lewis, this is the most logical and consistent option if we consider his teachings corroborated by miracles and the Resurrection.

This argument, while showing the reasonableness of our faith, does not prove it conclusively. It presupposes, among other things, the fundamental historical credibility of the Gospels. This issue, which is also reasonable, cannot be addressed here. For now, it is sufficient to state that Jesus' high claims are not presented as isolated assertions, but permeate every page of the Gospel, often implicitly in his works; if we rejected them, it would not be easy to explain the historical origin of the stories reported by the Gospels.

6. The Resurrection and the revelation of Jesus' divinity

Jesus' words had a similar effect on his contemporaries as the one described by Lewis. His followers were willing to give up everything for him, but those who did not believe him considered him a dangerous blasphemer. Denial prevailed and Jesus was crucified. This end refuted all of Jesus' claims, for there was nothing more contrary to the expectations of the people than a messiah easily defeated and humiliated by oppressive power. He died rejected, abandoned and crucified as a cursed man; the immediate conclusion would be that his cause was not divine and therefore his message was false. The end of his movement was predictable. Yet, against all odds,

Jesus' cause did not end with his crucifixion but re-emerged with new momentum and spread throughout the world.

The Resurrection is important not only in itself but also because of its significance. Among other things, the Resurrection was a sign that God is with Jesus, backing his cause and supporting his message: it is the divine confirmation that guarantees Jesus' truthfulness. If God resurrected Jesus, then Jesus is who he said he was. In this sense, the Resurrection is the sign by which the Father confirms that Jesus is his Son and our Lord (cf. Rom 1:4; Acts 2:22, 36; 3:12).

The Resurrection is thus one of the foundational events of the belief in Jesus' divinity. It is a necessary factor but would not be significant enough without its connection to earlier teachings: even Lazarus was seen alive after his death but was not considered Messiah, Lord or Son of God. Without Jesus' statements in his earthly life, the Resurrection would never have been understood as a revelation of his divinity. Finally, the New Testament emphasizes that the understanding of Jesus' words and signs, including the Resurrection, is attributed to the action of the Holy Spirit sent upon his disciples: it is the Paraclete who guides the disciples to the full truth about Jesus (cf. Jn 16:13).

7.   The witness of the saints and the imprint of their teachings.

Jesus, throughout his ministry, did not hesitate to challenge the religious teachers of his time and propose a radical ethic that went beyond what the Scriptures prescribed. His teaching was not limited to mere observance of the law but called for a demanding inner transformation and total giving to God and neighbor. This ethical

challenge has resonated throughout the centuries, inspiring countless men and women to live according to the Gospel, even in the
midst of adversity and against opposing tendencies, internal and external.

The saints, true disciples of Christ, are living witnesses to the authenticity and transforming power of Jesus' message. Their exem-
plary lives and their lasting impact on the world are eloquent testimony to the quality and enduring relevance of Christ's teaching.
These testimonies show that the doctrine of Jesus cannot simply be
rejected as the product of a confused man or a failed revolutionary
on the cross. As Lewis notes, Jesus' teaching cannot be attributed to
a liar or a madman. The example of the saints invites serious consideration of the truth of Jesus' identity as the Son of God and Savior.

8.   A faith with a solid foundation

Ultimately, the question of Jesus' divinity is a matter of faith, but
not a blind or irrational faith, but a faith that can find support in
reasonable arguments and historical evidence. The manifestation of
Jesus' divine *status* did not consist only in his works and words, but
was endorsed by the Father in his Resurrection and can be fully understood and fully received only through the inner action of the
Holy Spirit. Contemplation of Jesus' life, teachings and influence
provides a solid basis for belief in his divinity. However, this faith is
not simply the result of an intellectual exercise, but involves openness of heart and free response to divine grace.

What certainty do we have that Christ is risen and therefore is God? Could not the apparitions narrated in the Gospels be hallucinations due to autosuggestion? Luke's Gospel says that the apostles "believe they see a ghost" (Lk 24:37)

(Daniel Arasa)

There are different kinds of certainty. On the one hand, there is physical or material certainty, that is, the one that tells me that I am certain about something because it is here, I see it, touch it, hear it, feel it. But there is also moral certainty, that is, the one whereby I am convinced of something because someone I trust has told me so or, put in journalistic terms, because I have authoritative and reliable sources about what happened (direct witnesses, scientific studies, and whatnot). For example, I am certain that my mother is such (moral certainty) without the need for DNA evidence (material certainty), which I could also obtain.

In Christ's case we have both certainties, both material and moral. Let me explain.

Let us begin with the material certainty about Christ being resurrected. It is true that we have no witnesses (at least human ones!) of the instant or moment of the Resurrection. No one has come forward to say, "I saw how Christ was resurrected!" So we start at a disadvantage. There is a "however" at this point: instead, we know that many people, followers and non-followers of Christ (soldiers, apostles, Pharisees, women in his retinue) saw him alive before the crucifixion, then saw him die on Calvary, lay his corpse in the tomb, and finally then saw him alive a few days later. And the encounter with Christ "alive after death" happened not once or twice, but many times, and it was not one or two people who saw him, but many. Therefore, if you agree with me that the word Resurrection means coming back to life after death, there is nothing else but to admit that Christ is risen, and that we have a material certainty of His Resurrection.

Let us now turn to moral certainty, which is very much related to the material certainty of those who saw Christ alive after his passion and death. For them, the conviction was so strong that they bore witness to it to the point of transmitting, over the centuries, a conviction (moral certainty) in hundreds, thousands, millions of people, who did not see Christ physically, then extending the Christian religion *urbi et orbi*.

Some might say that the certainties we have been talking about, material and moral certainties, are human certainties, and therefore subject to the limits of fallible human nature. Certainly, but this does not take any value away from them, in fact it adds to them, because – you will agree – a certainty that is maintained for so long over time, indeed strengthened over time, has more than one motive to be considered a *real* certainty, that is, one that corresponds to reality, to the true.

At this point I would like to point out that almost all our knowledge (i.e., our certainties), in whatever sphere (historical, geographical, cultural, spatial, etc.), are acquired not because of personal material certainty, since we cannot experience everything, but because we trust (moral certainty) what our parents, teachers, books teach us and say... This trusting is therefore an absolutely necessary human faith that is consonant with our existence and without which it would be impossible to do anything. I am now given the example of an uncle of mine who, when I went out for walks with him as a child, used to say, "Do you know why we cross the street when the light is green? Because we trust those coming the other way who, seeing the red light, will stop and not run us over." *Dixit.*

One more piece is still missing: supernatural faith, that is, the gift of God whereby we believe what God has told us and his Church proposes, not so much because of our understanding of what they tell us, but because of God's authority that cannot (and will not!) deceive or be deceived. Faith is a virtue that Christians receive with baptism and it gives that "plus" of certainty, of security to believe what is affirmed in the profession of faith, when we repeat every Sunday that Christ "suffered under Pontius Pilate, was crucified, died and was buried," and, after descending into hell, "on the third day he rose from the dead."

If then someone does not want to believe, that is another matter. We are all free and, hopefully, respectful of the beliefs of others. In fact, there are even those who don't believe that man landed on the moon or think the Earth is flat. Most of us think they are dead wrong, but that does not lead us to despise them.

This brings us to the second, and legitimate, question about "hallucinations" and "ghosts." Personally, I have never seen a ghost and I believe I have not had any particular hallucinations, but I will try to answer the question.

In the Gospels, the Acts of the Apostles, and many later books about the life of Christ, we are told that after his death, the Lord appeared bodily to the disciples. Obviously, it came as a shock to them. "But wasn't he dead!" As I see it the initial surprise and disbelief of those present seems perfectly normal: "How is it possible that one who has died just a moment ago is now here, alive and talking to us?" More than one must have rubbed their eyes or wondered if it was their own imagination (hallucination). But the fact is that this has happened several times implies that the doubt that sleep or imagination has deceived them does not hold.

And then, there is a rather significant and illuminating episode, which Luke's Gospel in chapter 24 recounts very well when, in one of these appearances, it says that the apostles "for great joy, still did not believe and were astonished." Faced with this attitude, Jesus stepped forward and said, "Do you have anything to eat here?" They "offered him a portion of roasted fish; he took it and ate it before them."... I don't know about you, but if I am offered fish (which I am not particularly thrilled about), surely out of courtesy I would eat it but leaving the head and the fishbone. Surely that is what the Lord did, leaving the plate a little dirty. So, it is obvious that everyone knew that there was that fish before, and without any of them eating it, then that fish was gone. Only Jesus had taken it, leaving some remains.

Even more striking is the case of the apostle Thomas. He was absent during the first appearance to the apostles and did not want to believe the testimony of all his companions. But he had to surrender to the evidence when for the second time the Lord appeared to them and invited him to introduce his finger and hand into the wounds caused by the nails and spear on his body.

That the apostles and other disciples do not recognize Jesus the first time he appears to them after the Resurrection, as is the case with Cleophas and one of his companions on their way to Emmaus, is explained by St. Paul with the special qualities of the resurrected bodies: while they may retain certain earthly characteristics and prerogatives (e.g., the wounds proper to the passion and crucifixion), they include other supernatural qualities such as non-subjection to time and space (which allows the Lord to enter the closed room or move around Galilee without having to walk).

In short, there are many testimonies, handed down subsequently from generation to generation and in the Tradition of the Church, that have always affirmed the real Resurrection of Christ. This very certainty has led hundreds of thousands of people to bear witness, even at the cost of their reputayion, fortune and, in many cases, their lives. If the Resurrection were not true, as St. Paul says again, the Christian faith would be nothing but useless folly.

If the Church is founded by Christ and supported/guided by the Holy Spirit, how is it possible that there are so many errors, scandals, crimes... committed even by its representatives?

(Gianfranco Calabrese)

Christ not only founded the Church during the time of his earthly mission – as can be gathered from the Gospel writings of the New Testament – but, after his Ascension, continually founds it with the gift of his Spirit from the day of Pentecost. It is the same Holy Spirit, the gift of the Father and the risen Lord, who makes the Lord present, who is the head of his body the Church, in the sacraments of faith and, in a special and unique way, in the sacrament of the Eucharist, the "memorial" of the Paschal Mystery, and in the sacrament of the brothers and sisters, welcomed and loved in the charity of Christ and in the space and time of history: "And behold, I am with you all days, until the end of the world" (Mt 28:20). This promise is the foundation, first of all, of the Gospel proclamation of the gift of faith, expressed to Peter and with him to the entire community of his disciples by the Lord Jesus himself: "And I say to you, you are Peter, and upon this rock I will build my Church, and the powers of hell shall not prevail against it" (Mt 16:18). This is the experience from the very beginning of the community of Christians in the faced of the perceived absence of the Master, the betrayal by Judas, and the potentially and truly divisive and arduous experiences of the early days of the Church. Strong in them was the awareness of the presence of the risen Lord and the promised and implemented gift of the Holy Spirit. This is the Kingdom of God brought about in the risen Christ and given to the believers gathered in his name by virtue of the action of the Holy Spirit: "Those therefore who were with him asked him, 'Lord, is this the time when you will restore the kingdom for Israel?' But he answered, 'It is not for you to know times or moments that the Father has reserved for his power, but you will receive power from the Holy Spirit who will come upon you, and you will be witnesses of me in Jerusalem and in all Judea and Samaria and to the ends of the earth'" (Acts 1:6-8).

This faith, tempted and professed, in the Lord's guidance and presence and in the action in the Church, which is indefectible though not impeccable, of the Holy Spirit has enabled believers to live through and overcome persecutions, divisions, multiple difficulties, internal and external, and epochal transitions, always with their eyes fixed on the Lord Jesus, the only Master, and trusting in the action of the Holy Spirit. In every historical period the community of Christians has kept faith with the kerygmatic proclamation, witnessed by the apostles from the day of Pentecost. This is the center that justifies faith in the Lord's effective presence and action, which is radiated in the Spirit's action in the Church. It is this faithfulness in the assistance of the Holy Spirit in the Church that legitimizes not sin but mercy, not sinfulness present in the members of the Church but the power of Christ's redemption and sanctification through the action of the Holy Spirit: "I have told you these things while I am still with you. But the Paraclete, the Holy Spirit whom the Father will send in my name, he will teach you all things and bring to your remembrance all that I have said to you" (Jn 14:25-26). And again, "When he, the Spirit of truth, comes, he will guide you into all truth, for he will not speak from himself, but will tell all that he has heard and will announce to you the things to come. He will glorify me, for he will take from that which is mine and proclaim it to you" (Jn 16:13-14). The Lord's words at the Last Supper have been the foundation of the journey of doctrinal and moral deepening and inculturation of the faith that has taken place from the post-apostolic period to the present. The unfailing faith of the Church and its magisterium, rooted through the assistance of the Holy Spirit in the profession of faith, has made it possible to combat heresies and defend communion and unity, despite schisms, moral infidelities, personal and institutional inconsistencies, and compromises with economic and political powers. The history and life of the Church have manifested a profound truth of faith: it is possible to receive and cherish revelation and develop it through legitimate theological, ecclesiological and moral reflection if one walks with Christ and his Revelation and allows oneself to be guided and enlightened by the light of the Holy Spirit.

In this sense, it is the Pentecostal gift of the Holy Spirit that is the foundation, legitimizing the theological reality of the Church in its complexity, in its paradoxical mysterical tension, in its sacramental reality(cf. LG 8). The mystery of the Church is manifested in its very hierarchical and ministerial constitution, in its pastoral, liturgical, charitable and missionary action. The human and institutional dimension, which must never be separated though it is distinct from its transcendent dimension, can undergo and has undergone in its development historical and cultural conditioning. This cultural-historical rootedness has certainly allowed the development of the Church's theological, magisterial, and moral teaching, its very institutional, juridical, and social organization and structuring, but also the inevitable risk of falling into sins and infidelity with respect to the Gospel of the Lord. In this sense, the presence of sin, error, scandals and crimes committed even by its representatives cannot be denied in the life of the Church. Each and every one of its members by the gift of the Holy Spirit and by baptism in the faith are called to participate in the very life of God, but they remain and can, because of their human nature, be conditioned by the confines and ambiguity of time and space, the limitation of their own human knowledge and the vulnerability and frailty of their own will. This does not justify sin but reaffirms the Gospel truth that everything is gift and free election. The divine call challenges human freedom and responsibility, which is always personal and communal. Man, in spite of everything, can reject the gift of grace and the action of the Holy Spirit.

The Second Vatican Council embraced, reaffirmed and proclaimed the mystery and sacramental dimension of the Church, its indefectible holiness and its close relationship with the redemptive presence of the risen Lord and the life-giving action of the Holy Spirit: "The Church, whose mystery is expounded by the sacred Council, is in the eyes of faith indefectibly holy. For Christ, the Son of God, who with the Father and the Spirit is proclaimed 'the only Holy One,' loved the Church as his bride and gave himself for her in order to sanctify her (cf. Eph 5:25-26), united her to himself as his body and filled her with the gift of the Holy Spirit, for the glory of God. Therefore, everyone in the Church, whether they belong to the hierarchy or are governed by it, is called to holiness, according to the

Apostle's words, "Yes, what God wants is your sanctification" (1 Thess 4:3; cf. Eph 1:4). Well then, this holiness of the Church constantly manifests itself and must manifest itself in the fruits of grace which the Spirit produces in the faithful; it is expressed in various forms in each of those who tend to perfect charity in their own line of life and edify others; and "in a manner all its own it is manifested in the practice of the counsels which are customarily called evangelical. This practice of the counsels, embraced by many Christians through the impulse of the Holy Spirit, whether in a private capacity or in a condition or state sanctioned by the Church, bears and should bear in the world a shining witness and example of this holiness" (LG 39).

At the same time, the Council also reaffirmed the necessary and constant journey of conversion and reform, which must characterize the historical-temporal journey of the community of believers: "Fully incorporated into the society of the Church are those who, having the Spirit of Christ, fully accept its organization and all the means of salvation instituted in it, and who moreover, through the bonds constituted by profession of faith, sacraments, ecclesiastical government and communion, are united in the visible assembly of the Church with Christ who directs it through the Supreme Pontiff and the bishops. That man is not saved, however, even though he be incorporated into the Church, who, not persevering in charity, remains, yes, in the bosom of the Church with the "body," but not with the "heart." Let all the children of the Church remember well that their privileged condition is not to be ascribed to their merits, but to a special grace of Christ; wherefore, if they do not correspond to it in thought, word and deed, not only will they not be saved, but on the contrary they will be more severely judged" (LG 14; cf. CCC nos. 825-827).

This is why the Kingdom of God is present in history and in the Church, the sacrament "in Christ" of the unity of the human race (cf. LG 1) but always in the fragility of the path of history, in the fatigue of faith, in the drama of sin and in the expectation of the full and final manifestation of charity, when the Lord will come at the end of time to establish the defined Kingdom and deliver it to the Father: "Then comes the end, when he delivers the kingdom to God the Father after destroying every rule and every authority and power. For he must reign until he has put all his enemies under his feet. The last enemy to be destroyed is death. 'For God has put all things in subjection under his feet.' But when it says, 'All things are put in subjection under him,' it is plain that he is excepted who put all things under him. When all things are subjected to him, then the Son himself will also be subjected to him who put all things under him, that God may be everything to every one." (1 Cor 15:24-28). This is the perspective of the pilgrim Church, of the people of God on the way, which emerges from Pauline theology and is taken up by the Second Vatican Council: "Already therefore the last phase of the times has come to us (cf. 1 Cor 10:11). The renewal of the world is irrevocably acquired and in a certain real way anticipated in this world: in fact the Church already on earth is adorned with true holiness, even if imperfect. However, until the new heavens and the new earth, in which righteousness has its dwelling (cf. 2 Pet 3:13), the pilgrim Church in her sacraments and institutions, which belong to the present age, bears the fleeting figure of this world; she lives among creatures, who still groan, are in the labor of childbirth and sigh for the manifestation of the sons of God (cf. Rom 8:19-22)" (LG 48).

The presence of sin in the members of the Church does not nullify the holiness of and in the Church, but places it in relation to God's faithfulness, to the sole source of holiness, which is God. He is the Faithful One. The holiness of the Church refers back to the gift of covenant and grace, which is realized in the Church by the action of the risen Lord, the head of his body, the Church, and by the life-giving and sanctifying action of the divine person of the Holy Spirit. In tradition, patristic theology and the magisterium of the Church, holiness, as the presence and gift of God in Christ Jesus by the Holy Spirit, is not annulled by the presence of sin. This consciousness of ecclesial faith, which was expressed through the Nicene-Constantinopolitan profession of faith, made it possible to condemn both the Donatist and Pelagian heresies, which conditionally linked the efficacy of salvation to the holiness of its ordained ministers and the holiness of believers to their consistent ascetic life. In this perspective, one must understand certain expressions used in patristic and theological reflection, which were intended to highlight the paradoxical character of the mystery of the Church and affirm the possible co-presence of both the holiness of the Church and sin in the Church. The affirmation, *simul iustus et peccator*, sought to express the personal and anthropological dimension of the call of every believer to participate in and experience the holiness of the Church and, at the same time, the dramatic possibility of rejecting its free and gratuitous gift. The other statement, *casta meretrix*, which must be understood within the theological-biblical reflection of the bishop of Milan, St. Ambrose, sought to highlight the beauty of

God's call addressed to the Church to welcome as a Bride the gift of nuptial communion, the divine Love of the Bridegroom, who is Christ the Lord (cf. G. BIFFI, *Casta meretrix. An Essay on the Ecclesiology of St. Ambrose*, Casale Monferrato 1996). Such a call refers back to God's faithfulness and, at the same time, challenges the free response of man, who must never isolate himself so as not to fall into temptation, into unfaithfulness and, on some occasions, into allowing himself to be attracted and conditioned by false forms of worldly love (cf. M. SEMERARO, *Mystery, Communion and Mission*, Bologna 1997, pp. 147-149).

In this sense, one should not confuse the indefectibility and holiness of the Church with impeccability. Everything is God's gift, the faithful are collaborators with his grace, and every fruit points back to Christ's redemption, to God's holiness and charity, to God's life of unity and communion of Love. It is the communion of the Father, Son and Holy Spirit, communicated to all people in the paschal mystery of the Lord and in the Pentecostal and memorial gift of the Holy Spirit, the living source of the Church's holiness, while its rejection is the reason for the drama of sin in the Church. The community of the Lord's disciples in its mystery participates in this divine gift and through the action of the Holy Spirit welcomes it in faith, lives it in the sacraments and offers it to all people in the evangelical and missionary proclamation. Holiness is the fruit of the personal, sacramental and witnessing free response of believers. In addition, through the universal gift of the Holy Spirit, all those "who through no fault of their own are ignorant of the Gospel of Christ and his Church but who nevertheless sincerely seek God and with the help of grace strive to fulfill by works his will, known through the dictate of conscience, can also participate in the unique vocation to holiness. Nor does divine providence deny the aids necessary for salvation to those who have not yet arrived at the clear cognition and recognition of God, but strive, not without divine grace, to lead a righteous life. For all that is good and true in them is held by the Church as a preparation for accepting the Gospel and as given by him who enlightens every man, that he may have life at last" (LG 16).

It is the one salvation that in Christ Jesus through the proclamation and life of the Church and through the action of the Holy Spirit is offered to all people by the one God. In this sense, both faithful Catholics and non-Catholic Christians, and those belonging to different religions and all men and women, who by following the light of right conscience seek to live in truth and goodness, can experience the unique of the holiness of Christ and the Church (cf. LG 14-16). It is the one universal call of God, which despite its rejection by believers and men, remains rooted in history and in the Gospel proclamation of the Church and which continues, in all times and every place, to illustrate the faithfulness and gratuitousness of God's Love, his election and his covenant, which, revealed in his incarnate Son, who died and rose again for us and for our salvation, continues, despite everything to be offered to all mankind. This universal call to holiness addressed to all people, which shines forth in Pentecost and in the history of the pilgrim Church, must be constantly welcomed, guarded, proclaimed and transmitted in missionary proclamation, in the tension of witnessing and in constant reform by all the baptized faithful (cf. LG 40-42). This is why "gifts of holiness have been deposited in the Church, making her an effective sign and instrument of salvation for all people [...]. Although holiness is a gift from God, it requires a free response from those whom he has called [...]. In the Church there are also those who, not persevering in charity, do not possess the Spirit of Christ. These, by virtue of the baptismal character, do not cease to be part of the Church [...]. For the sin of Christians will never be able to overcome the victorious grace of Christ, which is deposited in it and which guards against the sin of its members" (M. SEMERARO, cit., pp. 149-152).

In this perspective the statements of the Second Vatican Council about the Church, the people of God, shine forth: "As she is to extend to the whole earth, she enters into the history of men, and at the same time, however, transcends the times and boundaries of peoples, and in her journey through temptations and tribulations she is sustained by the power of God's grace promised her by the Lord, so that through human weakness she may not fail in perfect fidelity but remain a worthy spouse of her Lord, and may not cease, with the help of the Holy Spirit, to renew herself, until through the cross she comes to the light that knows no sunset" (LG 9).

Couldn't the Resurrection of Christ be a myth as there are similar ones in other religions?

(Marco Vanzini)

Around A.D. 180, the philosopher Celsus, in his defense of traditional religion against Christianity, which he saw as a dangerous innovation, compared the Christian doctrine on the Resurrection of Christ to one of the myths or legends that circulated about heroes or characters who had returned after death from the realm of Hades. According to Celsus, the Christian belief regarding the Resurrection of Jesus was basically not very different from the resurrection or pseudo-resurrection myths associated with the Pythagorean Zamolxis, the Egyptian Rhampsinit, Orpheus or the Greeks Protesilaus and Hercules. He also insinuated that, as with some of those stories, a deception could probably be exposed with regard to Jesus as well: he might not really have died, but would have kept himself hidden from men for a while, only to reappear as "resurrected" and thus bind a handful of suggestible and deluded followers to himself for good.

In times closer to us, in the 18th and 19th centuries, similar criticisms to those of Celsus were raised by scholars with a rationalist orientation and within the framework of research on the history of religions. Various attempts were thus formulated to explain the emergence of Christian belief in the Resurrection of Jesus in mythical terms. The Christians of the first generations, convinced of the glorification and deification of their teacher and *leader*, would have expressed this belief by assuming concepts and figures from the surrounding cultural and religious environment. In Greco-Roman religion there were myths about heroes or gods dying and rising again. For example, the apotheosis of Roman emperors expressed the widespread belief in their *post-mortem* deification. Could not such conceptions have offered abundant material to clothe the figure of the "historical Jesus" with a divine character and transfigure his earthly experience, which ended in death by crucifixion, into a glorious "resurrection," into the heavenly exaltation of the "Christ of faith"? This is a suspicion still in the minds of many, including Christians, circulating on the web and in discussion forums on the historicity of Jesus and the Gospels.

But the fact is that the hypothesis that the Christian proclamation of the Resurrection of Jesus of Nazareth is the result of a mythical transfiguration of historical reality has long since lost all credence in the scholarly community of historians and theologians dealing with the issue. And there are several solid reasons for this.

1. The similarities... are little alike

First of all, the supposed similarities between pagan mythological literature and the Resurrection of Christ, as narrated and interpreted in the Gospels and the New Testament as a whole, are not similar at all. Profound differences can be seen in the literary style, the figures and the fundamental meanings expressed in one case and the other. Take for example the Greek myth of the exaltation of Hercules or the figure of the emperor's apotheosis among the Romans. Well, the Greek hero is exalted and welcomed into heaven while his body, now seemingly worthless, burns on a pyre. Similarly, the deification of the Caesars in imperial times was imagined as an ascension to the realm of the gods, reserved for those who had acquired great merit. Again, the bodiliness of the emperor declared *divus* was of no importance; his body continued to lie in the tomb, unlike what Christian sources attest about Jesus. His body is no longer in the tomb. He has risen bodily and, precisely because of his bodily presence, he can be recognized by his own as the one who had been crucified and is alive in a new way: he is the Risen One (cf. Mt 28:9; Lk 24:36-43; Jn 20:19-20.26-29). Also significant is the comparison with the story of Alcestis as told by Euripides. Alcestis, wife of Admetus, sacrifices herself for him and dies, but she is snatched from the realm of the dead by Hercules to be restored to her husband's affection, returning to a completely normal life. In this, as in similar mythological narratives such as that of Protesilaus, the underlying theme is the reunion of affections, a private affair as it were. Other myths, about deities who descend into the realm of the dead and rise again, are instead linked to fertility cults and express the cyclical reawakening of the earth's energies in spring: think of the myth of Demeter and Persephone. Totally different are the context and meaning of the Resurrection of Christ, whose exit from the tomb took place once and for all and has eschatological and universal value: the Risen One inaugurates a radically new condition of life; he has definitively overcome death and in his glorified bodiliness (cf. Rom 1:4) we see humanity fulfilled, brought to fullness, which in him is promised to every human being (cf. Rom 8:11; Phil. 3:20-21).

The great differences between the Christian conception of the resurrection and mythology are, moreover, understandable if one remembers that Christians appreciated the philosophical culture of the Greek world, as well as its *pietas* – authentic religiosity – but they sharply criticized its polytheistic view of the divine exalted by myth and its morally corrupt forms of worship. So too, it is difficult to seriously think that they could have taken from Roman politico-religious customs such an idea as the apotheosis of the Caesar to express their faith in the risen Christ, since it was precisely for their refusal to worship the deified emperor that they were persecuted and put to death.

2. A myth created too quickly

Perhaps an even more important reason for rejecting the hypothesis of a myth-making process as the origin of belief in Christ's Resurrection is that the formulation of a myth takes far longer than the few years that separate the historical event of Jesus of Nazareth's death and the first written accounts of his Resurrection, that is, between about the year 30 and the early 50s – the time of St. Paul's first letters – and the years 60-70 in which the final writing of the first Gospels is placed. Contrary to the early rationalist and enlightenment critics, who thought they were written relatively late, dating to the mid-2nd century, the Gospels were written during the time of the generation of eyewitnesses to the historical events of Jesus. Therefore, there was absolutely no time for a significant accumulation of legendary elements prior to the written Gospels. More importantly, for a myth to work there needs to be a considerable distance in time between when it is created and elaborated and the time of the events it is intended to represent. This distance is practically zero in the case of the Gospels and the Resurrection of Jesus.

3.   So much historical information for a myth!

A third fundamental reason, related to the previous one, allows us to recognize as unfounded the mythical hypothesis of the formation of the resurrection traditions. The Gospels, together with the entire New Testament, provide an impressive amount of historical data, precisely placing the events of Christ's life, death, and Resurrection in space and time, in the geography of Palestine, and in the general course of human history, particularly that of Israel and Rome. Prominent public figures and witnesses to the events well known to all are mentioned, with precise references to places and circumstances that could be verified by those who received the announcement of the Resurrection. All this prevents us from seeing in the Gospel narratives of the finding of the empty tomb and Christ's appearances a "myth" constructed to convince unsuspecting and gullible listeners. On close examination, the very narratives of the Gospels, even with their character of extraordinariness – an encounter with the risen Christ is not a "common" experience! – appear not as artifacts created and elaborated a posteriori by the Christian community, but as very ancient and genuine testimonies. In fact, the texts do not contain any theological considerations about the event of the Resurrection, or allusions to the fulfillment of Scripture or doctrinal teachings, all of which would indicate in them the presence of reflection and attempts at understanding that had already taken place earlier within the early Church. Rather, the Gospel narratives appear to be genuine attestations of concrete experiences, reported as such. A striking fact, in this sense, is that all the traditions that flow into the Gospels unanimously point to women as the first witnesses to the event, as the first to have encountered the Risen One. If one keeps in mind that in Jewish society women had no legal capacity as witnesses, one understands that their presence and their fundamental role in the Gospel accounts is a strong indication of the absence of "manipulation" of the truth of the facts, on the part of the Christian community and the evangelists. It is significant that the apostle Paul, when writing in the early 50s of the first Century AD and wanting to provide a list of the only authoritative witnesses to the Resurrection, does not mention women (cf. 1 Cor 15:3-8).

It may be useful in this regard to report the result of a recent investigation conducted with a rigorous historical method on the Resurrection of Jesus. Examining all the data obtainable on the basis of the New Testament sources, M.R. Licona (*The Resurrection of Jesus. A New Historiographical Approach*, Downers Grove 2010) comes to the conclusion that only the resurrection hypothesis – that is, the claim that Jesus really did appear alive after his death to a number of people, presenting himself to them in his resurrected body – is capable of meeting all the criteria of historicity, leaving all alternative explanations, including the mythological one, far behind.

In his response to the criticism of the pagan philosopher Celsum, the Christian writer Origen ends his refutation with the argument that he considers most decisive and which is worth placing at the conclusion of these considerations of ours: "I believe that the manifest and obvious proof comes from the behavior of his disciples, who devoted themselves entirely to a teaching that involved a danger to the lives of men. Had they invented the resurrection of the dead they would not have so vigorously imparted this teaching" (Origen, *Contra Celsum*, II, 56; tr. it. P. Ressa, Brescia 2000). A teaching that they imparted not only in words, but with the witness of their lives, even to the point of martyrdom, so that we too might receive the great news – the Gospel! – that in Jesus, for all of us, Life has once and for all defeated death.

If Christ is God, why did he not avoid being betrayed and by one of his own apostles?

(Amedeo Cencini)

1. **This one of the questions or perplexities or doubts with which a certain image of God is bound to clash.**

Indeed, several themes are evoked here at the human and even more strictly theological level and it may be problematic to interpret them: such as the freedom and dignity of man, the divine risk taken by the Creator who gives life to a free creature (free to the point of rejecting his love), the risk again of the Redeemer who – in an act of extreme freedom – delivers himself into the fragile hands of his disciples before handing himself over to the high priests and finally into the great and sure hands of his Father, and in turn is "betrayed" by the disciples (those who deny him, those who abandon him, those who sell him), while the Father exalts him as a son who has totally trusted the Father, entrusting himself to him.

2. **The meaning of *tradere* in Latin**

It is perhaps worthwhile to clarify at the outset that when we use the word "betray" here, we are translating the Latin word "*tradere*," which means both to deliver/consign and to betray. Such ambivalence of meanings also throws light upon our question and allows us to glimpse a possible answer or at least a basic direction so as to unravel what at first glance seems to be a contradiction or a dark point. We see it in the two relational movements that inspire Jesus' acting during his passion (and not only then), toward man and toward his Father: his direct acting and as the motivation behind his acting:

- Jesus put trust also in who was betraying him, that is, he believed to the last, he hoped in him, in the disciples, in Judas, in Peter, in the people... (this is his direct action)

- and when entrusting his life to the Father he also placed it in human hands, indeed, he explicitly decided so to do: "no one takes it from me, But I lay it down of my own accord" Jn 10:18), for he was so certain of his relationship with the Father that he did not hesitate to allow himself to be judged, condemned, scourged and crucified, confident that Abba would not abandon him (this is the motivation that explains his action).

3. Precisely because he is a son of the Father...

We might already attempt, then, to construct the answer on the basis of these elements. If the question that forms the title of our reflection finds Christ's divinity irreconcilable with allowing himself to be betrayed even by his disciples, we could answer that – *precisely because he was the Son of the Father-God and God himself* – Jesus had the freedom to put trust even in man, continuing to believe in the sinful and treacherous human being even until the last moment!

Put another way: it is typically human to trust in a calculated way, to give trust drop by drop and never with eyes closed and to just anyone, lest one be proved wrong and betrayed in trusting any other person, starting with so-called friends, more or less intimate companions or business associates or fellow diners. Indeed, there are believers who find it entirely right and wise to distinguish carefully between faith in God and (not) in man. A popular expression of this diverse and contradictory trust is the joke of those who say they "believe entirely in God the Father Almighty, little in men and in women not at all." And they do not realize that a faith in God (at least in the Christian God) that does not also open its heart toward its brother, and does not somehow have faith in him, trusting, hoping, and being certain that he can be better, provoking him – in the end – to be so, is not credible at all.

4. Typical Christian pearl

In God, instead, it is typical to believe in man, in his dignity and lovability. Does not Creation reveal this faith of the Eternal in the small and limited creature? Is not Redemption the expression of this divine faith that does not fail even when man denies both his dignity and his lovability?

It can indeed be said that this truth deserves to be remembered rather as a specific feature of the Christian faith: that man believes in God is indeed quite normal, all religions say so. But that the Creator believes in the creature is a typically Christian pearl, as part of the belief of the follower of Jesus Christ, contemplated particularly in his cross.

5. "If you are a son of God, come down from the cross... "

Actually, the objection with which we started and which we are trying to answer is not new, nor only of our days so critical and skeptical of everything and everyone. It was already made – in fact – to Jesus himself, though formulated differently, even ironically and scornfully, as a challenge. At the most dramatic moment of his life and also the most revealing of his divine identity: when he was on the cross. And in the form of a question resounding again and again on the lips of various characters: ordinary people and members of the Sanhedrin, soldiers and one of the evildoers hanging like him on the gallows of the cross: "Are you not the Christ, save yourself and us!" (Lk 23:39).

All of this tells us that we are facing a decisive point in our faith option, and/or a recurring doubt, an ever re-emerging request from our little faith: the request for the sign, and the formidable sign, the one that will definitively drive away all resistance and make faith strong and without fissures of doubt (at least so we delude ourselves!).

Just think what would have happened if Jesus with a spectacular "coup de théâtre" had come off the cross gliding down before those people! Certainly, he would have won the challenge big time and filled those who had provoked him with holy terror. But let us ask: would he have obtained faith from those people? Only apparently, for it would have been a *faith born of fear* in the face of so much power, therefore full of guilt, perhaps even of prostrations and requests for forgiveness, contrition and repentance... But this is not the faith the Lord looks for and for which he ascended the cross: faith as

a *free* act, springing from love, from love received and somehow reciprocated, and engendering trust; not faith as won by the unequiv-
ocal sign of power, which somehow imposes itself on the so-called
believer, but arouses fear in him (of the almighty deity); not trust,
but compulsory (often servile) obedience, nor joyful and filial abandonment.

6. The highest theophany

That is why the cross represents the highest point of God's un-
veiling, or his brightest theo-phany, where he manifests something
that is exclusively God's. *Only God, or the Father revealed by the Son,*
could have climbed up on a cross, though he could have chosen not to
do so. Just as only God could have chosen not to come down from the
cross, though he could have done so.

That is, it is not power that is the central element, the one that
distinguishes the God of Christians, but love or the freedom of love.
Or, to return to our question, Christ could have chosen perfect disciples, who would never betray him, but then first and foremost he
would not have founded the Church, but rather an unlikely society
of the perfect, incapable of betraying him, but not because of their
own personal free choice dictated by love, but because so pro-
grammed by another, be it even the Creator. Perhaps perfect, then,
but not free. As if he himself had been afraid of the freedom of his
disciples, and was therefore himself less free.

And here we touch on another point relevant to answering the
question we started with.

7. Is God (all)mighty?

I do not think that I am far from reality if I perceive in questions similar to the one from which we started, a very precise idea of God, indeed a concern – perhaps a bit excessive – to safeguard a certain image of God, the classical one, which comes to us from the first catechism, of the almighty God who makes all things out of nothing and, once he has "become man" (for the salvation of man), is careful to avoid contradictions, uncertainties, frailties, and pettiness that are typically human, choosing – when it comes to forming the group to which he will entrust the Church – the best that was around, albeit accepting human reality as it is, even identifying with it.

In short, it is clear that God is all-powerful (as all religions affirm), but it is equally clear that at least the Father revealed by the Son Jesus does not use this prerogative as mere power, but as a means to manifest something that is much more central and expressive of his identity, namely love: he is all-powerful in love. His is *the omnipotence of love*, not because it is limited by benevolence toward the creature who is weak, but because it is resignified by it, as if it were love that gives it meaning.

What does this mean in concrete terms? It is important to try to understand this, otherwise this adjective ("all-powerful") becomes ambiguous, even misleading, giving an image of God that may not correspond to what the Son, the only one authorized to speak to us about the Father, has revealed to us, and it is probably also at the origin of the question/doubt we are trying to clarify. And since this divine appellation has literally invaded liturgy, prayers (think how many Collects in the Eucharistic liturgy begin precisely by calling

God so!), catechesis, sacred art representing the divine..., it is worth trying to distinguish in order to understand better. To purify the way we think and say God.

The mystery of divine vulnerability

While all religions profess belief in the almighty God, it is only Christianity that speaks of vulnerability in God and of God. That is, of vulnerability as a divine condition, not so much as an exception determined by the parenthesis of the Incarnation and made evident in the crucifixion and death of the Son, but as God's way of being! It is clear that this is a mystery, before which to stop and take off one's sandals, as if it were holy ground, burning bush (cf. Ex 3:1-6).

But mystery full of light, of light so dazzling that it prevents our poor eyes from immediately understanding everything, from seeing clearly; and mystery that desires to unveil itself, to make contact with those who seek it.

And we seek such contact in Salvation History, that history which is God's history and ours as well, where man's vulnerability not only meets but is saved by God's vulnerability. History that reveals to us a vulnerable God in the three fundamental moments that mark the mystery of salvation.

8. God's vulnerability in Salvation History.

(a) In the Creation: the weakness of one who loves.

God creates out of love and, with absolute consistency, he creates a free creature. Free also to the point of letting itself be loved or rejecting the love that created it. This is the radical vulnerability of

God the lover! God is vulnerable *out of love,* because, inevitably, the one who loves is weak, and no one is as weak as he. Indeed, it is *he himself who places* himself *in a position of weakness*; for if he truly loves, he leaves the beloved free, he respects him in his dignity as a free being, he does not impose himself nor impose his own benevolence on the beloved by a subtle blackmail, but exposes himself, if anything, to possible rejection.

Creation not only expresses and entails this risk as a possibility, but shows it immediately, from the very beginning, in its dramatic fulfillment in Adam's rejection.

(b) In the Incarnation: God takes upon himself human vulnerability.

The most significant difference between divine and human vulnerability is that while we are in some way subject to vulnerability, as a fact of our creatureliness, in the God of Christians, on the other hand, it is a *choice.* We cannot not be vulnerable, whereas in God it is he himself that decides to be vulnerable. We often experience our vulnerability with fear or shame or simply endure it. God chooses it and motivates it, embraces it and does not hide it or even less is ashamed of it. Nor is he ashamed to rely on vulnerable instruments.

This is made manifest in the mystery of the Incarnation, where God always out of love *chooses to take on his shoulders all our vulnerabilities,* taking them with him to the cross, in what is the most... powerful and mysterious theophany of the *omni-weakness* of the God of Jesus Christ. The Incarnation is so real that it goes so far as to assume totally all human vulnerability: an assumption that is

anything but apparent or merely symbolic, see the night of Gethsemane with that extreme and yet very human sweat of blood and
that supplication that reveals all the vulnerability of the praying person ("Father, if you are willing, take this cup away from me!...," Lk
22:42a). It is interesting, and it says a lot about our resistance in the
face of the mystery of divine vulnerability, that, faced with this heart-
felt plea of Jesus, we do not spontaneously pause and meditate on
his fear expressed in no uncertain terms, but we immediately rush
to the second part of the verse, where the Son entrusts himself to the
will of the Father (cf. Lk 22:42b)! As if the first part of the verse
causes us problems, while the second part is more... *theologically correct.*

(c) In Redemption: the restlessness of God.

Finally, God is vulnerable and continues to be vulnerable in our
daily salvation history not only because he exposes himself to man's
free response, but because he himself takes the initiative, and *always
and forever has been seeking his creature, as he once did with Adam.*

It is what we might call the *restlessness of God*! We Christians
believe and experience the restlessness of our heart, made by God
and for God, until it rests in him, as Augustine reminds us (*Confessions* I,1,4). But the astounding thing is that God first is restless until
he finds rest in the heart of man. It is divine restlessness at the origin
of human restlessness. And it is truly amazing, dazzling light, great
mystery!

In that restlessness is told the whole mystery of Redemption, and even before that the mystery as well of the Creator-creature relationship, or the love of the Eternal!

9. The Father delivers the Son – and every son

If we return then to the initial objection, we find that it is already ambiguously posed. When Jesus says, "The Son of Man is delivered into the hands of men..." (Mk 9:31) we are not here confronted with the disciple who betrays the Master, much less the Christ who would choose his disciples badly, but we are, if anything, confronted *with the Father's plan to deliver the Son to mankind*: it is the Father-God who is the subject of this operation. The Word, who has been with the Father from all eternity, allows himself to be delivered into poor human hands precisely because he knows that nothing and no one will ever have the power to break that unity of love. Or he trusts his Father's love so much that he has the freedom to entrust himself to those who will seem to want his death.

And it is beautiful then to think that now, in the same way, the Father also delivers each of us, to life, to others, to death....

Blessed are those who allow themselves to be delivered with the same freedom and trust as the Son!

If Jesus is God, why did he not manage to convince his people that he was the Messiah?

(Gonzalo de la Morena)

During his ministry, Jesus manifested that he was the messiah, at first discreetly, but then more and more clearly. It was during the last week of his earthly life that this revelation reached its climax. Jesus entered Jerusalem on a donkey, thus fulfilling an ancient messianic prophecy (cf. Mark 11:1-10 and Zech 9:9). Some people recognized him and acclaimed him as "son of David," that is, Messiah. Jesus' movement did not go unnoticed by the Jewish authorities who, concerned about political repercussions and possible Roman reprisals, decided to distance themselves and reject Jesus (cf. Jn 11:45-53). The fundamental question we now want to clarify is therefore:

1. **Why did the authorities of the people reject the one who presented himself as the Messiah?**

The reasons for Jesus' rejection are not simple, as they involve both historical and theological reasons. From a historical perspective, it is important to understand the political and religious context in which Jesus preached. A plausible reconstruction of some of the motivations behind this decision might be as follows.

Some Jewish authorities longed and even hoped for it with religious motives, for the coming of a savior who would deliver the people from the foreign power, that of Rome. It is essential to understand that, in that historical context, the political and the religious were intrinsically linked: the enemies of God's people were the enemies of God himself. An exclusively religious liberation, therefore, did not fit into their mental picture. The Scriptures contained promises and norms whose nature was both religious and political such as, for example, the law that a foreign king should not reign over God's people (cf. Deut. 17:15). All of this fed the hope of God intervening to give his people a kingdom, independent of foreign powers.

Most likely, these ideas were also current among Jesus' followers. However, his teaching encouraged attitudes that did not fit with a political insurrection, such as meekness, forgiveness, love for the enemy, and a radical trust in God. In addition, Jesus welcomed into his circle tax collectors, seen as collaborators with the oppressive regime, and surrounded himself with humble and poor people and sinners rather than those who could have influenced or manipulated the levers of power. Clearly, Jesus' movement was not aimed at gaining the power and strength needed to confront the enemy power. However, its messianic nature made it a social danger: it could generate popular enthusiasm that threatened to drive the population out of control.

Those in positions of power had reason to see Jesus' movement as a danger to the nation's interests: this powerless group would have no hope of success and Rome's reprisals could have been devastating. In this context, it was understandable that the authorities should choose to distance themselves from a movement perceived as a threat to the stability and security of the people.

Moreover, Jesus' message at times openly challenged the Jewish authorities of the time, both the Pharisees and the Sadducees. What he taught challenged the authority of the Pharisees, who probably saw their influence over the people threatened. Jesus' opposition to the Sadducees was even more evident, manifesting itself not only in words but also in actions that seemed to challenge the power of those who ran the Temple. Any triumph of Jesus' movement could have disturbed the balance of power and influence existing among the authorities of the time. Resistance on the part of those who benefited from this state of affairs was therefore understandable.

We should point out that although the decision to reject Jesus prevailed among some authorities, it would be unfair to attribute this rejection collectively – much less unanimously – to his people. Jesus' movement consisted entirely of Jews and was even welcomed by some influential Jews, such as Nicodemus and Joseph of Arimathea. Moreover, early Christianity soon welcomed into its midst "a great multitude of priests" (Acts 6:7), as well as "some of the sect of the Pharisees" (Acts 15:5). In other words, Jesus' rejection was neither universal nor exclusive to his people; rather, his ministry provoked a variety of responses and attitudes within the Jewish society of the time.

However, it is undeniable that Jesus was not recognized as the Messiah by his people, which led to his surrender to the Roman authorities for crucifixion. From the perspective of our faith, this is deeply scandalous because it implies the rejection of the incarnate Son of God himself. Faced with this puzzling reality, one wonders why Jesus did not use his power to assert his position and thus secure the acceptance of the people.

2. The mystery of human freedom

From a theological point of view, the first consideration we must make concerns the mystery of freedom. God gave human beings free will, the ability to choose between good and evil, and he wanted to count on it to bring about their salvation. As St. Augustine says, "God, who created you without you, will not save you without you." For reasons known to him, God does not want to impose salvation unilaterally, but offers it to our freedom. Salvation is a liberation from bondage to make us sons, in Latin, *liberi* (that is, "free"). It is logical that a true relationship of love cannot be established unilaterally, but requires the freedom of the beloved. Hence, God offers in Christ a gift that can be accepted or rejected.

With signs and words, Jesus announced that he was bringing about God's plan of salvation, but this fulfillment was presented as a call to freedom for those involved. Some believed in him, followed him and left everything for his cause. Others chose to reject him. It is true that there were influential men, such as Nicodemus or Joseph of Arimathea, who wanted to accept Jesus. However, the final decision of the Jewish authorities was to reject him and hand him over to the Roman power. The freedom to accept or reject Jesus was genuine, and salvation history was shaped by the decisions of men: ultimately, those in power made a negative decision.

3. The "failure" of the Son of God in God's plan

A second theological reflection brings us into the mystery of evil within the plan of salvation. It should not be forgotten that Christ's rejection, although the result of truly free human decisions, was mysteriously integrated into the divine plan of salvation. The political failure of the Jesus movement was not simply an unexpected twist, but was providentially foreseen in God's plan. This is possible by virtue of divine eternity, whereby God simultaneously knows all of history. We cannot imagine it, but God's eternity does not consist in an infinite succession of time, but in a simultaneous and ever-present possession of all time. For this reason, he can consider, from his eternal perspective, the free choices made by creatures in time.

In this mysterious way, the free response of creatures is mysteriously included in the plan of salvation willed by God in his eternity. Man's "no" caused God's unconditional self-giving to man to reach its culmination on the cross. God eternally willed his Son to fulfill his mission of salvation through man's "no," thus transforming failure, suffering and death into God's chosen way to assume our sin and redeem us.

Christ himself takes into account the negative outcome of his earthly journey, and makes rejection an opportunity to give us his life: "No one takes it [life] from me: I give it of myself" (Jn 10:18). In this way, Jesus makes the cross a supreme revelation of his love: "No one has greater love than this: to lay down his life for his friends" (Jn 15:13).

It was not Jesus' mission to be recognized and triumph as the temporal king of Israel, but to offer himself as a sacrifice for our salvation. His rejection and suffering are part of the plan of our redemption and, in this sense, were caused not only by the negative response of the historical figures of the time, but also by the sins of all people throughout time. Thus, the mystery of Christ's suffering is united with the mystery of evil, making it possible for the victory of the Resurrection to emerge from the apparent failure.

In conclusion, the authorities' renunciation of Jesus as Messiah is part of the deep mystery of divine love and human freedom. Christ's suffering and cross are not simply tragic events in history but take on new meaning in the light of the Resurrection and manifest the very heart of God's redemptive love. In his total gift of himself, Jesus transformed human failure and contempt into a path to full life, but only faith in the Resurrection allows us to accept this truth.

If Christ came to save all people, why did he not manifest himself in a more obvious way and instead lived 30 years in a remote village in one of the poorest countries at that time?

(Antonio Ducay)

In his novel *The Diary of a Country Priest*, Georges Bernanos paints the life of a parish priest, grappling with multiple challenges in his rural parish of Ambricourt. As he engages in his pastoral role, he must confront indifference, hostility and suffering in his community. In a world permeated by despair and disappointment, the priest strives to offer spiritual comfort to his parishioners, remaining steadfast in his faith despite his own struggles and limitations. At the end of his life, the priest finds himself seriously ill and in a situation that is anything but idyllic. He may appear to have failed in his religious mission, but the protagonist judges otherwise. He dies with the knowledge that "everything is grace." The difficulties, hardships, and struggles he encountered along the way did not lead him to "nonsense," but enabled him to discover God's presence in everything and to understand that God can infuse a sense of salvation into every situation.

The novel highlights a fundamental aspect of everyday Christian experience: the human heart is slow to know itself, to listen, to be converted and to trust. This is why the coming of Jesus into the world was preceded by a long journey. Christians have not only the

New Testament, but also the Old Testament, for the new life brought by Jesus does not fit into a theoretical or idealized world, but into a concrete world, made of flesh, which has experienced all the greatness and miseries of being human.

It took a long time for a small portion of mankind to be ready to receive the Savior. First there was rebellion, idolatry, indifference and injustice on the part of mankind, even among the chosen people blessed with a particular calling. There were encouragements, demonstrations and blessings, but also threats, punishments and curses from God himself. Only after this long journey, which explored the entire sphere of the human spirit and reactions, did mankind begin to understand God, to recognize how to relate to him and to perceive the importance of its connection with God in order to achieve true happiness. It was only at this point that the fullness of time could be fully manifested in the world with the arrival of the Son, Jesus.

Overall, Old Testament history teaches us that nothing that happens in the human world is unimportant in God's eyes. As the book of Wisdom states, addressing God, "For you love all things that exist and have loathing for none of the things you have made; if you had hated something, you would not have made it" (Wisdom 11:24). The Lord, through his Providence, sustains all things, whether great or small. What may seem insignificant in the eyes of the world may instead be of great value in the eyes of God, who despises nothing he has created, but rather loves everything he has made.

In a famous inscription on the tomb of St. Ignatius of Loyola, we read, "Not to be limited by the greatest and to be contained in the smallest is divine." The aphorism reminds us that God is so immense that he is not limited by the greatness of the world, but also is so loving that he can reside even in the smallest things. This last concept is embodied, as it were, in his own birth in Bethlehem, which took place in a manger, surrounded by the local shepherds, and enfolded in the love of a young mother and her husband. While human beings tend to be attracted to efficiency and spectacle, by what arouses clamor and wonder, God prefers simplicity and humility.

This inclination of God toward what the world considers negligible and insignificant has its own coherence. Life does not consist only of major events or spectacular phenomena, but is made up of a wide range of small, often repetitive and seemingly common moments. In particular, human life is interwoven with numerous gestures that are of modest value when considered individually, but together can create a fabric of great value.

A caress to a child, a gesture of kindness to an elderly person, advice given to a friend, a task performed with tender care: even if they do not make media headlines, they can bring joy and happiness to those who receive them. When such gestures become part of the daily routine, society is enriched with human value and becomes a reflection of God's presence. Conversely, in the absence of such actions, environments are impoverished and interpersonal relationships become difficult.

Much of the Christian life is focused on this area of the ordinary, the everyday. We do not have many opportunities to express our love of God and neighbor through striking gestures, but we can do so by carefully attending to our relationship with God and other people in the small, everyday things, such as those mentioned above.

Jesus came into the world with the goal of redeeming us from sin and teaching us how to live as God's beloved children And so he spent many years living a life similar to ours, immersed in the routine of a small village in a remote region of the world, as most people do. Jesus learned to obey his parents, performed small family services and exercised a trade for many years. As he grew up, he matured as any human being does. Although he was similar to us in these daily experiences, inwardly Jesus always lived in communion with the Father's love, distinguishing himself from us who often act out of selfish motives. Through this ordinary life, Jesus sanctified the everyday and taught us to do the same. As St. Josemaría Escrivá pointed out, "Jesus, growing up and living like one of us, reveals to us that human existence, ordinary everyday activity, has a divine meaning" (*Christ is Passing By*, 14). He had to live a human existence similar to ours in order to bring it back to love, showing us how to live in God's presence and granting us the grace to do the same.

It is clear that the Gospel message Jesus brought to the world and the mission of salvation he was to fulfill were not exhausted in these first 30 years of his life, during which his identity remained hidden from the eyes of the people. He still had to carry out in full the mission entrusted to him by the Father: to announce the coming of the times of salvation and the Kingdom of Heaven, and to bring salvation to completion through his cross and Resurrection. He had to reveal himself as what he was: the Messiah and the Son of God, the true "sign of contradiction, so that the thoughts of many hearts might be revealed" (cf. Lk 2:33). However, the importance of this "public" phase of his life and his passion and death does not detract from the relevance of the years of his "hidden" life.

During those 30 years, Jesus chose to live an ordinary life, made up of small everyday realities, to give full meaning and to make the normal condition of humanity's life, too often made burdensome because of sin, pleasing to the Father. The world needed our Lord to confer full meaning to the common and ordinary circumstances in which it spends its existence, to redeem them from their subjection of sin. Therefore, Jesus fully immersed himself in the most basic aspects of life: family, work, society, and fulfilled, as any Israelite would have done, the prescriptions and regulations of the Law of Moses.

He wanted to remain within the laws given by God to the world, to creation. He wanted to bring them to completion by giving them meaning. The Fathers of the Church – and in particular St. Irenaeus of Lyons – saw in Jesus' taking up of all these human realities, the basis of a *recapitulation*, that is, of a process by which, in Jesus and thanks to him, creation is given a new beginning, takes a new course, different from the one lost with the sinful Adam, a course fully in accordance with the divine plan. This is possible because Jesus always lived these realities in filial obedience to the Father's will.

We can conclude by recalling the words of the Second Vatican Council in the Pastoral Constitution *Gaudium et spes*: "By the incarnation the Son of God united himself in a certain way with every man. He worked with man's hands, he thought with man's intelligence, he acted with man's will, he loved with man's heart" (no. 22). This formulation, "Christ worked with man's hands, thought with man's intelligence...," effectively represents what we have just explained: the fact that Jesus took on the entire experience of human life and condition. The hands, the intelligence, the will, the heart:

these are the spheres of practical life, spiritual life, affectivity; the whole human being with its complete life. Jesus made all this his own, and therefore his hidden life contains, in its apparent silence, a very eloquent message: every noble aspect of human life was sanctified by Jesus and is therefore for us an opportunity for filial obedience to the Father, a means for our sanctification.

Why did Jesus agree to die on the cross to save men and reconcile them with God? Could he not have saved them in a less cruel way?

(Nicolas Massmann)

Those who ask this question have realized one important thing: Jesus' death on the cross is difficult to understand and explain. In fact, there is a sort of gap that reason on its own cannot bridge. For there will always remain a certain percentage of mystery. It is what St. Paul calls the scandal of the cross, which is actually the scandal of love.

To question the cross, in fact, is to peer into an abyss that provokes our intelligence and challenges our sensitivity: Why so much suffering? Could it not have been otherwise? Did God need the suffering of his Son to make up for our offenses and restore justice? And how to reconcile this with the Christian God of love, mercy and forgiveness?

Actually, we have before us one of those deep realities, like so many in life, that can only be understood through a new logic: that of love and freedom. In other words, to love differently from the way we love, to love even if one is not loved.

In order to give an answer, we will first have to take a few steps back and gain perspective. Then we will slowly begin the ascent. The path, like any mountain, will not always be linear. We will have to make a few more turns, but eventually the goal awaits us.

1. At the origin we always find love

The first and most important thing to remember is the reason for the Son of God's coming into the world. Perhaps the best answer is found in John's Gospel: "For God so loved the world that he gave his only begotten Son, that whoever believes in him should not be lost but have eternal life" (John 3:16). In other words, God sends his Son to reveal his love to us and to save us by his love. Christ comes to remove the chains of sin and to help us to enjoy something much better: the freedom of God's children.

Jesus is aware of his mission and makes this clear several times: his *food* is to do the Father's will (cf. Jn 4:34); he did not come to be served, but to *serve* (cf. Mk 10:45); he does not want his own will to be done, but that of the one who sent him (cf. Lk 22:42).

In other words, Jesus is clear that his task is not only to proclaim that God loves us, but to *become himself* the concrete revelation of God's love for people. He knows that his mission will be to make this love transparent and close to us, for only then will the world believe in him and have eternal life.

2. The Father's most precious gift

We also know that God the Father not only sent his Son but also *delivered* him. This is more than sending: it means making available, handing over, even submitting the destiny of his own Son to human freedom. In Gethsemane Jesus could have asked the Father for twelve legions of angels to come immediately to protect him (cf. Mt

26:53) but he does not do so because, precisely, he was *handed over* to men.

In fact, God *gave* his Son as the most precious gift he could give us. And Jesus, as a gift of infinite love, expresses this love through all his words, actions, silences, looks and reactions. In other words, through the totality of his existence. Everything in Jesus' life speaks the language of love.

This already is bringing us slowly closer to the mystery of the Passion. In fact, Jesus is not delivered into the hands of men only at the moment of his arrest in Gethsemane, his interrogation before the High Priest or his trial before Pilate. Jesus is delivered long before: from the very moment of the Incarnation, of his birth in Bethlehem, Jesus is already to some extent delivered to men. He is already in our hands. He chooses the path of vulnerability, weakness and humility, so that what converts our lives and transforms our hearts is only the witness of his love. In other words, nothing but love will have to be the real cause of what God wants to accomplish in human hearts.

What should be most surprising, then, is not the fact of death on the cross, with all its suffering and injustice, but the very fact that God gave his Son and that this handing over entails the reality of dying, like any human being. Jesus is handed over to the circumstance of death from the moment the Word becomes flesh. This is what is truly amazing!

Now, did Jesus come *only* to die or exclusively to die *on the cross*? As the Catechism of the Catholic Church says, it is true that "his redemptive passion is the raison d'être of his incarnation" (no. 607). But, on the other hand, it is also true that the heart of Jesus' message is the Kingdom of God. His main purpose was for us humans to open ourselves to the coming of the Kingdom of God, and this implied accepting the full revelation of God's love through our conversion: "Repent and believe in the Gospel" (Mark 1:15) are the words with which the evangelist Mark introduces us to Jesus. "In his appearance in Galilee, Jesus did not begin with the message, *I will die on the cross for God's people*. Rather, he preached the Kingdom of God as the powerful newness and fulfillment of all promises. He wanted nothing more than to live entirely for the coming of the Kingdom of God" (G. Lohfink, *All meine Quellen entspringen in dir*, Freiburg 2023, p. 276).

But opening oneself to this new Kingdom, believing this good news and converting one's heart also meant something very specific: accepting him as the Son of God, the Messiah, the one sent. And this forces us to take the next step.

3.   Our response and his reaction

We all know how things turned out: his message, but also his very person, were rejected. "In the Lord's public action there is an ascent: the more Jesus shows his love for Israel, the more obstinate these people become" (H.U. von Balthasar, *Kennt uns Jesus - kennen wir ihn?*, Freiburg 1980, p. 22). And this rejection finally took the form of the cross. The cross was mankind's great "no" to the Son whom the Father *delivered* to us.

This was man's response to the invitation of the Son who had been sent. Now, how does Jesus react in the face of rejection? What is his attitude to the cross? This is where the most surprising, truly revealing and moving thing happens: Jesus not only continues to love unconditionally, but makes even more explicit and evident the love he came to manifest to the world. Let us not forget: the cross was a brutal punishment for great criminals. And what Christ does is to transform the meaning of the cross from within: from being a place of hatred, of forsakenness and of denial of love, it becomes *the expression of the greatest possible love.*

Surely, the key to understanding what happened during the passion and on the cross was given to us by Jesus himself: "No one takes [life] from me: I give it of myself" (Jn 10:18). That is to say: men will believe that they are taking my life away, but they do not know that it is I who am voluntarily giving it out of love. We get a glimpse of the new logic, what God means by love: giving ourselves even to those who do not accept us and even hate us.

It is as if Jesus, at the moment of the crucifixion, was saying, "No matter what they do with me, where they take me and how they want to end my life. I will continue to love and I will continue to love you. Only words of love and forgiveness will come from me. This is why I came into the world: to witness to the Father's unconditional love. If it was necessary to go this far, to the cross, to give this message, I will carry it, I will embrace it, and from it I will continue to witness to the one thing for which I came into this world: the love of God that forgives, transforms, heals and gives life."

In other words, man's rejection does not cause Jesus to walk away or turn his back on us, but it causes his self-giving and love to shine through even more. Because Jesus' giving himself out of love is stronger than man's capacity to reject.

In the hour of crucifixion, even the last cell of Christ's body reveals his love for mankind. This is why St. Josemaría Escrivá said, "On the Cross, all his gestures and all his words are of love, of serene and strong love" (*Way of the Cross*, Station XI). And before him, St. Cyril of Jerusalem: "God extends his arms on the cross to embrace the whole universe."

Many people passed by Jesus during the crucifixion on Golgotha, but very few were aware of what was really happening. Why? Because it takes other eyes to understand the true meaning of the cross. They are the eyes of faith.

4. A love story

In fact, although at first glance it may not seem so, the cross is the most beautiful love story ever told. What we see there is *the ultimate expression of the greatest possible love*. Calvary is the place and the moment when God's love is fully manifested, making itself maximally close and visible. The cross is the synthesis and, at the same time, the revelation of God's love story for mankind, which began with creation, matured and developed over the centuries until the handing over of his own Son. All of Jesus' life is beautiful and saving, but all of it is made present and manifested to us in its greatest grandeur at the moment of the cross.

So how does God save us and how does the cross save us? We could answer with one word: *by converting us*. But not through an acknowledgement of guilt for our injustices and sins, but through the manifestation of all the love we contemplate in the scene of the cross. It is what Jesus always knew: "And I, when I am lifted up from the earth, will draw all to myself" (Jn 12:32). It is the attraction of revealed love that moves our affections and converts our hearts.

On the cross we see close up the wickedness and cruelty of sin, which Christ confronted, overturning it, teaching us to love in such a way as to change ourselves and the world around us.

5.   Pain is not the protagonist

I hope that by now at least one idea should be clear: only love is capable of saving man. As Pope Benedict XVI has written, "Man is redeemed through love" (*Spe salvi*, 26). This means that pain and the intensity of suffering are not the cause of our redemption, much less the central theme of the cross. "It is not the suffering of Jesus that saves us, but the love with which he lived this suffering" (Y. Congar).

It is important to emphasize this, because sometimes we get the impression that the cross redeems us, because the sum of suffering and torment there has reached the highest level imaginable. But it is not the quantity of pain, but the quantity and quality of love that is decisive. On the cross there is more divine obedience and patience than human hatred and sin.

And this is because pain and suffering in themselves, if they are not an expression of love, are meaningless. More: they can quickly become an insurmountable barrier to love and begin to fill life with sadness and bitterness. "Only love gives direction and meaning to pain" (J. Ratzinger). Pain is a secondary element, which can only be understood against the background of unconditional love.

6.   The answer that makes sense of everything

However, we still need to add a fundamental consideration: how does God the Father respond? What is his response to the death of his Son? Does all the love poured out on the cross simply remain there? The answer is a profound No. Indeed, the answer has a very specific name: *Resurrection*. We can never separate the cross from the Resurrection. It would be like leaving a story without its ending and what gives meaning to it all.

The Father does not want the death of the Son. He cannot be said to send him into the world desiring that he be crucified. Of course, God *cannot not know* that it will be so, and indirectly we can say that Jesus' death on the cross is part of his will. But his main will is life, not death. And this is precisely how we understand Jesus' Resurrection, as the response of a Father who does not allow death to be the last word. Neither Jesus' death, nor that of any of his children "At the center of the New Testament is undoubtedly the cross, which finds its meaning in the resurrection" (H.U. von Balthasar, *Kleine Fibel für unversicherte Laien*, Einsiedeln 1989, 68).

7.   God's freedom and the path of our salvation

Before concluding this long answer, it would be good to add an observation, which actually goes beyond the mystery of the cross:

God is not compelled to anything, nor bound by anything. That is, God was not obligated to save us by sending his Son, much less by bringing him to die on the cross. God *does not need* the cross to save us, any more *than he needs* the sacraments to bring us into communion with him.

But at the same time, in the event of the cross we see an important part of the wisdom with which God wanted to arrange the way to save us and to give us his love. St. Thomas Aquinas teaches that one of the reasons *it seemed appropriate for* Jesus to suffer for us on the cross is "to give us an example of how we should act." Indeed, the Christian life would consist in nothing more than "despising what Christ despised on the cross and desiring what Christ desired. In the cross we find the example of all the virtues" (*Ex Collationibus sancti Thomas de Aquino, Collatio 6 super Credo in Deum*).

But none of this contradicts the initial truth: God is not subject or obligated to anything. Consequently, on a purely theoretical level, we can say that Jesus' outcome *could* have been different. Jesus *could* have ended his days in this world in another way, the love of God the Father in his Son could have manifested itself to us in another way, and man's affirmative response to this love could have conditioned the shape of our redemption in a different way.

However, we do not know this hypothetical way, nor will we ever know it, because the only path we have, the only one that has remained open to all, is the speciic one of the cross. This is and will be the specific path of our salvation. The path in which each of us can understand the true meaning of those key words "God so loved the world" (Jn 3:16). Words that *explain* the *folly* of the cross and show us that God loves seriously and to the last consequences.

If Christ is the only savior, redeemer, mediator of salvation, how then can non-Christians be saved?

(Antonio Ducay)

The discovery of America in the late 1400s profoundly changed the way the world was viewed. This event also influenced missionaries from Spain and other countries, who traveled to these new lands to spread Christianity. Many of them noticed that the locals enthusiastically welcomed the Christian message and were eager to convert. Around 1530, Bishop Juan de Zumárraga, the first bishop of Mexico, was impressed by the moral behavior of the natives, which seemed to be even better than that of many Spaniards who had come to Mexico to make their fortunes. While some of these Spaniards behaved none too honorably, the natives seemed genuinely interested to change their lives for the better. Zumárraga went so far as to say, "You see how good they are, so much so that I believe many of them will have been saved even without baptism." This opinion, rather bold for the time, shows that Zumárraga believed that the good deeds of the natives would be rewarded with eternal life on judgment day.

1. Christ offers grace and salvation to all men

This account makes us realize that, even at that time, the idea that Christ's grace could operate outside the strictly sacramental sphere was alive. Indeed, it was noted that people who were not sufficiently instructed in the faith still managed to lead honest and upright moral and religious lives. This opened up the possibility that Christ's grace could reach everyone, since he is the mediator and Savior of all mankind.

In more recent times, the Second Vatican Council has explicitly stated that God offers salvation to every individual. The Constitution *Gaudium et Spes*, in no. 22, sets out the reasons for this. It affirms that despite the difficulties of life and the inevitability of death, Christians are united to the paschal mystery of Jesus and, consequently, will also participate in his Resurrection and glory. Then, the Council also addresses those who are not Christians, declaring, "And this applies not only to Christians, but also to all people of good will, in whose hearts grace acts invisibly. For Christ died for all, and the final destination of every human being is the same: the divine one. The Holy Spirit offers everyone the possibility of being united, in a way that only God knows, to the paschal mystery of Christ."

The Council highlights two basic reasons why salvation is offered to every person, Christian or not: first, that "man's ultimate vocation is indeed one, the divine one," and second, that "Christ died for all." We will examine these two ideas in more detail.

(a) The Council affirms that "man's ultimate vocation is indeed one, the divine one," that is, that the true purpose of human life is not just to achieve an earthly happiness, but a higher, divine happiness: to live forever in communion and friendship with God. St. Augustine expressed this idea by saying, "You have made us for yourself, O Lord, and our heart is restless until it rests in you" (*The*

Confessions I,1,1). This means that God created man out of love and called him to live in a loving relationship with him. The true happiness of the human being is found in responding to this divine call, for this is how man's ultimate purpose is fulfilled.

However, human history did not go in this direction because, from the very beginning, the first human beings turned away from God. Had they remained faithful, their descendants would also have been able to live in communion with God. In this sense, there is one plan for all human beings, which began with creation and, after sin, was reopened through Christ's saving mission. As St. Paul explained, if Adam, by sinning, brought death to all, Jesus Christ, the only righteous one, brought justification and salvation to all (cf. Rom 5:18).

(b) The Council also affirms that "Jesus died for all." This is one of the fundamental truths of the Christian faith: Jesus redeemed mankind from sin and brought salvation through his sacrifice on the cross, which was completed with his glorious Resurrection. The crucifixion is seen as an act of immense love by Christ, the Son of God made man, who *gave his life not only for his friends or his people, but for all mankind.*

From the very beginning, the Church has interpreted Jesus' sacrifice in this way, that is, as a sacrifice of universal value. St. Paul, in his letter to Timothy, says that Jesus, as mediator between God and men, "gave his life as a ransom for all" (1 Tim 2:5). St. John, speaking of Christ's sacrifice, also says that Jesus cleansed the sins of the whole world (cf. 1 John 2:2).

We confess that Jesus is our Savior because, as human beings, we are unable to fully respond to God's love because of sin, which has

been present in us since the fall of Adam and Eve. This inability always to do good and love God is something we can all experience in
our daily lives. We do not have the necessary strength for such perfect love, which is why we needed to be freed from our condition of
sin.

Jesus, by his sacrifice, did what no human being could have
done: full of obedient love, he gave his life on our behalf. Through
this, he erased our sins and introduced into our lives a new strength,
grace, which enables us to respond to God's love. When we accept
Christ into our lives we are united with him, we are able to truly love
and therefore we are saved.

However, Jesus' work does not eliminate our freedom. Although
he gave his life for everyone, this does not mean that everyone will
be saved automatically. To have friendship with God, it is necessary
that we also sincerely want to respond to his love with obedient
faith.

2.   The problem of salvation of the unevangelized

Union with Christ the Savior is achieved through faith in him
and the sacrament of Baptism. Faith is a divine gift that impels us to
believe in Jesus, his word and teaching, recognizing him as Lord and
Master and accepting his divinity. Baptism introduces us into the
life of Christ, making us participants in his Cross and Resurrection,
and adopts us as children of God, making us brothers and sisters of
other believers in the Church family. Baptism marks a decisive moment in the life of those who receive it: before it we are in some way
subjected to the power of sin and the devil, but through sacramental

grace we are freed from it, being led into the true love that is in Christ. After Baptism, it is no longer the devil who dominates us, but it is Jesus our Lord, who guides us inwardly in life and uses pastors and brothers in the Church to accompany us on our spiritual journey.

These conceptions have been consistently upheld by the Church, which has also reflected on Jesus' words recorded at the end of Mark's gospel. When sending his disciples out to preach, Jesus tells them, "Go into all the world and proclaim the gospel to every creature. Whoever believes and is baptized will be saved, but whoever does not believe will be condemned" (Mark 16:15-16). It seems to follow from these and similar words of Christ that baptismal faith is an essential condition for salvation. In other words, it seems that without physical baptism, the individual is not spiritually united with Christ and, as a result, remains in bondage to sin and the devil.

If this were so, however, no one could obtain salvation without receiving baptism, which would mean that all those to whom the gospel was not proclaimed would have no chance of being saved. However, this perspective would defeat the two statements of the Second Vatican Council that we have previously explained. In fact, many would not be able to arrive at the communion with God for which they were created, nor would they be able to benefit from the salvation obtained by Jesus through his sacrifice.

For these reasons, the Church has always strongly emphasized that the saving power of Jesus' cross and resurrection actually extends to all human beings. In other words, Christ's offer of salvation is able to manifest itself in mysterious ways in the heart of every individual. Returning to the text of *Gaudium et Spes* 22 cited at the beginning, we note that it is clearly stated that participation in the salvation obtained by Jesus "applies not only to Christians, but also to all people of good will, *in whose hearts grace works invisibly.*" This calls attention to the good will and the invisible action of grace. The basic idea is that Christ's grace is not denied to anyone so that he can lead a righteous life; it works and bears fruit to the extent that the person, even if unknowingly, opens himself to it.

Of course, those who have not been evangelized usually know little or nothing about Jesus and his grace; nevertheless, this grace exists and works, and if the person does not direct his or her freedom toward evil, it guides him or her to live honestly and justly. Thanks to the action of the Holy Spirit, who communicates the grace of Jesus to every man and woman, the Council concludes, "we must hold that *the Holy Spirit gives everyone the possibility of being associated, in the way God knows, with the paschal mystery.*" This means that every person, even if he or she has not been evangelized, has the possibility of coming into contact with the source of grace and salvation, which is the life of Jesus.

But then, does Baptism not become superfluous? If a person can receive the grace of Christ even without being formally Christian, what is the point of Baptism? The answer becomes clear when we consider that the grace received by those who are not baptized is nevertheless oriented toward Christ and the Church. Conversion to Christianity is often an inner process that requires time and gradual steps. Immediate conversions, such as that of St. Paul, are rare exceptions. However, if a person is sincere and seeks the truth, the Holy Spirit guides him or her toward the Christian faith. This journey may lead to Baptism, but even if it does not end with the sacrament, the important thing is that the person is cooperating with grace, moving toward a more righteous life and responding to the Spirit's call.

In this sense, we can say that such persons are already on the way to the Church. They are not yet formally part of the Church, but they are "in the courtyard," close to entering it, because they are following the illuminations that the Holy Spirit offers them.

In this context, the ancient statement of many Church Fathers, already found in St. Cyprian of Carthage, that "outside the Church there is no salvation," reveals a profound truth. This statement was meant to emphasize that those who leave the Church or reject it after knowing it will not find another way of salvation, for there is no other. As St. Paul taught the Ephesians, there is one Body, one Spirit, and one hope of salvation, for there is "one Lord, one faith, one baptism, and one God the Father of all." With the coming of Jesus and the founding of the Church, God has manifested his ultimate and final will for the salvation of humanity, offering no other alternatives.

The only path to salvation is the result of the earthly life of Jesus, His incarnate Son, and the gift of the Holy Spirit. However, in his infinite mercy, God also embraces those who sincerely seek the Truth, even if, due to the manifold circumstances of life, they sometimes do not succeed in fully understanding it or manage to become incorporated into the Church through baptism before the end of their lives.

3.   One way or many ways of salvation?

What can we say about people who follow other religions, such as those who rely on the doctrine of Muhammad, or who are Buddhists or Hindus? Does the religion of those who are not Christians have any relevance to salvation? Can we consider these religions as ways or paths to communion with God and salvation? The Second Vatican Council reflected deeply on these questions. It stated that religions often bring with them ways of life, precepts and doctrines which, though different from those of the Church, "not infrequently reflect a ray of that truth which enlightens all men" (*Nostra Aetate*, 2). Not everything found in other religions is to be discarded. The Holy Spirit often uses elements found in these faiths to develop the religious sense of their followers, instilling in them a thirst for truth and a search for the ultimate meaning of life. In this way, these religions can keep alive a longing for transcendence, which God can use to draw people to himself.

However, this does not mean that these religions are in themselves paths to salvation, nor that they can be considered alternative paths to Christianity for reaching God. There is a fundamental difference between such religions and Christianity. These religions have arisen from human religious experience in different cultural-historical contexts and represent various forms of expressing religiosity. They arise out of man and his aspirations, to which the Spirit of God is never a stranger, since he is always present in man's attempts to reach transcendence. Christianity, instead, has a different origin: it does not arise from man, but from above, as the fruit of divine Revelation, for Jesus came into the world, "not of blood, nor of the will of the flesh, nor of the will of man, but of God" (Jn 1:13).

It is therefore natural that, from the moment God revealed his Word to the world with the coming of Christ, this is the way man is called to follow to achieve salvation. To this end is directed the invisible work of grace in the heart of every individual, regardless of the religion to which he or she belongs. Therefore, the Church has a permanent mission in the world: to proclaim in every age the Gospel of salvation. The Church seeks to dialogue with other religions to promote a culture of peace and transcendence, and to walk a common path together as far as it is possible. However, she remains faithful to Jesus Christ and, therefore, cannot refrain from proclaiming the truth about God and man to the world.

The greatest gift Christ left us is the Eucharist. The Church's Magisterium states that "transubstantiation" takes place (cf. CCC, no. 1376) in the consecration, that is, the bread and wine become the body and blood of Christ, even though what science sees (molecules, atoms) of the bread and wine remains unchanged. How is this possible? Is it not contradictory?

(Giovanni Zaccaria)

God's desire to be with us, to live with us, to infuse his own life into us is so great that no obstacle deters him.

It is precisely this desire that drives him to take on our very nature, becoming man: from infinite he becomes finite, in order to be able to show us with words and actions this aspiration of his; from immortal he becomes mortal, in order to be able to show us that his love is always there and never fails: from the height of the Cross he tells us, with deeds, something beyond words: "I love you and I will love you always; no matter what happens, I will continue to love you; no matter if you turn away, I will be with you; no matter if you insult me, I will continue to seek you and tell you of my love."

The Bible is full of expressions describing this attitude of God. To give but one example, Psalm 139 says:

"Lord, you scrutinize me and know me,

    you know when I sit down and when I rise up,

    you understand from afar my thoughts,

You observe my path and my rest,

    all my ways are known to you.

    My word is not yet on my tongue

    and behold, Lord, already you know it all.

    Behind and in front you surround

    me and lay your hand upon me.

    (...)

    Where shall I go from your Spirit?

    Where to flee from your presence?

If I ascend to heaven, there you are;

    if I descend to hell, there you are.

    If I take the wings of the dawn

    to dwell at the end of the sea, even there your hand guides

    me and your right hand shall hold me."

It is one of so many ways in which God makes us know that he is near us ("Behind and in front you surround me"), and understands the depths of our hearts ("...all my ways are known to you").

When we are are in love we know perfectly well that we would like to tell our loved one "I love you" a thousand times a day, and even more if we could, and we would not get tired of saying it or hearing it. We would like to say, "I will always be at your side, no matter what," and would not only like to say it, but also to have this wish come true: we would like to be with the person we love all day and all night long.

Yet, we know perfectly well that this is impossible: our desire is unlimited, but we are limited when it comes to effecting it.

Jesus at the Last Supper spoke words and performed actions that manifest his boundless love: "Having loved his own who were in the world, he loved them to the end" (Jn 13:1). Then, on the Cross, he showed us that that "to the end" was not just words. Truly he reached the end, to the extreme of dying for us, because he was in love with every human being, of every place and time.

However, the infinity of God's love does not end there: the Resurrection of Jesus from the dead opened a new dimension of this "love to the end." For his love does not remain confined within the space and time of Jesus' earthly life. It acquires an additional dimension. It transcends the barriers of space and time.

The Eucharist is precisely the presence, manifestation and communication of this love that knows no limits.

All of us have had the experience of having to depart from a loved one; the reasons may be the most diverse, but it is normal not to be able to be together all the time.

Then, before we leave, we exchange an object, and every time we look at that object we will be reminded of our loved one and the times we spent together, our hearts will beat faster and the desire to spend time together will be awakened in us.

Or we will scroll endlessly through photos we keep on our phone. Or we will reach out to our loved one on the phone, with a video call or just a text message, and without being sure that we will see them or that they will respond immediately.

We cannot do more, because our power does not match our will. "What we cannot do, our Lord is able to do. Jesus Christ, perfect

God and perfect Man, leaves, not a symbol, but reality itself: he himself stays with us. He will go to the Father, but he will also remain among men. He will leave us not simply a gift that will make us remember him, an image that will tend to become blurred with time, like a photograph that soon fades and yellows, with no meaning except for those who shared that loving moment. Under the appearances of bread and wine, He is here, really present: with his Body, his Blood, his Soul and his Divinity." (J. ESCRIVÁ, *Christ is Passing By*, no. 83).

How is this possible?

Jesus during the Last Supper gives his disciples bread, saying, "This is my body" (Mk 14:22; Mt 26:26; Lk 22:19); then he gives them wine, saying, "This is my blood" (Mt 26:28; Mk 14:23) and invites them to eat and drink what they have received. He is performing a gesture of disruptive force because of what it means; when he had foretold it, speaking of it in the synagogue at Capernaum some time before, the people listening to him reacted with violent bewilderment: it seemed to them an absurdity: "How can he give us his flesh to eat?"

But Jesus does not retract what he said, he does not try to make things easier; on the contrary, he goes even further: "Truly, truly I say to you, unless you eat the flesh of the Son of Man and drink his blood, you do not have life in you. He who eats my flesh and drinks my blood has eternal life, and I will raise him up on the last day. For my flesh is true food and my blood true drink. He who eats my flesh and drinks my blood abides in me and I in him. Just as the Father, who has life, sent me and I live for the Father, so also he who eats me will live for me" (Jn 6:52-57).

These are strong words, which Jesus turns into reality at the Last Supper: he gives the apostles his own body to eat and his own blood to drink.

Therefore, what Jesus is saying and accomplishing during the Last Supper is not symbolic in nature. Jesus does not say "This is as it were my body" or "This represents my blood." The reality of the bread is transformed by Jesus' word into his body and the reality of the wine into his blood.

It is precisely the power of Jesus' word that works this mysterious transformation. Just as his word had raised Lazarus, who had been dead for four days, so it is his word that transformed that bread into a body and that wine into blood.

Jesus' word is a living, effective word because it is God speaking, just as, at the beginning of time, "God said, 'Let there be light'; and there was light." (Gen 1:3).

Our daily experience tells us that when something is transformed, our senses pick up the change. The first knowledge comes through the senses.

If I take a wooden chair and throw it into a fire, the chair will burn and eventually I will no longer have wood but ashes; likewise if I take eggs, mix them with flour and sugar and put them into the oven, I will no longer have eggs, flour and sugar, but a cake.

Sight, touch, taste and smell do not miss these changes; in fact, it is those very senses that tell me that something has happened, that a transformation has taken place.

In the case of the Eucharist, however, exactly the opposite happens: the senses do not perceive any change. The bread we used for the celebration tastes the same before and after the consecration, has the same weight and color.

The Eucharistic change takes place on another level, a level that lies beyond physics, chemistry and all experienceable dimensions; the bread and wine change on a metaphysical level, that is, on a plane that lies beyond what I can perceive with my senses.

This plane is that of the identity of things, of their deep reality, which does not depend on the shape or color or what I think or experience of them, but on the very nature of the thing; it is the plane of being itself.

For example, a person changes over time: from being a baby in his mother's arms he becomes an adult person, grows in height, in knowledge, and in countless other aspects. Practically all the cells in his body change several times over the years, yet he always remains the same person. That person is still himself, even though he changes so much. He might even lose one or more limbs, yet he will always remain himself; he might lose the ability to express himself or to interact with his surroundings, but that will not make him another person or turn him into an object. When two people love each other, they continue to love each other even if the years pass, even if wrinkles increase or it becomes difficult to walk.

What makes that person who he or she is lies on a different plane from what we can experience with our senses.

This is the plane in which transubstantiation takes place. It is the plane that defines things for what they are, regardless of the characteristics they have on the sensory plane.

In the case of the Eucharist an absolutely unique change takes place because the bread and wine, by virtue of Jesus' words and the power of the Holy Spirit, change what they are in themselves, while retaining all other outward characteristics.

But what is even more extraordinary is that, when we stand before that bread which is no longer bread but the body of Christ, and before that wine which is no longer wine but the blood of Christ, we are in the presence of the body and blood of Jesus, that is, of his person, in his entirety.

When we are in the same room with other people, their presence is mediated by their bodies: it is through my body and the other person's body that I realize that a person is next to me; through sight or hearing, touch or smell I perceive the fact that there is another person next to me.

Christ's presence in the Eucharist, on the other hand, is not at the level of what is perceptible by the senses, but this does not detract from the truth of his presence: it is a real, true, full presence precisely because it at the level of what things are in themselves.

So when we are before the Eucharist, we are before Christ, who died and is risen, alive in his glorious body. A body that – we deduce from the evangelists' narratives – has qualities that our bodies do not possess, qualities that make it a body fully available to the will and power of Jesus' spirit. Consequently, it can make itself present in a way that is not according to the space-time mode, the only one we know of for a material body. In the Eucharist, therefore, our senses do not perceive him, but thanks to faith we know that we are before that person who has loved us and continues to love us "to the end."

We are not dealing with a sacred object, but with a person: the same person who worked for thirty years as a craftsman, who walked among the men and women of his time, who preached and healed.

And this presence is not a static presence, because the presence of a person is never like that of an object: he is present with his love, with his history, with his humanity and his feelings. That is why thanks to the Eucharist that true and profound personal encounter that is given between persons, an encounter of hearts before an encounter of bodies, can take place with Christ.

If Christ is God who came to this world to enlighten all people, how can it be that after 2,000 years there are so few true Christians?

(Emanuele di Marco)

The gospel is for everyone

The question posed may have several possible avenues of answer. The mystery of God is revealed to all peoples: in Jesus Christ it is shown in a humanity that surprises us. The Old Testament is the time in which the people of Israel are chosen as the custodians of a particular relationship between mankind and God the Father. In Jesus this relationship is opened to all peoples. *Lumen Gentium* voices the hope that "the light of Christ, reflected in the face of the Church, will illumine all people, proclaiming the Gospel to every creature" (LG 1). The Gospel message is thus proposed as a way forward for everyone. This "universality" of the call to the way of the Gospel led the first apostles to enthusiastically proclaim the good news. But what is this good news? The so-called *kerygma* is defined by Benedict XVI as follows: "He who was crucified, and who thus manifested God's immense love for man, is risen and is alive among us" (*General Audience*, Nov. 5, 2008). It reveals the heart of the Christian message. A message that is proposed not imposed, because Christianity, by its very nature, is a free response to a call. Pope Benedict and then his successor Francis had already affirmed this in the first pastoral document of his pontificate (Apostolic Exhortation *Evangelii gaudium*, 2013, here no. 14): "Everyone has the right to receive the Gospel. Christians have the duty to proclaim it without excluding anyone, not as one who imposes a new obligation, but rather as one who shares a joy, signals a beautiful horizon, offers a desirable banquet. The Church does not grow by proselytism but 'by attraction.'"

This premise helps us to understand right away that the way of the gospel is presented as something good, true, valid. But not exclusive. And, above all, it is not imposed.

To a few, but for all

Already in the words of Jesus we find important indications showing in which direction an answer to the question may lie.

Jesus' call reaches a few disciples, chosen from many other possibilities (Mk 1:16-20 and 16:15-20; Mt 4:18-22; Lk 5:1-11). "Come after me...." By its nature, the call is addressed to some: the universal call thus passes through a particular call: concrete faces and lives which are willing to begin this new Gospel way, based on friendship with Jesus.

Further words of Jesus help us to understand even better how the call is expressed. The Master, referring to the disciples' role in relation to the world, tells them, "You are the salt of the earth [...]. You are the light of the world; a city that stands on a mountain cannot remain hidden, nor do you light a lamp to put it under the bushel, but on the candlestick, and so it sheds light on all who are in the house. So let your light shine before men, that they may see your good works and give glory to your Father in heaven" (Mt 5:13-15). The theme of salt and earth necessarily points to the particular being at the service of the universal. That which is small at the service of that which is great.

A demanding call

As well as Jesus' more general address to his disciples, there are also dialogues in the Gospel with very specific protagonists who are faced with the dilemma of whether or not to accept the proclamation of the Kingdom of God. This is the case of the disciples who, after Christ's teaching in the synagogue at Capernaum, hear his question, "Do you also want to leave?" (Jn 6:67).

The progressiveness of the proclamation of the Gospel leads us to reflect on a fundamental conviction: the Church will shine forth fully at the end of time. Until then she "constitutes for all humanity a most valid seed of unity, hope and salvation" (LG 9). This salvation reaches every man who is redeemed in Christ. Even those who do not know the Gospel itself, but who with a sincere heart seek justice, goodness, and love: hence, God.

The fragility of those who carry the proclamation

Those, therefore, who are committed, perhaps unconsciously or without all the elements of a mature faith, to the good of neighbor and mankind already participate in a search for God that becomes an attraction toward salvation. The Letter to the Hebrews (11:6) reminds us of this when it states, "Without faith it is impossible to be pleasing to him; for those who draw near to God must believe that he exists and that he rewards those who seek him." The official sending to all nations is made explicit in clear words at the end of Matthew's Gospel (28:19): "Go, therefore, and make disciples of all nations, baptizing them in the name of the Father and of the Son and of the Holy Spirit, teaching them to observe all that I have commanded you." The CCC reminds us, however, that Jesus entrusted the proclamation for every man and woman to frail disciples who must constantly refer to the Holy Spirit, who makes up for the weakness of those who are bearers of the works of God's love (cf. Second Vatican Council, Pastoral Const. *Gaudium et spes*, 43 and Decr. *Ad gentes*, 2). Jesus Christ's decision to engage frail men and women to spread this proclamation is emphasized by St. Paul: "we have this treasure in earthen vessels, so that it may appear that this extraordinary power comes from God and not from us" (2 Cor 4:7-8).

The weakness of those who carry the proclamation is an incessant call to conversion and penance, so that no one feels that they are the exclusive owner of the Gospel, which is immensely great and can never be owned. In this dynamic, there are some who abandon the way of the Gospel, as seen above. Still others, however, show signs of inconsistency that undermine the proclamation itself. It is a risk Jesus himself took: of having a pinch of salt, of having a light. But it is for everyone.

Friendship, by its very nature must be personal

The foundation of Christian faith is relationship: with God and with people. Christ's coming to this world brought about a renewal of human relationships. To be a Christian is to enter into this new dynamic that heals brokenness and leads to a peace that passes even through suffering. The inconsistencies of the Church's faithful do not detract from the holiness of the Church, which remains "one, holy, catholic and apostolic" (cf. CCC 867-870). In a recent document entrusted to young people, Pope Francis goes into the theme of friendship, referring to human friendship for a description and experiential reference, but then assumed by Christ who perfects this friendly relationship by conferring on it uniqueness, fidelity, and reciprocity. "Friendship is not a fleeting and passing relationship, but a stable, steadfast, faithful one that matures with the passage of time. It is a relationship of affection that makes us feel united, and at the same time it is a generous love that leads us to seek the good of the friend" (Ap. Exh. *Christus Vivit*, 152). Moreover, the category of friendship is used by Jesus himself, who recalls, "I no longer call you servants, but I have called you friends" (Jn 15:15). A new relationship has arisen by his initiative, which also heals the infidelities and perplexities of the human approach.

From communities to Communities

The challenge for the Christian faith therefore does not lie in having rising statistics or the demonstration of sinlessness in its members. Instead, the challenge of the Christian story lies in having a community that proclaims the Risen One from personal encounter. An encounter with him that generates a community of those who have encountered him. In him then the Christian community becomes a proclaimer and can bring riches to all peoples. The only truly evangelical strategy is to have encountered Christ and to desire to encounter him constantly in one's neighbor. "It is no longer I who live, but Christ who lives in me," says St. Paul in Gal 2:20. In an age strongly marked by the fragility of relationships and the fleetingness of encounters, in which it is easy to simply seek out those who have the same opinion, the contribution of Christianity is precisely the restoration of relationships. Recognizing ourselves as part of a community that has something to bring to the whole world in a "renewed Pentecost" that re-proposes the challenge of the cenacle (cf. John Paul II, *Address to the Assembly of Delegates of Episcopal Conferences*, Feb 12, 2000). A small group of the Lord's friends who, moved by the Spirit, will be faithful and convinced heralds in a world that will not fail to show coldness or perplexity, as St. John recalls in the priestly prayer, "I gave them your word, and the world hated them because they are not of the world, just as I am not of the world. I do not ask that you remove them from the world, but that you guard them from the evil one. They are not of the world, as I am not of the world" (Jn 17:14-16). But it is precisely the diversity of this community constantly nurtured by the Spirit that can make a difference and bring about the fascination that the early Christian communities were already able to inspire in those who encountered them. To be bearers of a Truth of relationships is the great ecclesial challenge of this time, with constant reference to the roots of the

Christian experience: "Every day they all attended the temple together and broke bread at home, taking their meals with gladness
and simplicity of heart, praising God and enjoying the sympathy of
all the people. Meanwhile, the Lord daily added to the community
those who were saved" (Acts 2:46-48).

Growth in the ecclesial journey

"The Church is the people whom God gathers into the whole
world" (CCC, 752). In its progressive realization in history, all can
recognize in the Church a continuous process of growth and self-
understanding, in the vicissitudes of history and time, tending to the
encounter with the Master, when he will come in glory. In this dynamic we understand the intertwining of human affairs and the sac-
ramentality of the Church itself. Resuming the question posed here
("If Christ is God who came to this world to enlighten all people,
how can it be that after 2,000 years there are so *few true* Christians?"), it will therefore not be a matter of reflecting on the quanti-
fication of the *few* (after all, the experience of friendship with Christ
starts with a dozen called), nor on quality control over the *true* (frailties and weaknesses are the best guarantee of a continuing need for
conversion and return to the Lord). Instead, it is a matter of grasping
the challenge of the authenticity of the relationship in Christ, who
sits the sinner, the enthusiastic but fragile Peter and all the others,
next to him. With this awareness, always striving for the ultimate
encounter with him, the Church is truly herself and can rejoice in
the "I go and prepare a place for you" (Jn 14:2) entrusted to anyone
who seeks him with a sincere heart. One of the temptations of the
Church is precisely to rely on human categories to define its success.

To understand the Church's story, however, we need the gaze of Christ, who even at the moment of almost total abandonment of all, on the Cross, meets John, his Mother and some other women In them he sees the whole Church. They were few, confused. But it was the Church.

If Christ has already given us the fullness of Revelation, why have there been so many apparitions and messages down the centuries from Christ, Our Lady or the Saints?

(Manfred Hauke)

Jesus Christ, the eternal Son of God, incarnated among us, has communicated to us everything necessary for salvation. This message intended for the whole Church of all times is called "Public Revelation". It is divinely revealed content proposed by the Church for the faith of its members. "Any person questioning God or desiring some vision or revelation would be guilty not only of foolish behaviour but also of offending him, by not fixing his eyes entirely upon Christ and by living with the desire for some other novelty." These words from St. John of the Cross, a great mystic and Doctor of the Church, are quoted approvingly in the CCC (no. 65) and in the "Norms for Proceeding in the Discernment of Alleged Supernatural Phenomena" of the Dicastery for the Doctrine of the Faith, published in 2024, and in oher places too.

At the same time, however, there are also prophetic phenomena that accompany the journey of God's people from the beginning of their history. Prophecies are authoritative messages on behalf of God. The apostle Paul writes in this regard, "Do not quench the Spirit, do not despise prophecies" (1Th 5:19f) and the book of Proverbs can formulate, "Without [prophetic] revelation the people become unbridled" (Pr 29:19). According to St. Thomas Aquinas, prophecies after the apostolic time are given "not to promote a new doctrine of faith, but for the direction of human acts" (*Summa Theologiae* II-II q. 174 a. 6 ad 3). Therefore, the CCC, followed by the recent "Norms" just quoted, stresses, "Down through the centuries there have been revelations called 'private,' some of which have been approved by Church authority... their role is not to 'improve' or 'complete' the definitive Revelation of Christ, but to help one live it more fully in a given historical epoch" (CCC, no. 67).

There were, for example, prophetic revelations to St. Margaret Mary Alacoque (1647-1690) that prompted her to promote the worship of the Sacred Heart of Jesus, introducing the devotion of the first Fridays of the month and the corresponding liturgical feast. The importance of the Heart of Jesus, a sign of the divine and human love of our savior, is well founded in Sacred Scripture, but the prophetic revelations of the mentioned saint emphasize the love of Jesus in a time of lukewarmness, when – in Jesus' words – "because of the spread of iniquity, the love of many will grow cold" (Mt 24:12).

Another example is Fatima. The Marian apparitions there reiterate, among other things, the concern to save us from the danger of eternal damnation (well present in the message of Jesus), the importance of the Rosary (in which Jesus' life is meditated upon and our supplications are inserted), the consecration to the Immaculate Heart of Mary, and a spiritual commitment for the conversion of Russia in the same year 1917 in which the Bolshevik revolution took place.

We speak here of "private revelations" not because they have no importance for the Church, but to reiterate the essential difference

between them and "public Revelation" (Benedict XVI, Apostolic Exhortation *Verbum Domini*, no. 14). The "private" revelations recognized by the Church are prophetic events that help us to understand
the "signs of the times" (Lk 12:56) and to find for them their proper
context in the Catholic faith. Instead of stressing the difference between Revelation *tout court* or public or general Revelation on the
one hand and "private revelations" on the other, we could usefully
distinguish foundational Revelation from "particular revelations"
that continue to come in diverse times and places.

It is the task of ecclesiastical authority to assess the credibility of
a prophecy and apparition of Mary. In his famous work on the processes of beatification (and canonization), canonist Prospero Lam-
bertini, later elected Pope with the name of Benedict XIV, points
out, "To such revelations, even if approved, we must not nor can we
give an assent of Catholic faith, but only of human faith, according
to the rules of prudence, by which the Church discerns whether the
aforementioned revelations are probable and piously credible" (*De
servorum beatificatione* 2,32,11). In his commentary on the publication of the "third secret" of the Fatima message (in 2000), Cardinal
Ratzinger describes three elements inherent in ecclesial approval:
"the relevant message contains nothing contrary to faith and good
morals, it is licit to make it public, and the faithful are authorized to
give to it their prudent adherence" (Benedict XVI also expressed this
view in *Verbum Domini*, 14).

The "Norms" of 2024 describe the need for discernment among
alleged supernatural phenomena: "the Church will be able to fulfill
its duty of discerning: (*a*) whether signs of a divine action can be
ascertained in phenomena that are alleged to be of supernatural

origin; (*b*) whether there is anything that conflicts with faith and morals in the writings or messages of those involved in the alleged phenomena in question; (*c*) whether it is permissible to appreciate their spiritual fruits, or whether they need to be purified from problematic elements, or whether the faithful need to be warned about potential risks arising from them; (*d*) whether it is advisable for the competent ecclesiastical authority to make an assessment of their pastoral value." (I, no. 10).

The supernatural origin is confirmed by miracles and prophecies. An example is the Fatima apparitions: Mary announced to the seers on July 13, 1917, that there would be a great miracle at the same place (Cova da Iria) and at the same time (noon) where Our Lady had already appeared to them in the previous months, and in fact the "miracle of the sun" occurred on October 13. For the miracles that occur at Lourdes, there is a medical commission that ascertains the scientifically inexplicable character of a healing that occurred instantaneously and completely, although the decision to recognize the miracle then rests with the ecclesiastical authority (a decision that has occurred in no less than 70 cases so far!). Then there are the Eucharistic miracles that underscore the truth and importance of the real presence of the body and blood of the risen Christ. The soon-to-be-canonized Charles Acutis, though very young, was able to gather important documentation of these prodigious Eucharistic miracles. In the miracle that occurred in Bolsena in 1263, for example, during the Holy Mass celebrated by a priest who doubted the real presence of Christ's body, the host began to bleed. The relics of the miracle, recognized as such by Pope Urban IV after careful study, are preserved to this day in the cathedral of Orvieto.

For alleged miracles, however, one has to be very careful, as even the devil can cause extraordinary physical phenomena such as levitations, flows of blood and stigmata, although their deceptive origin will tend to be recognizable in each case. As for messages, the subjective susceptibility of the seers, which can influence the communication, will also need to be examined. It would be wrong, however, to ascribe all heavenly apparitions to a purely subjective view. When it is an entire group of visionaries that convey a message (as at Fatima), discernment of the objective message is easier. There are also experiences that demonstrate a physical reality independent of the subjective perception of the visionaries, such as during the apparition at Knock (Ireland, 1878), which took place in the rain, while the place of the apparition, attested by many witnesses, remained dry.

God's signs in history and prophecies are to be valued, after due discernment. The "Norms" cited above reiterate the bishops' duty to obtain information when cases arise and to set up a competent commission to investigate (II, Art. 7-12) and to be able to make a prudent evaluation (II, Art. 13-17).

The charism of prophecy has an important role in the Church, but the exceptional character of apparitions and visions should also be emphasized. The fact is that the Christian religion is based on the hearing of the word, while the face-to-face vision of God is reserved for the blessedness of those who are received into Heaven, as Jesus said, "Blessed are those who, though they do not see, will believe" (Jn 20:29).

To better understand the importance of apparitions recognized as authentic, we can give some examples of pseudo-appearances. Among the oldest are those reported by the Montanists in Asia

Minor (in Phrygia) beginning in the mid-2nd century. The founder of this spiritual current, Montanus, presented himself as a representative of the "paraclete" announced by Jesus (of the Holy Spirit, therefore). Montanus was in close association with two alleged prophetesses, Priscilla (or Prisca) and Maximilla. Allegedly, the heavenly Jerusalem would descend on the tiny village of Pepuza in Phrygia, in present-day western Turkey. The "new prophecy" was characterized by alienation of the senses during a trance (so the seers did not know what they were enunciating), a trait compared by contemporary observers of crisis in the possessed. Early church synods in second-century Asia Minor had to oppose the Montanists because they questioned the authority of the bishops.

Among the alleged contemporary apparitions we can mention those in Bayside, New York (1968-1995). The phenomenon began, when the seer, Veronica Lueken, smelled a miraculous odor of roses and an "inner voice" that dictated a pious poem to her. The lady announced cosmic catastrophes, which never came about, and received the "message" that Pope Paul VI would be secretly put in prison and replaced by a person physically similar to him. Supporters of the phenomenon were enthusiastic about photographs with the new Polaroid cameras that manifested seemingly pious phenomena that could not be explained humanly (such as the name "Jacinta," little seer of Fatima). This does not mean, however, that it was the good God who caused these phenomena. Even the "father of lies" is capable of it (Jn 8:44). Therefore, careful discernment is needed which, in this specific case, also took place. As early as 1974, the Diocese of Brooklyn issued a critical warning, and in 1986 the bishop concluded his research by stating that these phenomena were not supernatural.

A similar thing happened recently in Trevignano Romano (Italy, province of Viterbo). The alleged seer had brought from Medjugorje a statue of Our Lady that allegedly shed tears of blood. Then there were problematic messages (which still continue), partly corrected by the seer herself. On March 6, 2024, the bishop of Civita Castellana, after a careful investigation, published his assessment, acknowledging that this was not a supernatural event.

The first authentic, historically ascertainable Marian apparition is that experienced by St. Gregory the Wonderworker (in Greek, Thaumaturgus, died c. 270), bishop of Neocesarea (province of Pontus, today in northern Turkey). This is testified by one of the Cappadocian Fathers, St. Gregory of Nyssa, who reports that the autograph of the Wonderworker on this event was still preserved in the episcopal house in Neocesarea. Gregory the Wonderworker was very concerned about heresies invading his young flock. The evangelist John appeared to him to "reveal the truth of the pious faith"; and the Blessed Virgin Mary also appeared. Both spoke to each other about the true faith, thereby instructing Gregory the Wonderworker. Then the bishop received a Trinitarian symbol that later was of great help in maintaining the faith (itself already present in the New Testament word of God) in the one God, Father, Son and Holy Spirit. Authentic prophetic revelations, such as this one, help us to remain faithful to the Revelation that was given forever in Jesus Christ and not let ourselves be confused by the errors of our time.

Among the major Marian apparitions recognized by the Church are those of Guadalupe in Mexico (1531), La Salette (1846), Lourdes

(1858) and Pontmain (1871) in France, Dietrichswalde (Giertzwald) (1877) in East Prussia (now Poland), Fatima (1917) in Portugal, Beauraing and Banneux (1932-33) in Belgium, Finca Betania (1976-84) in Venezuela, Kibeho (1981-89) in Rwanda, and Saint Nicholas (1983-90) in Argentina.

Questions about the Church

How to prove that the Church was founded by Christ?

(Isabel Troconis)

After the first and second parts of this book, devoted to faith in the one God and in Jesus Christ, his incarnate Son, it is time to delve into the truths of faith concerning the Church.

By now you will have deepened your certainty that Jesus is not just another character who has existed in the course of history, but that he is endowed with a unique characteristic that distinguishes him from all others: he is the only begotten Son of God made man. In this chapter, we will try to show the same thing, but in relation to the Church. That is: we will give the reasons why Christians believe that the institution that preserves and transmits the memory of Jesus' earthly words and deeds is not simply a human institution but was founded by Christ and is therefore also divine. It is human and divine, like its founder.

Throughout history many have wondered whether the Church was willed by Christ as it exists today (at least in its essential features) or whether it is instead a human invention. It is clear that the key to this question lies in the content of Christ's mission, that is, in the answer to the question of what Jesus really came to do on earth.

Reading the synoptic gospels (i.e., the gospels of Matthew, Mark and Luke), it becomes immediately clear that the content of Jesus' mission was to announce that the time had come when God would establish his Kingdom in this world: "Jesus walked in Galilee, proclaiming the gospel of God, and said, 'The time is fulfilled and the Kingdom of God is at hand; repent and believe the gospel'" (Mark 1:14-15).

On the basis of the interpretation of this message in the writings of St. John and St. Paul, for a long time the great part of Christians understood that the establishment of the Kingdom of God had its beginning in the person of Jesus Christ himself – in his existence of loving and filial obedience to the Father – and that, starting from him and through him, it had spread throughout the world, thanks to the fact that many people had joined him through faith, love and the sacraments.

However, this way of conceiving the Kingdom of God in the world has faced radical challenges, especially since the 19th century. In the previous centuries, under the influence of the rationalist Enlightenment, the way of interpreting the Bible had been changing, especially among Protestant theologians. Eager to offer a presentation of the figure and message of Christ that was more acceptable to reason and to the common experience of the time, some theologians began to interpret the Bible as if it were simply a historical document, leaving aside its supernatural elements. As a result, this approach led to a merely human view of Christ and his message about the Kingdom of God.

Thus, for example, some authors (belonging to the current of liberal theology) began to assert that Jesus was a man who had, yes, a divine mission, but that this mission had been simply to preach the message of universal love among all men To this end, Christ had founded a moral brotherhood – the Kingdom of God – in which men, united by love, would exercise their dominion over the world through work and by helping one another to achieve moral perfection.

Others (the theologians of so-called "consistent eschatology") argued that Jesus was a man who believed, mistakenly, that God was about to break into history and bring it to an end, establishing his eschatological Kingdom. A Kingdom in which he, Jesus, would be elevated to the glorious status of "Son of Man" (Messiah). However, his announcement had not been fulfilled: Jesus had died crucified and history quietly continued its course. These authors alleged that the doctrines of the divinity of Jesus Christ and the Church as a divine, visible, hierarchical institution charged with prolonging his presence in the world were the creation of early Christians to give meaning to and justify Jesus' failed project.

I tell you these things because perhaps your questions about the Church are related to these theories. Perhaps, like the authors of the first group, you hold (or have heard) that the Church should be an exclusively inner and invisible reality (the moral or spiritual fellowship of believers) and that its external aspects (hierarchical structure, communal and visible worship, etc.) were created by humans and, therefore, can change. Or perhaps, like the authors of the second group, you think that the Church is an entirely human invention and that we would do better to leave it aside and strive to relate directly to God.

To answer these questions, the best thing is to look, once again, at how Jesus' mission is presented in the Bible.

As we have already seen, Jesus inaugurated his mission by announcing the good news that the fullness of time had come, when God would finally establish his Kingdom. If one traces the history of the people of Israel before Jesus Christ, one realizes that this announcement was something the Jews had been awaiting for centuries, as a fulfillment of the salvation God had promised them.

As you may know, the history of the relationship of the people of Israel with God is essentially the history of their covenants. To understand why, it is necessary to recall the purpose for which God created man and the world. The Book of Genesis tells us that God made man in his own image and likeness (cf. Gen 1:27). How can we interpret this expression? What makes a certain object an image is the fact that it refers back to something else, either because it resembles it (as in the case of a painting or sculpture) or because it reflects it (as in the case of a mirror). Thus, man can be said to be the image of God because he is able to know and love him, and in this way God can make himself present ("reflect") in him while at the same time maintaining his transcendence. But to the extent that it refers back to him and reflects him, an image is also something that evokes its object and makes it present. From this point of view, it can be said that for man to be the image of God means he is God's representative in the world and thus is at the head of creation (cf. Gen 1:28). All this reveals the divine design for creation: God created man so that he might live in communion with Him and so that, through man, the cosmos might also participate in this communion with God (cf. CCC 760).

This explains why when Adam and Eve committed the first sin - that is, when they rejected to be in communion with their Creator - God immediately promised them a savior (cf. Gen 3:15) and set to work to restore the damaged relationship: because the very meaning of creation was at stake. First, God called a man, Abraham, with a promise to make him the father of a great people and to give him a fertile land (cf. Gen 15). Next, he chose and sealed a covenant with his descendants, the twelve tribes of Israel. By this covenant God pledged to be their God (to guide and protect them) and they pledged to be his people (to obey and worship him alone) (cf. Ex 24). But throughout history the people of Israel broke their word many times and fell into the sin of idolatry. That is why God sent them prophets who, by their preaching and punishments, helped them to become aware of their sins and to announce to them the establishment of a new covenant, by which God would permanently restore communion with his people (cf. Jer. 31:31-34; Is. 55:3). This is the Covenant that Jesus came to establish and by which he established the Kingdom of God in the world. The Church is precisely the new People of God that emerged from this new Covenant and, because of this, is also the seed and instrument through which God builds his Kingdom in history.

The way the Church extends the Kingdom of God is not external but internal. It is the communion of people whom God has summoned in Christ through the Holy Spirit as his new People or family. This means that, as we read in St. Paul's letters (cf. 1 Cor 12; Col. 1:18, 24; Rom 12:5; Eph 3:6), it is an organism or body that receives its unity and vitality from mystical union with Christ through his Word and sacraments (especially Baptism – cf. Rom 6:3-4; Col. 2:12; 1 Cor 12:13; and the Eucharist – cf. Gal. 6:56). This is why recent theology explains that Christ founded the Church not simply by organizational or declarative actions, but by its entire existence of union with God, since what constitutes the Church as such is precisely its participation in that existence. In this sense, it can also be said that the foundation of the Church is not an event of the past, but something that is taking place permanently insofar as the Church's existence depends on its constant participation in the mystery of Christ (cf. R. PELLITERO, *Eclesiología* (ch. 6), Pamplona 2019, 61).

At the same time, within this framework it is possible to point to some concrete acts – theology usually divides them into four types – by which Jesus prepared, configured and constituted his Church.

First, there are the so-called preparatory acts by which Jesus gave his community a permanent structure (cf. CCC 765). In the course of his public ministry, Jesus formed a large community of disciples (cf. Lk 10:1). From among these disciples, he chose twelve, with Peter as leader (cf. Mk 3:14-15), to be the seed of hierarchy in the Church. In the Bible, the number twelve is filled with symbolism: twelve were the patriarchs of the tribes of Israel and twelve are the foundations and gates that the book of Revelation says the heavenly Jerusalem will have (cf. Rev. 12). Therefore, the fact that Jesus wanted the foundations of his Church – the apostles – to be twelve shows that this new community he was creating was foreshadowed in the Old Testament and was oriented toward a future consummation that would include the entire cosmos (PELLITERO, 2019, 62). As the Catechism reminds us, these twelve (cf. Mk 6:7), as well as the entire community of disciples (cf. Lk 10:1-2) participate in Christ's mission, his power, and his destiny (cf. Mt 10:25; Gal 15:20 and CCC 765).

Secondly, there is the Last Supper, which occupies a central place in the founding of the Church, not only because in it Jesus promulgated his main commandment (the commandment of love, cf. Jn 15:12, 17) and instituted the priesthood (cf. Lk 22:19), but especially because in it he instituted the Eucharist (cf. Mt 26:26), which is the sacrament by which God continues to gather his Church into the unity of one Body. In fact, by presenting the bread and wine of that Passover supper as his body and blood that would be delivered the next day on the Cross for the salvation of all people, Christ constituted the Eucharist as the sacrament of his Body and as the sacrifice of the New Covenant by which God continues to gather his People in every age. For this reason, along with St. John Paul II, it can be said that "the Eucharist builds up the Church" (*Ecclesia de Eucharistia*, 2003, no. 26).

Third, there are the acts by which, after his Resurrection, Christ conferred various powers on the members of the Church: on all the apostles, the power to forgive sins (cf. Jn 20:2) and to go into all the world to preach the Gospel, to make disciples and to baptize (cf. Mt 28:19-20); to Peter, the power of primacy, that is, the commission to shepherd his Church (cf. Jn 20:15-17) and to be his vicar on earth (cf. Mt 16:17-19).

The final act by which Christ configured and built up his Church was the sending of the Holy Spirit to the apostles on the day of Pentecost (cf. Acts 2). With this sending, God sanctified and strengthened them to carry out their mission. As the Second Vatican Council's decree on the Church's missionary activity explains, it was on the day of Pentecost that "the Church officially appeared before the multitude and began through preaching the spread of the Gospel among the Gentiles" (*Ad Gentes*, no. 4). Since that time, through his permanent presence in the Church, the Holy Spirit continues to build and direct her, endowing her with various hierarchical and charismatic gifts (cf. *Lumen Gentium*, no. 4).

In the light of all these facts, attested in Scripture, we can conclude that the Church is not a human invention, but that its existence and its essential elements – still present today – were explicitly intended by Jesus. As far as we have been able to see, Christ had the explicit intention of founding it as a community that, gathered in the mystery of its union with God, would prolong it in history through its faith, charity and worship. Consequently, this foundational intention of Jesus did not remain an abstract idea, but developed into concrete forms that, with their rich symbolism, reveal to us that the Church is not simply a moral association, but rather the manifestation, the seed, the instrument of the Kingdom of God and the fruit of the redemption wrought by Jesus.

Christ at the Last Supper prayed for the unity of the Church. How then did so many divisions arise in it?

(Philip Goyret)

1. Introduction

"That they may all be one, even as you, O Father, are in me and I in you, that they also may be one in us, so that the world may believe that you have sent me" (Jn 17:21): these are words of Jesus during the Last Supper, addressed to God the Father in the presence of the apostles, that have the flavor of a testament; words of the greatest theological significance, for they indicate how the unity of the apostles – and in them of the whole Church ("all of them," the text says) – must actually be a participation in the unity between God the Son and God the Father and, in them, of the whole Trinity. These words are echoed in 1 John 1:3: "What we have seen and heard, we proclaim also to you, that you also may have fellowship with us. And our communion is with the Father and with his Son, Jesus Christ"; words that lead us to understand that ecclesial communion is nothing other than participation in the Trinitarian communion. Since God is One, even though he is also Triune, so the Church cannot but be one, even though it is present and operating in many local churches: a unity of communion, which entails, as in God, simultaneous unity and diversity.

Unity was understood in this way from the very beginning of the Church's life. As soon as the Church gained a space of freedom, in the fourth century, the ecumenical councils of Nicaea (a. 325) and Constantinople (a. 381) were celebrated. From them comes the Nicene-Constantinopolitan Creed, in which we profess our faith in the one, holy, catholic and apostolic Church. A unity consisting simultaneously of internal cohesion (bonds that keep it cohesive) and oneness (there is only one Church, although the expression "Churches" is legitimately used to refer to different dioceses).

But in fact we know that the reality is not so straightforward, because alongside the Catholic Church there are also the Orthodox Churches, the Lutheran, the Reformed, the Anglican and others, which are not the legitimate "local churches" just mentioned, but real and distinct communities that have separated from the Catholic Church. Has the founding will of Jesus therefore failed? How can we profess our faith in *Unam Ecclesiam* (the one and united Church) when we observe that there are different Churches in the world? This is the question we will attempt to answer as convincingly as possible. We will do so by first considering the origin of the divisions, and then move toward the authentic path of restoring unity, which involves perceiving how it can subsist even in the midst of divisions and of so many legitimate diversities. We will conclude by looking toward the future, drawing on the lessons of history.

2. Origin of divisions

Since the Trinitarian communion – in which the Church participates – is a communion in love, the theological virtue of charity,
which perfects our capacity to love, acquires a central position.
When charity is truly alive, unity is preserved and strengthened; sin,
on the other hand, which is always contrary to charity, breeds division. The deepest reason for divisions in the Church lies in the sins
of Christians: more than attacks from outside or difficulties in evangelization.

Then follow, in order of importance, theological reasons. Although all Christians accept revelation as it is contained in Holy
Scripture and summarized in the Nicene-Constantinopolitan Creed,
the interpretations of it can differ in a way that makes them incompatible. For example, among the oldest divisions still subsisting today we find those of the Nestorians and the Monophysites, who understood the mystery of Christ's Incarnation in ways that were incompatible with the Catholic faith and opposed to each other. For
the Nestorians the two natures of Christ are separate, while for the
Monophysites there is only one nature in Christ, the divine nature.

However, theological motivations have not always been the
main cause of divisions. Often the divisions have had a strong cultural component, in the sense that the formulation of faith made
with categories from one culture may eventually seem incompatible
with revelation when that formulation is read with categories from
another culture. To a large extent, this happened with the Latin

Creed's phrase about the Holy Spirit "proceeding from the Father and the Son," which was not accepted in the Orthodox East.

To this is often added a political component. Although church-state separation often prevails in the Western world today, it should be kept in mind that in the ancient world and even in the modern age, the configuration of society was much more unified, such that religious positions also entailed political positions. In that era, church division seriously damaged the unity of the state, and division in state matters could give rise to a schismatic situation.

Naturally, a negative situation of the Church in the moral sphere makes the ground slippery, greatly facilitating division, especially when immorality takes root strongly among ecclesiastical authorities. Although there was no lack of deep theological motivations, it was such a situation that led to the Reformation of the 16th century on the European continent. In the British Isles, on the other hand, the circumstances were somewhat reversed, in the sense that it was an ethical motivation – the marriage issue of the king of England – that led to the Anglican schism.

At the origin of splits among Christians there have also been misunderstandings, wounded pride and attitudes not always permeated by fervor for the truth and honor of God; but if we limit ourselves to strictly theological causes, it can be said that at the basis of many departures from Catholic communion there is, paradoxically, a desire – at least implicitly – for fidelity to the substance of the gospel, a substance that is seen to be compromised and whose defect is sought to be remedied. The history of many divisions could be summarized as a different appreciation, depending on the parties involved, of what in the Church is substantial and what in it is secondary, incidental, changeable according to the circumstances of time, place or culture.

Finally, it is worth noting that the motivations behind splits are not usually unique motivations "in their pure state," but a set of circumstances that fatally come together at a given historical moment. This can make the road to reunion more complicated, as there is a need to deal at the same time with several different aspects of the split in question.

Without pretending to describe the entire history of the divisions (of those still in force), it may be useful to report here, in outline, their origins and names, so that those who are not expert may have an initial idea of what we are talking about. The fifth century is that of the Christological heresies. Nestorius and his followers did not accept the doctrine of the Council of Ephesus (a. 431) on the uniqueness of the person of Christ (and thus on the divine motherhood of Mary) and on that account remained outside the ecclesial communion (they are called, though improperly, Nestorians). Twenty years later came the Council of Chalcedon, on the two natures of Christ, human and divine, persisting in him "without confusion, without mutation, without division, without separation." Those who refused to accept the decisions of Chalcedon are therefore called "non-Chalcedonians," although they are better known (incorrectly) by the name of "Monophysites."

In the 11th century, the Eastern Schism that gave rise to the Orthodox Church (in reality, "Orthodox Churches") was formally consummated; the term "formally" is a must, because the circumstances that incubated it (linguistic incommunicability, non-navigability of the Mediterranean, the Church's alliance with the Franks and the

Romano-Germanic Empire) had been going on for several centuries and produced its most divisive effects only in the 13th century.

The 16th century was the century of the Reformation, the main protagonist of which was the Saxon monk Martin Luther, with his doctrine of salvation by faith alone, which spread throughout much of Germany and the Nordic countries under the name Lutheranism (whose followers were also called "evangelicals"), eventually reaching the American colonies. Almost at the same time there developed, first in Switzerland and then in the Netherlands, Britain and the United States, the more radical views of John Calvin, whose followers took on the name Reformed (on the European continent) or Presbyterian (in Scotland and the New World), although the teaching is sometimes referred to as "Calvinism" (more as a system of thought). Still in the first half of the 16th century appeared the "Church of England" or "Anglican Church" (a name assumed in the Commonwealth countries), which in the United States, after independence, became the "Episcopalian Church."

The 17th, 18th and 19th centuries were the centuries of the "Reformation of the Reformation" (in the strict sense, that is, divisions not directly from the Catholic Church), with the Congregationalists, Baptists and Quakers (17th C), Methodists (18th C) and Adventists (19th C). Not connected to the Reformation were the 19th century Old Catholics, who did not accept the First Vatican Council. Finally, the 20th century was the century of more cross-cultural phenomena, such as Pentecostalism and evangelicals, which took followers from different Christian denominations (including from the Catholic Church).

3.   The road to unity

Other divisions have been overcome, either by the gradual ex-
tinction of non-Catholics (as in the case of the Donatist sect), or by
their conversion (as happened with the Arians, the followers of Ar-
ius), or even by the reestablishment of unity (Western Schism). With
those that still exist (mentioned in the previous section) the Catholic
Church has entered into dialogue (there is dialogue also among
those communities with each other), with a view to restoring unity,
also through the current ecumenical movement. It should be recalled that the beginning of the latter can be traced back, symboli-
cally, to the 1910 Edinburgh International Missionary Congress, in
which Christians of different denominations participated. There it
was noted that divisions among Christians were a major obstacle to
mission. This prompted – first among non-Catholics – a desire to
restore the unity of the Church. In the Catholic Church, this same
desire developed strongly following the Second Vatican Council
(1962-1965).

Limiting ourselves here to essentials, we may recall that it was
stated then, for the first time, that the Church of Christ "subsists in
the Catholic Church, governed by the successor of Peter and the
bishops in communion with him, even though outside its body there
are found several elements of sanctification and truth, which, belonging properly by God's gift to the Church of Christ, impel toward
Catholic unity" (*Lumen Gentium* 8), thus paving the way for the
recognition that "even in them (non-Catholic Christians) he (the
Holy Spirit) works by his sanctifying virtue through gifts and graces"

(no. 15). Vatican II's Decree *Unitatis redintegratio*, which is entirely devoted to ecumenism (i.e. all the various efforts to restore the unity of the Church), calls for "the elimination of words, judgments and works which do not reflect with justice and truth the condition of separated brethren." It encourages engagement in "dialogue conducted by competent experts, in which each expounds more fully the doctrine of his own communion and clearly presents its characteristics". It urges them "to cooperate more extensively in any duty required by every Christian conscience for the common good," and "on occasion, (to) come together to pray together." Finally, it initiates a process in which "all examine their fidelity to Christ's will concerning the Church and, as is their duty, vigorously undertake the work of renewal and reform" (no. 4).

The doctrine enacted by this council on the "elements of sanctification and truth" that also exist among other Christian denominations, which "push toward Catholic unity," is of great importance for the methodology to be followed in the process of restoring unity. What is required of everyone – including the Catholic Church – is not a renunciation of their own identity, but on the contrary, a deepening in fidelity to the ecclesial elements they already possess. Indeed, these elements work reciprocally towards unity. At the end of the process there should come about the possession of all ecclesial elements, united in their fullness, in one sole Church.

Thus the initial question is also answered. According to the Catholic faith, "the elements of this already-given Church exist, found in their fullness in the Catholic Church and, without this fullness, in the other communities" (John Paul II, encyclical *Ut unum sint*, 14). Consequently, non-Catholic ecclesial communities and

Churches do indeed exist as such, though not in the fullness of the Catholic Church, which holds that the totality of the ecclesial elements (Scripture, sacraments, ordained ministry, prayer, virtuous life, missionary zeal, etc.) entrusted by Christ to the apostles "subsist in the Catholic Church, governed by the successor of Peter and the bishops in communion with him," as noted above.

However, this does not constitute a "boast" for Catholics but, on the contrary, a greater responsibility. St. John Paul II did not hesitate to add that in non-Catholic Christian communities "certain aspects of the Christian mystery have sometimes been more effectively brought to light" (*Ut unum sint*, 14). Vatican II had already boldly stated that "the Church, which includes sinners in her bosom and is therefore holy and at the same time always in need of purification, continually advances along the path of penance and renewal" (*Lumen Gentium*, 8): not only at the level of individual persons, but also in the human aspect of her institutions, which do not always reflect the authentic spirit of the Gospel.

4.   Importance of catholicity

The Catholic Church not only "calls" itself Catholic, but believes it is "Catholic," as professed in the Creed. Catholicity as a theological characteristic of the Church certainly entails the universal destination of the gospel entrusted by Christ, and also possession of the universal salvific heritage (all the ecclesial elements, as already explained). But it also entails an intrinsic openness of the proclamation of the gospel to all people of all times and cultures. In order for all the ecclesial elements to reach all people, they must be proclaimed, celebrated and lived out, in a way that all can understand, welcome and experience. Therefore, Pentecost is the most paradigmatic event of the catholicity of the Church, when the one gospel was proclaimed in a way that everyone could understand it.

We should remember that each of the great historical Churches possesses its own cultural context: Orthodoxy moves in the Eastern orbit; Lutheranism is configured as a typically German phenomenon; Anglicanism is deeply imbued with the British mentality. This constitutes a wake-up call for the Catholic Church, which cannot afford to be exclusively a "Western," "Latin" Church. It is not by chance that the name of the Church headed by the Bishop of Rome is called "Catholic": a denomination not imposed at a table, but born naturally, because it is aware, before God, that it must evangelize all without discrimination of language, culture or nationality. It can never be a sectoral Church, and that is precisely why it has ecumenism at the center of its heart.

Why is Mary so important
in the Catholic Church?

(Carla Rossi Espagnet)

Just another girl?

"I would like to know Mary as she was at my age, to know how she lived, what her relationship was with her family, what she dreamed for her life, how she behaved." The girl in her 20s who made this wish would be surprised to know that by her age Mary of Nazareth had already had a child, had had to flee abroad to save his life and keep him safe from persecution by a tyrant, and had probably recently returned to her homeland after several years of forced stay in a faraway and unknown country, Egypt. She had gone through all this together with Joseph, the young man to whom she was commited and whom she had married. Their relationship was guided by the Holy Spirit, who had inspired both of them to unite in marriage while guarding their virginity. In contrast to what happens today, when sexual relations are often experienced without any real personal commitment, Mary and Joseph loved each other deeply, following a divine inspiration not to include sexual union in their affection for each other.

The God of Mary and Joseph

In fact, the great protagonist of their story is God, a constant interlocutor in their choices and decisions, a point of reference in all circumstances. A God who is present and near, powerful lord and just judge, reliable but not predictable. A far cry from both the condescending and reassuring God, always ready to legitimize all kinds of behavior, the "God made to measure" we tend to portray today; and from the stern and punitive, wrathful and intransigent God who loomed over some Christian souls in ages past. The God of Mary and Joseph acts with strength and gentleness. He, knowing the inner weakness of men and women in the face of evil, and the difficulty they experience when they try to understand what is really good or evil in various circumstances, has agreed to approach us men by becoming himself a man so as not to leave us alone in the difficulties of life. And he chose human beings as collaborators: first Mary and Joseph, then the Apostles and a variety of disciples, both men and women His was a grandiose project that revolutionized the course of history, and his collaborators are still being talked about: Mary of Nazareth over the centuries has become one of the best known and most influential people. It is no accident that Pope Francis called her "God's *influencer*" (World Youth Day in Panama, 2019); and the others also know a fame that does not wane.

A faith that has changed the world

But why has Mary become so famous throughout history and her prophetic words "All generations will call me blessed" (Lk 1:48) not remained an empty vaunt but have in fact come true? The answer is that her task had a priority over that of the others and, in a sense, was generative of all the other events. For she was asked to believe in Jesus when he was yet to come into this world, while the Apostles and other disciples at least had him before their eyes. Of course, they too had to make the leap between seeing in him a mere teacher, and believing in him as in the incarnate Son of God, and for this reason their faith was also an act of courageous placing themselves in God's hands. But Mary's faith was the inner certainty of what really could not be seen and could not even be remotely imagined: the Son of God who would become incarnate in her. Her faith has been fruitful. The Holy Spirit was able to act because she allowed him to (cf. Luke 1:38), and she conceived Jesus with her decision to cooperate in the Lord's work. A new story had begun that would change the world, and she was there to put it on track.

Mother of disciples in the Church on the way

Her faith made her mother of Jesus physically, and spiritually of Jesus' disciples, who with the help of her encouragement at Cana ("Do whatever he tells you" Jn 2:5) began to believe ("And his disciples believed in him" Jn 2:11). So important is her presence for the disciples that Jesus' thoughts, at the last moment of his life, now on the cross, went not only to his eternal Father to entrust his soul to him and ask him to forgive his murderers, but also to the disciples who had strayed. To recover them and help them overcome their sense of guilt and inadequacy, he wanted to leave them a mother, and he entrusted her with a new task: "Woman, behold your son!" (Jn 19:26). He said this to John, the beloved disciple, in whom all believers are represented. Still today her motherly figure powerfully expresses the closeness and love of God who chose her so as to make our journey toward him more trusting and easier, especially at times when we are discouraged or feel incapable.

Thus, after becoming a widow on Joseph's death, Mary, at the age of almost 50, lost her only Son and found herself surrounded by his disciples. From that day on she became a point of reference for them and kept them united in faith and common prayer (cf. Acts 1:14) as they awaited the Holy Spirit to open their minds to understand what Jesus had taught over the years (cf. Jn 14:16-26). At that point, the disciples would no longer have needed her on this earth, and Jesus took her up to be beside him in the glory of Heaven At that moment she entered upon her definitive communion with the Persons of the Most Holy Trinity to whom she had already been united all along on this earth. So intense was that embrace, that her body too – transformed by divine glory – entered to enjoy the goods of heaven. She who, as we said, had been the first to believe, was also the first to go to Heaven in body and soul. But her happy lot was not for her alone. As a good mother she opened the way for us, and at the end of time our bodies too will be in glory and we will enjoy God's love not only spiritually but also physically, as the true men and women that we are, and we will be imbued with deep happiness in every fiber of our being.

Why her?

One final note we take from the Gospel: in anticipation of this universal maternal mission of hers, God prepared Mary in a fitting manner. In fact he does this with all men and women, who come into the world with a mission, perhaps seemingly small and unimportant, but always significant and useful for other people as well as for themselves. He envisions and creates people with some gifts and not others. He brings them into being in one historical and geographical context instead of another, and no one is the result of chance, but always of the Creator's love (cf. Eph 1:4-7). This was also the case with Mary, and Christians from the earliest centuries have thought that God bestowed appropriate gifts on her who was to be the Mother of the Redeemer and to accompany him in the fulfillment of his mission. Sustained by this inspiration, the people of God who are the Church have come with certainty to the conclusion that God preserved Mary from original sin, to make her fully receptive to the action of grace and to avert the dominion of the devil over her. It was not for nothing that, in greeting her, the angel addressed her with these words, "Rejoice, full of grace!" (Luke 1:28). After all, this was the condition that in the beginning God had foreseen for the whole human race, when he created man and woman in a "state of innocence and grace," as theologians say. Immaculate were Adam and Eve, and we all should have been, had they kept faith with their friendship with the Creator instead of falling into the deception of the evil one, coming to suspect God and seeking their own greatness behind his back (cf. Gen 3:4-6). At the moment when he decided to send his Son into the world to recover the original covenant and "re-found" the whole world he had created, he wanted the maiden who was to become the mother of the Word to receive the gifts of innocence and grace, so that already in her the Christian newness would be manifested: Mary, as the new Eve, accompanies Christ, the new Adam (cf. Rom 5:14-21), and we venerate her Immaculate Conception.

A beautiful but not easy story...

This, in a nutshell, is the story of Mary that we know from the Gospels, which constitute the only certain source on her life. But in order to answer our young friend's initial questions, it is necessary to stop and read between the lines of these interlaced texts, which, as if against the light, allow us to know her better and appreciate her human and supernatural depth. It is not a matter of giving free rein to the imagination, but of penetrating the sacred texts. Many *Lives of Mary* have been written with the intention of enriching the essential information offered by the Gospels, but in these lines we will be able to address only one aspect that may appear puzzling. Contrary to what is generally thought, Mary's friendship with God did not shield her from a difficult and at times harsh life. On the contrary, becoming the mother of Jesus exposed her to objectively risky situations that required supernatural faith and human courage.

It is important to pause for a moment and consider that Mary, like all of us, did not know how events would unfold or if and how the difficulties would be resolved. She faced them with faith and courage, as mentioned above, and today we can tell her story but without forgetting that for her the future was uncertain, just as it is for us. So, she knew that Jesus was coming from Heaven, and that he would fulfill the covenant with the house of David, but how and when this would happen she could not foresee, and at various times it seemed as if things were going in a totally different direction from what they were supposed to go. When she accepted the Son whom God had sent to her, she risked being rejected by Joseph, who might have disbelieved her and abandoned her, exposing her to precariousness and violence (cf. Mt 1:19). When she had to give birth far from home and in poor conditions, she might have feared that God had forgotten his promises and despaired at this abandonment (cf. Lk 2:7). When Herod decided to have all the newborn children killed in Bethlehem and she by a miracle managed to escape, she was not spared the discomfort of a long journey for which she had not prepared and along a route that was unsafe (cf. Mt 2:13-14). When she heard Simeon announce that a sword would pierce her soul, she understood that God would not protect her from trial and leave her quiet, but rather he would want her present at the decisive moment of her Son's mission (cf. Lk 2:34-35). When Jesus stayed on in Jerusalem without saying anything to his parents, throwing them into anguish, she heard words from her Son that she could not understand (cf. Lk 2:50). When she went to look for Jesus together with other relatives, she was seemingly put in second place behind the disciples (cf. Mk 3:31-35). Finally, she was present at the torture and death of her Son (cf. Jn 19:25) suffering unimaginably. In all these situations Mary was guided by the Holy Spirit who enabled her to believe, to hope, to love; and she did not turn away from this supernatural perspective, but overcame the temptation to close in on herself in pain and despair or rebellion.

We often hear people say: but she was full of grace, it was easy for her! Certainly the first statement is true, but the inference drawn from it is incorrect. For we know that God sends his grace in proportion to the trials people face in life, and this applies to all of us: no one is forsaken by God (cf. 2 Cor 12:9; Heb. 4:16; 1 Pet 5:10). Mary, too, received the grace she needed to sanctify herself through the difficulties she would encounter on her journey, and her greatness lies in the fact that she did not reject God's grace. She did not think that God should have followed her advice, she did not protest against situations beyond her littleness that came upon her life. She did not bewail the loss of the life she had expected together with Joseph... She opened herself to the divine plan for her, and the pole star in her life was faithfulness to Christ was. Her faith was not a passive acquiescence, and we should not mistake it for irresponsibility or recklessness. Her complete confidence that she was always in God's hands never constituted an excuse for her to avoid reflection and freedom in the decisions she made (cf. Lk 1:28-35; Jn 2:3-5).

How many "Madonnas" are there in the world?

Today we know Mary in many different aspects. Venerated in various places with particular characteristics, she seems almost an expert in transformism... There are hundreds of images of her that, although they are also very different from each other, do not prevent us from recognizing her in her identity: she is the mother of Jesus. This variety of representations has arisen from the experience of feeling her closeness that so many people have had in different parts of the world. There are even "Madonnas" that identify with a people, such as the Virgin of Guadalupe in Mexico, or the Virgin of Często-chowa in Poland, who seem to embody the soul of those peoples. In many cities, Marian shrines can be found on façades or street corners, and there are often pictures of her inside homes. Many people keep one of her little images in their wallets or pockets: almost a way of expressing gratitude and love for the one who does not forget her children, and succors them in their needs. Her shrines draw over the world a kind of "Marian geography" (cf. St. John Paul II, Encyclical *Redemptoris Mater* 28) that is an expression of her presence, of her apparitions, of her messages calling men to a true life of faith that in time and space God has asked her to address to believers, sending her as an ambassador of his fatherly and motherly Providence.

Queen in Heaven and on earth

Mary is often invoked as Queen, and although we know from the Gospel that her social status was that of a person of the people, in Heaven this title rightfully belongs to her because she is the mother of Christ, the true King and Lord of the universe. By invoking her as Queen, believers express their confidence in the power of her prayer before God and recognize the importance of her role alongside

Christ: although Mary was not necessary to the Redeemer's work, He wanted to rely on her (cf. Lk 1:26-38; Jn 19:25-27), and Jesus' example is a lesson for us to imitate.

It is difficult to think of another person who, like her, is in Heaven and at the same time so present on earth... Of course, we can never fully understand the great mystery of the Mother of God, but we can always contemplate it with wonder, as in all ages have done the saints and many artists, to whom Mary has inspired great masterpieces: "Virgin Mother, daughter of your Son, humble and high more than creature, fixed term of eternal counsel..." (Dante, *Paradiso*, 33.1 ff.).

The Church teaches that every man can be saved by seeking to do the good that his conscience indicates to him. Why then does she insist on the importance of baptism to be conferred as soon as possible?

(Graziano Borgonovo)

1) Let's start with the first statement: the Church teaches that every man can be saved by trying to do the good that his conscience indicates to him. Yes, that is indeed the case! But in order to understand this teaching properly – that is, according to its truth –and, above all, to understand the connection of this statement with the question of the importance of baptism to be conferred as soon as possible, we need straightaway to recall the clear word of Holy Scripture: "For in no other is there salvation; for there is no other name under heaven given to men in which it is appointed that we may be saved" (Acts 4:12). It is St. Peter who is here speaking to the high priests and elders of Israel, and he is speaking about Jesus of Nazareth, who died and rose again, whom Peter proclaims to be the only Savior.

2) Salvation, Savior: what do these terms mean? The Latin word *salus* can help us: we all know what health is and we all value our health. Humans invest energy and resources to preserve it and extend life as long as possible, which health guarantees. But there is an insurmountable limit, whether we want it or not, whether we think

about it or intend to censor it: it is the event of death. The limit of death contrasts strikingly with the desire for eternity and permanence in being, in life! Such desire and such contrast are experienced by man, acutely, within himself. Now: if indeed One has risen from death, it is He who proposes himself as the Savior, as the *salus*, the salvation, the "permanent health after death," for all.

3) This justifies the Church's perennial missionary task, founded in the last command given by the risen Jesus to his disciples: "Go therefore and make disciples of all nations, baptizing them in the name of the Father and of the Son and of the Holy Spirit" (Mt 28:19). Until the end of time, the Church is called to proclaim the salvation by Jesus – the salvation he brought to men and that he himself is – by personally making each one a sharer in his victory over death through baptism, to be conferred "in the name of the Father and of the Son and of the Holy Spirit." And this is so that each one may be happy, now already, through coming to know the One who is the full meaning of life, in order to be able to love him and respond to his love. It is therefore understandable why the Church insists on baptism as the source of new life to be made possible for each person as early as possible, from the beginning of his or her life.

4) Question: what if someone has not received the proclamation of Jesus, will he be able to be saved? Or if he has perhaps heard it but from a distance, not persuasively, without being able to adhere to it or being able to receive it by being baptized? How many such situations have occurred and will continue to occur in human history! It is a fact that, to this day, billions of people do not know Jesus. What about that? Are they inescapably "damned"? Can they be "saved"? Yes, the Church answers, they can be saved, precisely by seeking to

recognize and practice that good which their conscience points to. For, as John Henry Newman admirably stated, "conscience is the first vicar of Christ." And so we return to having to justify our starting point.

5) In this regard, it so happens that several misunderstandings need to be set aside. The first revolves precisely around the notion of conscience. John Paul II has written lucidly that in "certain currents of modern thought… the individual conscience is accorded the status of a supreme tribunal of moral judgment which hands down categorical and infallible decisions about good and evil. To the affirmation that one has a duty to follow one's conscience is unduly added the affirmation that one's moral judgment is true merely by the fact that it has its origin in the conscience" (Encyclical *Veritatis splendor*, no. 32). That is: it is one thing to say that each person is called to follow his own conscience, forming it in relation to the good to be recognized: this is a sacrosanct affirmation. It is quite another to say that any option is true (and therefore everything in the end is equivalent, possessing no value whatsoever in reality), posed on the sole condition that it comes from one's own individual conscience: this affirmation is false. To use Joseph Ratzinger's enlightening image: in such a case, conscience ceases to be the wide-open window on reality and becomes the shell in which subjectivity encloses itself and claims to become absolute.

6) The second misunderstanding, closely related to the first, emerges from what is an insuppressible reference point for understanding conscience: the good, precisely. In order to grasp the universal and absolute scope of the notion of "good," we might suitably turn to the so-called "golden rule," which we find also formulated

on the lips of Jesus: "Whatever you want men to do to you, do also to them" (Mt 7:12). This suggestion contains an obvious question that each person is called to ask himself first of all: I, what would I always want done to me? And the answer can only be one, for everyone, in whatever culture he is born, whatever religion he professes, whatever nation or social class he belongs to: the good. I would like – exactly as every one else would like – good to be done to me all the time. It is not conceivable and reasonable to desire evil for oneself, even at the moment when, unhappily, it would be inflicted by and/or on others. Conscience is the human "organ," the natural "instrument," to affirm, for self and others, the desired good.

7) It is worth reading here a beautiful page by Romano Guardini: "The living good beats at my conscience. Welcomed by the mind and heart, it presses to be translated into human action. The first and most important task of conscience consists in perceiving the imperious voice of the good, which wants to be implemented in a manner worthy of man. The good therefore demands and insists, 'Welcome me! Understand me! Want me! Implement me!' [...] Thus conscience is also the door, through which the eternal enters time. It is the cradle of history. Only from conscience does history flow, which means more than just a natural process. History means that, as a result of free human activity, something eternal is accomplished within time." The living cry of the good does not resound in nothingness, it can be caught, received and held: conscience exists for the reception and realization in time of such a work of good. In the contingency of time there appears a glimmer of the eternal.

8) "In the heart of each person, hope dwells as the desire and expectation of good things to come," Pope Francis wrote in the very

first lines of the Document with which he called for the Ordinary Jubilee of the Holy Year 2025 (cf. Bull *Spes non confundit*, no. 1). In biblical language, to say "heart" is also to say "conscience." The "good" is therefore originally desired and expected in the conscience of every human being, and it is from that hidden and sacred source that the hope of welcoming it springs forth, when and if it manifests itself. And if it is true that conscience is the door through which the eternal enters time – as we have just heard from Romano Guardini – , it is the Lord Jesus who is the only true "door" of salvation (cf. Jn 10:7, 9) of time to the eternal. He is the "our hope" (1 Tim 1:1). The proposal of baptism that the Church offers in the proclamation of salvation realized in Jesus of Nazareth therefore marks the fulfillment of the expectation of good inscribed in every man's conscience.

9) However, human action has a dramatic character: it is possible to do good and it is possible to do evil. Always. Even at the moment when the conscience is sincerely straining to listen to the voice of the good that "cries out" to be done. Even once one has received baptism. Everyone's experience is a witness to this. But for this very reason, the natural desire for the good – which persists, even after the fall into original sin and even after every evil committed, as conscience witnesses – needs to be sustained by the new life in Christ received in baptism through the Spirit's gift of grace. Left alone with ourselves we would succumb to the lure of evil. "Without me you can do nothing," the Lord admonished (Jn 15:5). Therefore, in order for conscience to remain under the light of the good and the true for which it is made, it needs indispensably a prior light, a prevenient grace, a constant support of the Spirit, which blows even beyond the

visible boundaries of the Church, into the heart of every man (cf. Jn 3:8).

10) Every man, by virtue of being endowed with intelligence and will, is called to do good, that good which we would always like to receive from our fellow human beings. It is a criterion of gratuitousness, the "golden rule," in the pursuit of holiness: "Be ye therefore perfect, even as your heavenly Father is perfect" (Mt 5:48). We have, all of us, the guidance of conscience. As Christians, we also have the grace of baptism. We have the responsibility of free adherence to the "good that cries out" and the "grace that grows." And we all need mercy so that evil does not prevail. A brief reflection on the conscience/baptism relationship such as the one offered here can then undoubtedly conclude with one of the profound and peacemaking invocations that the Church raises in her liturgy: "O God, source of all good, who answers the prayers of your people beyond all desire and merit, pour out your mercy upon us: forgive what conscience fears and add what prayer dares not hope for."

Is it really necessary to attend Mass every Sunday? At best, 10% go. Why does the Church continue to teach that missing Sunday Mass is a grave sin (cf. CCC, no. 2181)?

(Pilar Río)

Dear friend,

The number of Catholics now going to Sunday Mass is, in fact, very low. Statistics reveal a drastic and constant decline in recent decades. Between 1993 to 2019, at least one-third of mass goers disappeared, in part due to the Covid-19 pandemic that changed relationships requiring people to be physically present. In fact, many have got used to going to Mass online.

Of course, this irrefutable statistic can easily lead one to be doubtful about the duty to attend Mass every Sunday. Indeed, one may wonder why the Church continues to insist on the need to attend Sunday Mass, given the low attendance, a sign that we are no longer in a Christian society, but a pluralistic and tendentially pagan one. Moreover, to claim that not going is a grave sin could prove to be rather counterproductive.

The Church undoubtedly does not ignore, and does not want to ignore, social reality, but the sociological-type criteria that emerge from the examination of that reality, while very useful, are only indicative and they are inadequate to resolve a properly religious question. It is therefore up to the Church to listen to questions and objections and to explain the reasons behind what she establishes.

In this regard, I would like to come to you with other questions that can guide our dialogue toward the deeper meaning of what the Church believes, celebrates and lives regarding the Sunday Mass.

Why does the Church gather?

The answer to this question, which may be the first of your objections, is based on the meaning of the name "Church," which comes from the Greek *ekklēsía* (from *ek-kalein*: to call out). This word therefore means convocation, gathering, assembly of those who have been called out, and because of this it defined the identity of the early Christian community.

By choosing this term, not only linguistically but also theologically, the community of those who believed in Christ recognized themselves as heirs of the *ekklēsía*, the Old Testament assembly. *Ekklēsía* in fact is the word frequently used in the Greek version of the Old Testament (called the *Septuagint*) to refer not to any assembly, but to that of the chosen people summoned by God – revealed to Moses by the name of YHWH – with a religious purpose, for worship: the hearing of his word, the offering of sacrifices, the celebration of Passover or the reading of the Law. *Ekklēsía* serves to designate first and foremost the assembly that the Lord had summoned in the Sinai desert, where Israel received the Law and was constituted by God as his holy people (cf. Ex 19).

More precisely, this term indicates the time when the chosen people respond to the call of the Lord and come together to worship him. The reference to worship, to liturgy, which in the Old Testament is linked to the word *ekklēsía* is therefore essential and characterizing.

Recognizing itself as the heir of the Old Testament assembly and therefore self-designating itself as *ekklēsía*, the early Christian community wished to express both its relationship with Israel (continuity) and its profound awareness of being the new eschatological people, permanently summoned by the Father, through the redeeming blood of his Son Jesus Christ and the gift of the Spirit (newness), "to the praise of his glory" (Eph 1:14).

This awareness continues to be for the Church, and for us Christians who are her members, an obligatory point of reference, because it is based on a rule that has been present from the beginning. *Ekklēsía* therefore reminds the Church of all times of her identity as a holy assembly and exhorts her to be faithful to the vocation she has received, which is to be summoned by God the Father into the Body of Christ by the power of his Spirit as a universal community of believers. A community gathered in one place, in liturgical assembly, to worship him. In fact, St. Paul speaks insistently of the "convening," the gathering together of Christians. Ultimately, the Church gathers because in this way she fully expresses and implements her very identity as "Church."

Why gather on Sundays?

According to the testimony of apostolic tradition, the community of Christ's disciples gathered on the first day after the Sabbath, that is, the first day of the week (cf. 1 Cor 16:2; Acts 20:7-12). In fact, this custom that marks the very rhythm of the Church's life from the beginning is also confirmed by non-Christian sources. At the beginning of the second century, the governor of Bithynia, Pliny the Younger, reported in a letter to the Emperor Trajan that Christians were in the habit of "gathering on a fixed day before the rising of the sun and singing among themselves a hymn to Christ as to a god" (*Ep.*, 10, 96,7). Around the middle of the same century, St. Justin Martyr, in his first *Apology*, confirms this, reiterating that the assembly brings together all the members of the community who come from both the city and the countryside, on "the first day on which God created the world having transformed darkness and matter, and Jesus Christ our savior rose on the same day from the dead" (*I Apol.*, 67,7). This first day thus refers back to the first day of creation as well as to the day of the Lord's Resurrection, which inaugurates the new creation.

Since apostolic times and throughout its bimillennial history, the Church has never neglected to gather together every eight days on what she rightly calls the Lord's Day or Sunday, a term that comes from the Latin *dies dominica* or *dies Dominici* meaning precisely the "Lord's Day." She gathers as a community of those who believe in the risen Christ, and have been incorporated through his Spirit into his glorified Body. The Church thus continues to celebrate Sunday as a faithful expression of her faith, hope and love for her Lord Jesus Christ, who rose from the dead for us.

For Christians, therefore, Sunday is the primordial feast, a joyful recurrence of the day when Christ conquered sin and death and made us partakers of his immortal life. The day, consequently, on which we are called to remember and celebrate the gift of salvation that was offered to us in baptism where we were buried in Christ's death and with him raised and reborn to new life (cf. Rom 6:3-9).

In short, as St. Jerome writes, "Sunday is the day of the Resurrection, it is the day of Christians, it is our day" (*In die dominica Paschae*, II, 52).

Should we give it up?

Why the Sunday Eucharistic celebration?

The Church's faithfulness to this appointment is not only due to the desire to "remember" the Easter of her Lord, but above all to participate in this mystery from which she lives and draws life and strength for her mission.

Indeed, since apostolic times, the Sunday convocation has had an indispensable significance for Christians: Sunday is the day of the Eucharistic assembly. That is, the day when the community of the faithful gathers around the altar to commemorate the glorious death and Resurrection of Christ, hearing the Word of God and celebrating the Eucharist. In fact, the Church has always lived from and in the certainty that the celebration of the Eucharist is not a mere remembrance of the past salvific event, but a "memorial" of Christ's

Passover, that is, a sacramental actualization and re-presentation – that is, through signs – of the paschal mystery (Christ's death and Resurrection). All this is because Jesus Christ instituted the Eucharist to perpetuate the memorial of his death and Resurrection and to make it possible for us to participate in it.

The Sunday Eucharistic celebration is thus a celebration of the living presence of the risen and living Christ in our midst. In this way, the celebrating assembly, commemorating the paschal mystery from which it is perpetually recreated and by which it lives and acts together with its Bridegroom and Lord, also becomes a visible sign of the Church in a place, called to bear witness to her identity and mission in the world.

The Sunday Eucharist is no different from that celebrated on any other day of the week, because every celebration makes present Christ's Paschal Mystery and is an epiphany (i.e., manifestation) of the Church, but it has a special, solemn value because it is celebrated on the day when Christ's Resurrection is commemorated.

Moreover, we cannot overlook the fact that the Sunday Eucharist has always been considered and lived as a sign of communion and a source of concrete fraternal charity, both among the members of the community and among the neediest in society. In his first *Apologia*, to quote just one testimony, St. Justin describes the outburst of solidarity generated by the Sunday assembly in this way: "Those who are wealthy and willing to give, give freely each one what he wills, and what is gathered is delivered to him who presides, who assists orphans, widows, the sick, the poor, prisoners, foreign guests, in a word, succors all who are in need" (*I Apol*, 67:6). Now, if in the light of all this, the Sunday Eucharist appears as a qualifying element

of the Church and our Christian identity, how can we neglect it or
do without it?

Why the Sunday precept?

Since the celebration of the Eucharist is the heart of Sunday, of
the Lord's Day, it seems paradoxical that there should be a precept
that obliges the faithful to attend Sunday Mass (unless a serious reason prevents it): the Sunday Eucharistic assembly should be an indispensable appointment for Christians both because of the immense gift that is offered and in response to Jesus' command, "do
this in remembrance of me" (1 Cor 11:24).

In the early centuries, pastors reminded the faithful of the need
to participate, but in fact there was no binding norm. Believers in
Christ adhered wholeheartedly to this call, and even if at certain
times participation declined, the heroism with which Christians participated in the Sunday liturgical assembly, even in situations of danger and restriction of religious freedom, is a clearly observable fact
throughout the twenty centuries' history of the Church.

Well-known in this regard is the example of the martyrs of Ab-
itine, in Proconsular Africa, who, during Diocletian's persecution,
courageously defied the imperial edict forbidding the celebration of
sacred rites and worship assemblies, accepting death so as not to
miss the Sunday Eucharist. Moving is the dialogue between proconsul Anulinus and Emeritus, one of the accused: "'Were meetings
held in your house against the imperial edicts?' [...] Emeritus replied,
'In my house we celebrated the mysteries of the Lord on the Sunday

day.' 'Why,' asked the proconsul, 'did you allow them to enter?' Emeritus replied, 'Because they are my brothers and I could not prevent them.' 'But you should have!' retorted the proconsul. 'I could not,' Emeritus insisted, 'because we cannot live without celebrating the mysteries of the Lord'" (*Acta Saturnini, Dativi et aliorum plurimorum martyrum in Africa*, XI).

Indeed, the Christians of the early centuries followed their conscience, which made them feel so strongly the inner need to celebrate Mass: "Without Sunday we cannot live!" It is too great a good to neglect!

With the passage of time, the original aspiration gradually faded, and faced with the lukewarmness or negligence of some of the faithful, the Church felt obliged to make explicit and prescribe this obligation, most often through exhortations, but also through precise canonical provisions that have become a precept. In fact, the current *Code of Canon Law* reiterates this norm (cf. CIC, can. 1247); as does the Code of the Eastern Churches (cf. CCEO, can. 881 §1), a provision taken up by the *Catechism of the Catholic Church*: "Those who deliberately fail to comply with this obligation commit a grave sin" (no. 2181).

However, the Church is not a judge enforcing a penal code; she is a mother, aware that the precept serves to guard the value, to enlighten and guide the freedom of her children so that they are aware of the importance of welcoming the Lord's invitation.

The Church urges us to ask ourselves: how could we be faithful to our Christian identity, to our being *Ekklēsía*, without allowing ourselves to be met by the risen Lord in the Sunday Eucharist, without listening to his Word, without feeding ourselves at his table?

How could we live the Gospel and the precept of love without drawing from the inexhaustible source of charity in the Sunday Eucharist? More, how could we live as Christians in an openly hostile or indifferent or refractory environment, such as today's, without relying on the support of the community that gathers on Sundays to celebrate the Lord's Passover together?

In short, dear friend, the Church believes in, celebrates and lives the Sunday Eucharist and invites Christians to participate in it first and foremost because of a matter of identity: the Church is a convocation around the Word and the Eucharist, and she expresses and makes herself as such (*Ekklēsía*) when she gathers and becomes a visible sign of God's merciful action.

The Church teaches that there are actions that are intrinsically evil, that is, evil in themselves, which must never be done, regardless of intentions or circumstances, but Pope Francis says that in order to judge the morality of an act one must pay attention to "conditioning and circumstances." Is the Church's moral teaching changing?

(André-Marie Jerumanis)

"The kingdom of heaven is like a householder who brings out of his treasure what is new and what is old" (Mt 13:52).

Before answering the question of whether with Pope Francis the Church is changing its teaching in the moral field, it is necessary to recall the logic of Catholic moral teaching as set forth in the Catechism of the Catholic Church.

First of all, it is absolutely fundamental not to forget that it is *freedom* that makes the human being a moral subject. It follows that only *voluntary actions* that characterize the human being, and thus are human acts, can properly be considered moral actions, and can be good or bad (cf. CCC 1734). A correct anthropology of freedom is an irreplaceable prerequisite for engaging in moral discourse, particularly within the Catholic Church (cf. CCC 1731). If freedom were lacking, or the exercise of freedom were diminished, responsibility and thus the qualification of mortal or venial sin would be profoundly marked. For the pastoral care that characterizes the Catholic Church this nuance is fundamental. It is so, in order to come to a correct personal concrete decision, and for an authentic exercise of the sacrament of reconciliation, for personal examination of conscience, and for the pastoral and spiritual accompaniment of persons.

But what then defines, according to Catholic moral doctrine, the goodness or badness of actions performed? Is freedom the ultimate criterion of moral action? Is it enough for personal conscience to evaluate an action as good for it actually to be good? Is it enough to canonize one's subjective conscience? Is acting out of love enough to justify a decision? The Magisterium of the Church in the Catechism of the Catholic Church teaches that in order to consider an act morally good, it is necessary to take into account three basic elements: the chosen object that must be good, the intention and the circumstances (cf. CCC 1750-61).

We stress the importance of stating that it is necessary that the object be good, precisely because it is an indispensable element and it is today relativized by giving priority to the subjective point of view. Let us define the object in morality: it is the concrete action that is performed, the immediate content, the matter of a voluntary action (cf. CCC 1751). There are actions that are always evil and are called "intrinsically evil" because they oppose the essential demands of the virtues of justice or temperance, such as stealing, abusing a person, raping, exploiting another, lying or cursing... Today who would dare to say that abusing another person, especially if it is a minor, is an indifferent action? On the contrary, it is a profoundly, that is, inherently negative action and will be so, regardless of circumstances and intention. It is therefore true that we must maintain the objective dimension when defining the goodness of an action and maintain the existence of inherently evil actions.

When we come to assess the *imputability* of certain actions, we need to avoid remaining only at the level of the objective aspect (essential though it is) as, for example, a certain rigorist tradition of Christian morality does (cf. Jansenism). The Catechism takes into account the subject when it teaches that an act is morally imputable if it is directly willed (cf. CCC 1736). It also points out that "the *imputability* and responsibility for an action can be diminished or even nullified by ignorance, inadvertence, duress, fear, habit, inordinate attachments, and other psychological or social factors" (CCC 1735). We note that the impulses of sensitivity, passions, external pressures and pathological disorders can diminish the imputability of the act, decreasing freedom and thus guilt. "For a *sin* to be *mortal*, three conditions must together be met: 'Mortal sin is sin whose object is grave matter and which is also committed with full knowledge and deliberate consent'" (CCC 1857). Full awareness means having not only full consciousness of performing an act, but also sufficient knowledge of the moral value of the act in question. Today more than in the past, we realize that external conditionings (loss of acceptance of the argument from authority, development of the critical spirit, multiplicity of alternative truths, contradictory theological opinions) can make it difficult to know the moral value of certain behaviors. Even deliberate consent today is interpreted taking into account the contribution of the human sciences, which, better than in the past, highlight the psychological and social conditionings of freedom.

However, as Christians we cannot fail to refer to the *fulfillment of freedom in Christ*. The Church's discourse on moral action is not limited to pure philosophical reflection that leaves theology aside, falling into a form of extrinsicism between philosophical rationality and theological rationality. Thus it is necessary, in order to give a proper account of Christian moral logic, to bear in mind the fulfillment of human freedom in Christ. From a Christological perspective, one can speak of freedom communicated in the Son to the human being. Freedom is then the positive realization of divine sonship. In this sense, Christian freedom is a gift, which gives a specific note to Christian morality. The "you must" becomes by gift a "you can" in the Son.

The axiom "to act according to one's conscience," as the proximate rule of action, also receives a specific connotation when one reads it from a filial perspective. Freedom of conscience is the expression of divine sonship and a sign of human dignity. Inviting conscience to remain open to the search for truth stems from the conviction that the intelligence and the will that scan freedom and therefore clothe our conscience, lead the man of good will to discover, in a continuous journey in the Spirit of truth, the whole truth, according to which to orient his life and make the fundamental option of his life, which is concretely expressed in particular choices. It is the Spirit who enables the believer to experience his new filial status, and thus his filial truth, his immense dignity. The son's action thus flows from the "new heart" given by the Spirit, a heart that believes, hopes, and loves. Its *rationale*, its perception of truth, its ability to act according to the Father's will, its capacity to love, are profoundly shaped by it. It is in the Spirit that the son understands that there are intrinsically evil acts, understood as anti-filial and anti-fraternal actions. It is in the Spirit that man's conscience becomes capable of prudentially discerning how to embody in specific acts the truth of his being a son.

This lengthy introduction is absolutely essential in order to interpret correctly Pope Francis' Moral Magisterium and how to understand him when he states that in pastoral discernment attention must be paid to conditionings and circumstances (cf. AL 301-306), because, as emerges from the Catholic doctrine just recalled, they make it possible to evaluate the freedom of a person in performing a certain concrete action and to better consider the imputability of such an action, as well as to accompany fragile persons on the path of conversion toward holiness with pastoral benignity in the logic of pastoral mercy (cf. AL 307-3012). Does such a view contradict the previous teaching of the popes on the illicitness of positing intrinsically evil acts? The answer to this question requires some premises.

The greatest difficulty arises from the artificial separation between objective morality and subjective morality and, consequently, from a certain conception of conscience. One must actually start from the definition of the moral object that VS proposes, as the "proximate end of the deliberate choice of the will" (cf. VS 78). Intentionality is not something external, but is inherent in action and contributes to the determination of the type of act posed. M. Rhonheimer has pointed this out well with regard to questions of sexual ethics and the second chapter of VS, which is to be interpreted according to the ethics of St. Thomas, properly understood, considering the perspective of the acting subject (cf. M. Rhonhei-mer, *The Perspective of the Acting Person: Essays in the Renewal of Thomistic Moral Philosophy*, CUA Press, 2008). This is precisely the fundamental question: how to properly define the object, which can-not, according to VS, be limited to the external, physical or material description, but implies the proximate end of a choice of the will that necessarily requires the inclusion of circumstances and intention.

In fact, Pope Francis' ethical-pastoral perspective expressed in *Amoris laetitia* (=AL) does not negate the statements of *Veritatis splendor* (=VS). In the transition from VS to AL, *a correct hermeneu-tic* must be carried out to avoid a harmful juxtaposition. The two texts are looking at two distinct aspects of moral life, one more cen-tered on the objective dimension, the other on the subjective dimen-sion, and both need to be considered in order to avoid having a wob-bly moral theology. We also note the need to contextualize the two documents; each considers a particular aspect of the culture: the first the relativization of norms and the subjectivist drift of moral con-science; the other considers the increasingly complex situation of Christians themselves who are living married life with difficulty in a secularized and globalized world, which seems incapable of perceiv-ing moral absolutes and is more focused on individual freedom. Ac-tually, "*Veritatis splendor* was intended to have an essentially doctri-nal scope in order to solidly ground a Christian morality in its ob-jectivity. At stake was whether it is possible to formulate a morality common to humanity and make a well argued defense of the human person in the light of the Gospel. AL is based on this conviction, but from an essentially pastoral perspective, a perspective that helps us better understand the doctrine from which it does not wish to be separated" (A. Thomasset - J-M. Garrigues, *Une morale souple mais non sans boussole. Répondre aux doutes des quatre cardinaux à propos d'Amoris laetitia,* Cerf, Paris 2017, 52).

In order not to misunderstand Pope Francis, it is necessary to keep in mind that he stands in the line of St. Alphonsus Maria de' Liguori, Doctor of the Church, patron of moralists and confessors, for whom moral theology is all about practicality, practicality identified with pastorality, integrating the virtue of prudence in judging what is contingent. And theological-moral reflection aims at searching for truth, but a truth that saves the person and sets him on the path of Christian perfection, understood from the perspective of the excellence of love. The objective norm must be accepted by the believer's personal conscience, and this acceptance transforms objective moral truth into salvific truth; moral truth passes from the objective plane to subjective acceptance and leads to the moral, salvific transformation of the person. This dynamic of conscience is reiterated by CCC 1782: "Man has the right to act in conscience and in freedom so as personally to make moral decisions." It is the judgment of conscience, as John Paul II states, that "formulates the proximate norm of the morality of a voluntary act" (VS 59). Freedom is a precondition for the morality of an act. If responsibility is lacking, the judgment to be placed on a concrete action will have to take this into account.

Such *salvific orientation of Christian morality* proposed by St. Alphonsus allows for a better understanding of Pope Francis' Moral Magisterium. Pope Francis himself highlighted the importance of the Alphonsian perspective for morality on the occasion of the 150th anniversary of the proclamation of St. Alphonsus Maria de' Liguori as Doctor of the Church: "The Alphonsian theological proposal stems from listening to and welcoming the fragility of the most spiritually abandoned men and women The Holy Doctor, who had been trained in a rigorist mentality, is converted to 'benignity' through listening to reality. (...) Following the example of St. Alphonsus Maria de' Liguori, renewer of moral theology, it becomes desirable and therefore necessary to move close to, accompany and support the most destitute of spiritual aid on the path to redemption. Gospel radicality should not be set against human weakness. It is always necessary to find the way that does not drive away, but brings hearts closer to God, just as Alphonsus did with his spiritual and moral teaching."

In the light of the human sciences recent theological anthropology has come to appreciate, better than in the past, all the complex dynamics of even the righteous man. *The divine call finds already present a soil that has its own conditions.* To affirm this is not to diminish the power of God's grace. It is true that the Council of Trent affirms that "no one should make his own that reckless expression that the commandments are impossible for the righteous man to keep" (DH 1536), but this does not exclude that it is always man who must open himself, and this openness is often conditioned by complex elements, as pastoral experience and current knowledge show.

Pope Francis reminds us of two fundamental elements of the theology of grace: not only that it is grace that saves us, but also that grace presupposes our nature, the transformation of which is historical and progressive. This dynamism of grace and freedom – which requires the cooperation of the subject – leads to the formulation of the criterion of the law of gradualness. Let us resume Cardinal

Ratzinger's explanation of it after the 1980 Synod on the Family: "*The law of 'gradualness'* is a new idea of the Synod, which has become one of its deepest perspectives and which remains present in all particular questions. With this idea of 'gradualness' the theme of 'being on the way' is addressed, which is concretized at the level of moral knowledge and practice. The whole Christian way is a 'conversion' that takes place through progressive steps" (J. Ratzinger, *Lettre au clergé du diocèse de Munich*, Documentation Catholique, 1981, p 387-388). The law of gradualness is taken up by Pope Francis in AL 293-295. Let us recall that it is necessary to understand the law of gradualness correctly, not as the gradualness of the law, but where steps are evaluated, often in very complex situations, and where a certain good is present, always taking into account that it is a relative good of a subject on the way. In this regard, there is a theological and philosophical debate about the nature of relative good and possible good, terms that can be misunderstood, wrongly considered and lead to a relativization of truth, a trivialization of evil, but also a relativization of grace.

At the end of this reflection we are able to return to the original question and give an answer.

1. *Between St. John Paul II reiterating the importance of the existence of inherently evil acts and Pope Francis' pastoral focus there is no contradiction.* They are two perspectives that are not mutually exclusive but, on the contrary, complement and deepen each other. It is necessary to practice a hermeneutics of continuity, understood as *progress within the living tradition of the Church*, in order to best grasp the *novum*, seen as a going deeper. A statement by St. Thomas can illuminate the complementarity of the two perspectives. St.

Thomas distinguishes two modes of moral judgment: "There are two modes of judgment: a judgment of severity, and a judgment of mercy or equity. The first is exercised when one considers only the nature of the object and not the condition of the person: one must fear this judgment. The second is exercised by considering not only the nature of the condemnable fact, but also the condition of the person: 'The Lord has compassion on those who fear him, for he knows what we are made of' (Psalm 102:13-14)" (*Super Psalmos* 42:1).

2. The concept of intrinsic evil imposes limits on human freedom, keeps safe the objectivity of the moral law, implies that certain acts are always contrary to the dignity of the human person, to the dignity that derives from divine sonship, and is rooted in Scripture and Church tradition. It is an aid for the believer to discern between morally licit and illicit actions, it orients the conscience toward what is objectively good, it helps pastors to accompany the formation of conscience according to objective moral principles, without falling into relativism and laissez-faire compromise, but all this must always be carried out in the logic of pastoral kindness. It implies listening, mercy and understanding, offering hope in divine mercy.

3. Regarding the evaluation of the erroneous conscience, the Church's doctrine expressed in the CCC on moral conscience (cf. CCC 1776-1802) must be taken into account. A reflection on conscience by Benedict XVI (*In Praise of Conscience. Truth Questions the Heart*, 2009) is very enlightening. He indicates that conscience opens the way to the liberating path of truth, reminding us that one cannot identify man's conscience with the self-consciousness of the ego, nor with subjective certainty about oneself and one's moral

behavior. That said, the difficulty of moral conscience in a pluralistic society and, therefore, the possibility of the bona fide erroneous conscience cannot be denied today. The pastoral approach of Catholic moral theology has always stressed respect for the person's conscience even if erroneous, but also the duty to remain open to the truth. However, prudence is required on the part of pastors in correctly administering the truth in some situations, taking people into account in accordance with the teaching of St. Alphonsus as evidenced by the *Vademecum for Confessors on Certain Morality Issues Pertaining to Marital Life,* from the Pontifical Council for the Family, particularly in no. 8. Pope Francis' pastoral approach does not depart from this tradition, but strongly recalls it in his moral magisterium. Pope Francis' 14 *Catecheses on Discernment* (2022-2023) provide a better grasp of the way on the path of truth. His pastoral approach does not relativize that path in pastoral kindness. His Catecheses illustrate well the meaning of discernment, so important for conscience, in the light of St. Ignatius which has nothing to do with subjectivism or a certain situation ethics. "Discernment, however, is not done alone [...]. An indispensable first aid is the comparison with the Word of God and the doctrine of the Church. They help us to read what is moving in our hearts, learning to recognize the voice of God and distinguish it from other voices, which seem to impose themselves on our attention, but which ultimately leave us confused" (*Catechesis on Discernment* 13).

In the face of the enormous changes in the understanding of sexuality, why does the Church not adapt its moral teachings to current sensibilities?

(Juan José Pérez-Soba Diez del Corral)

For the Christian, the Church's moral teaching is a path towards God, not a series of prohibitions. The current changes in the area of sexuality actually stem precisely from the removal of God from this experience and the secularization of this dimension of the human being, which ends up impoverished and deformed. This change of approach goes back to Luther who came to regard marriage as a non-sacramental reality. This was reaffirmed by the French Revolution which, considering marriage as a purely civil fact, for the first time in human history removed any sign of sacredness from its celebration.

In this way sex, and the body itself, came to be regarded as something man could use as he pleased. This gave rise once more to the radical dualism with which early Christianity was confronted by Gnosticism and its sexual practices that were very similar to those of today, though Gnosticism still saw a connection between sacredness and sex.

Given this situation St. Paul taught that God's plan for sexuality was to be seen in the context of God's revealing himself to Israel in terms of human love and the requirements of faithfulness and exclusivity in that love, so much so as to portray the relationship between Christ and the Church as an image of marriage (cf. Eph 5:21-33).

The Church Fathers saw the need to affirm the radical goodness of sexuality in God's plan of creation, in opposition to the Gnostic rejection of the body – seen as a prison of evil matter that confines the soul – which brought with it widespread sexual licentousness.

St. Augustine saw the need to determine the goods that were proper to man as a sexed being in order to understand how he should live them. This was all in the context of man's vocation to love as one made in the image of God.

From the beginning, Christians understood, in faithful reception of Jesus' teaching, that this vocation could be lived both in marriage and in celibacy (cf. 1 Cor 7), which prevented the temptation to reduce sexuality to the level of mere biology or genital behavior.

This gave rise to some of the earliest insights that have then constantly characterized the Church's teaching, enabling Christianity to respond to the major cultural changes it has lived through in its twenty centuries of existence and that have so often affected the understanding of human sexuality.

Personal value

The first thing Christianity affirms about sexuality is that it is a dimension of human beings affecting them personally, and so the moral qualification is intrinsic to it because it touches and qualifies human intimacy. It is not something that man can use, because his intimacy is at stake, just as it is not consonant with his dignity that he should choose to be a slave.

Second, it must be seen as coming from the revelation of a God who is Love (cf. Jn 4:16) and who teaches man to love as an action that leads to the fullness of life, because man is created "in the image and likeness of God" (Gen 1:27), which includes the dimension of sexual difference.

Therefore, sexuality cannot be judged as a good external to man, as a reality that can be used or engaged in simply for pleasure. Christianity understands the mystery that surrounds sexuality and illuminates the innermost part of the human heart, and therefore invites us to live it as a love story to which God calls us.

As a result, man understands that in his being there is a wholeness of meaning that gives him an inner unity and is to be seen as a calling from God, who knows the heart of man and enlightens him (cf. Jn 2:25).

Bringing things together

This is the context that helps us understand the morality of sexuality on the basis of two fundamental principles that are in correlation with the person's action. Sexual behavior is not a matter of biological laws, but the proper object of deliberate action (cf. Encyclical *Veritatis splendor*, no. 78). We are dealing with the proper meanings of actions that have to do with our innermost desires.

The first principle is that the morality of sexuality must be evaluated from the perspective of the totality of the person insofar as it gives meaning to living. It is therefore not measured from the stand-point of mere pleasure or mere utility, which are interrelated reali-ties, but from the standpoint of a human meaning that has to do with a loving reality capable of filling the human heart with a fullness of life. This principle is very experiential and, if it is ignored, there comes the enormous emptiness that many experience in the very performance of sexual acts and the possibility of serious obsessions and addictions in this area.

The second principle shows us that to experience sexuality in an authentically human way requires the intention to unify the mean-ings it contains for one's life. To live sex in a human way presupposes an inner integration of the various levels in which human sexuality manifests itself, which clearly differentiate it from sexual behavior in animals. In humans there is a biological sexuality, a psychological sexuality, a personal sexuality and a spiritual sexuality. If sexuality is looked at only from the point of view of usefulness, these meanings break apart. If the only thing looked for is pleasure, with no other references, sexuality will be reduced to one of the psychological senses and be unable to integrate the others, and the experience of sexuality will be seriously threatened into falling into the narcissism of one's own emotions.

Meanings

These two principles make it possible to determine the human meanings of sexuality that enrich man. Paul VI referred to them in the encyclical *Humanae vitae* (no. 9), speaking of love that is fully human, total, faithful and exclusive unto death, and fruitful. In them we see a recognition of the personal value of an intimacy due to the profound unity of body and soul (cf. *Gaudium et spes*, no. 14).

These are the goods that St. Augustine identified to show the goodness of marriage (*De bono coniugali*): faith, offspring and sacrament. By faith he meant fidelity and by sacrament indissolubility.

Both are to be seen from the divine presence that sustains the experience of sexuality as a good for man.

The integrity we speak of is understood by love insofar as it has its own truth. No man wants to be deceived, because after all he loves the truth; to be deceived in love is a real tragedy, the source of the greatest pains experienced by man with regard to sexuality.

The personal meaning presented to us implies a deep union that is a communion of persons. This is the fundamental point that indicates the aim of all true sexual expression.

As far as sexuality is concerned, we are talking of a relational truth that requires the recognition of an affective language that guarantees the personal and spiritual understanding of union. It is what John Paul II explained as the language of the body and he related it to the fundamental human experiences that have a bodily mediation in order to know oneself.

Thus, one can speak of a grammar of the body in which the fundamental meanings of sexual difference are integrated, as a polar masculine-feminine reality that asks for freedom and fruitfulness as transcendence of a love that does not become closed in two, but opens to a third with the need to integrate the different generations. The first is one that guarantees an otherness in which one's sexuality is fully recognized only in the face of the other sex, and the second manifests the taboo of incest that demands a new otherness that defends a paternal and fraternal meaning in which there is no sexual surrender.

The bodily reality that is integrated into this dynamism is not merely biological, but generates through desire the intentionality characteristic of human action that is oriented toward a communion of persons in the participation of certain goods that comprise it, in this case a common bodily intimacy: that is, being "one flesh" (Gen 2:24). This is essential for the direction of affective dynamics that show themselves as modesty regarding bodily intimacy and jealousy regarding the uniqueness of the beloved.

The sexual revolution

In the course of history, various cultural changes have led to profound shifts in the understanding of the meanings of sexuality, which can be called sexual revolutions because of the radicality with which they have come about. This is the main factor in evaluating changes in the meaning of sexuality today.

The Church, in its 2,000-year history, has experienced some of these revolutions and has had to respond to them. Particularly important was the one that occurred with the Cathar heresy in the 12th century, which gave rise to courtly love and the emergence of clandestine marriages. The effects of this revolution lasted four centuries and strongly conditioned the concept of sexuality in the West (DE ROUGEMONT, *Love in the Western World*, Harcourt, Brace & World, New York 1940).

The current revolution emerged in the 1960s, especially in what was called the May '68 revolution. Actually, its origin dates back to the 1920s, with the fall of Puritanism after World War I. By that time radical feminism – which viewed sex as something purely cultural that could be changed for social reasons – and the first homosexual political pressure lobby groups had already emerged. All this exploded again in the 1960s, producing a pansexualist culture that modified the experience of sexuality.

Its content can be summarized in three principles.

1) Sex was reduced to genital arousal, this itself has been commercialized with pornography, and socially it is considered something good for coexistence because it liberates people and should be a principle of radical tolerance. It is an individualistic and fragmented consideration, separated from human intimacy, which is deeply affected. This is particularly due to a mystique of rejection of modesty, whereby sexuality is neither assumed nor integrated into human intimacy. This rupture leaves man very weak in the face of the various manipulations he may undergo in a cultural environment where social engineering is the order of the day: he is invited to experience everything without considering the consequences. Thus, the experience of sexuality has been separated from marriage by considering marriage as an external and rather repressive bond of love, as presented by romanticism since the 18th century.

2) Then sex was separated from fertility, as if fertility were simply a biological matter that technology could manipulate according to the couple's will.

3) Finally, it was separated from love itself, to avoid great expectations, and all that was required was simple mutual consent without any further obligation.

A light for the heart of man

The Church must teach the truth of human love as a call to the integration of the heart and the fellowship of people.

"He is bone of my bones and flesh of my flesh" (Gen 2:23). It is the first song of humanity, which recognizes the call to be "one flesh," that is, to experience a unity of persons which is fruitful. The joy of this recognition is linked to the light of love as awakening.

The Church, expert in the wisdom of the human heart, desires that each person should truly respond to the vocation to love that can fill his or her life. She does this not only with a message to be conveyed, but above all by accompanying people on the journey of life so that they can properly interpret their experiences of love in the light of a truth that promises them fullness in their encounter with Christ. Thus is fulfilled the mission of the good shepherd who came "that they may have life and have it abundantly" (Jn 10:10).

Why is the Church so critical of gender ideology?

(Antonio Malo)

Gender theories have been particularly concerned with aspects that refer to the differences between men and women determined by society, such as the roles assigned to each person and that influence the social, cultural and political functions they may assume. These roles also refer to society's expectations regarding the "typical" behavior of men and women in various areas of life: from play to work, from gestures to clothing, from language to behavior. In addition, gender theories show how some of the social roles assigned to men and women in the course of history, besides being conventional, have in many cases had a negative influence on the evaluation of women's role in society and culture.

Furthermore, these theories emphasize the personal character of human sexuality. Scientific studies reveal that human sexuality, in addition to being rooted in the body, needs to be personalized through psychological identification with one's own sex and inter-personal relationships, starting from those with one's parents.

Gender ideology

Therefore, the Church is not opposed to these theories, except when they are based not so much on science as on ideology. Benedict XVI had already warned against *gender ideology*, i.e., that current of thought which, in an attempt to bring about "man's self-emancipation from creation and the Creator" (BENEDICT XVI, *Christmas Address to the Roman Curia*, Dec. 22, 2008), aims to spread in society a libertarian approach – that is, an approach untied from any truth or norm – to sexuality, marriage and the family.

The opposition between sex and gender is a central element of this ideology, which emerged in some North American feminist circles in the 1960s and 1970s and has since spread through much of the world (see Congregation for Catholic Education, *Male and Female Created Them. For a Way of Dialogue on the Question of Gender in Education,* 2019). By "sex," gender ideology refers to what is *given* by biological nature, that is, bodily sex. By "gender," on the other hand, it means the social construction – based on patriarchy (i.e., the dominance of the father in the family) – of the different roles of men and women in all spheres of existence, starting with sexuality, which, being cultural, are necessarily subject to historical change. In its most radical expression, proponents of this ideology believe that, in each of the existential situations a person goes through, he or she should be able to choose the gender (LGBTQIA) they prefer, regardless of their body and the marital and parental ties that have undertaken.

Gender ideology has a negative influence on society at two levels. At the political and legislative level, through the pressure it exerts to change the nature of marriage and family through unjust laws. In the name of progress, tolerance and equal rights, it calls for the legalization and acceptance of new models of marriage and family, including the adoption of children by same-sex couples. However, this "progress" is not such and, unless corrected, will sooner or later lead to the self-destruction of the individual and society (cf. BENEDICT XVI, *Address to the Roman Curia on the occasion of the presentation of Christmas greetings*, Dec. 22, 2008). At the cultural level, gender ideology seeks a change of mentality to make citizens favorable to it, starting with those who are easiest to indoctrinate: children and adolescents. Under the guise of educating them to be tolerant, they are encouraged to "explore" and "experiment" all kinds of sexual behavior so that they can choose whatever they prefer.

Gender ideology can thus be understood as ideological colonization, as it seeks to impose by all means at its disposal an inhuman vision of sexuality, marriage and family that enslaves people (cf. Pope Francis, *Press Conference on Return Flight from Philippines to Rome,* Jan. 19, 2015). Gender ideology pretends to hide such manipulation, promising great freedom when in fact it denies it. It claims to help every person to discover their sexual identity, when in reality it prevents them from recognizing and accepting their status as male or female. It combats Church teaching that "Physical, moral, and spiritual *difference* and *complementarity* are oriented toward the goods of marriage and the flourishing of family life" (*Catechsim of the Catholic Church*, 2333).

The Church, teacher of humanity

The Church, which is ever watchful of all that concerns the good of men and women, denounces the evil inherent in gender ideology because it has the right and the duty to intervene when the natural and supernatural good of persons and society is at stake. The Church has received from God the "responsibility for creation" (Benedict XVI, *Address to the Roman Curia on the occasion of the presentation of Christmas greetings*, Dec. 22, 2008). Therefore, it promotes a human ecology that helps nations and states discern between what offers an opportunity for true progress and what, on the other hand, produces regression and disintegration in people and the social fabric.

On the basis of Scripture and the Magisterium, the Church defends that the differences between men and women, far from arising from an unjust structure, are a gift from God to mankind. The two creation narratives in the book of Genesis definitively confirm the importance of sexual difference. In the first we read that God created "man in his own image and likeness. In the image of God he created him. Male and female he created them" (Gen 1:27). In the second account, the man realizes that he is alone and God creates for Adam "a helper who is like unto him" (Gen 2:18). This help is mutual and does not imply any kind of inferiority of the woman with respect to the man. It refers not only to actions and roles, but to the very *being* of the man and the woman. Man and woman are complementary not only on the physical level, but also in their very existence: man offers woman something that only he can give her, and woman offers man something that only she can give him (cf. Congregation for the Doctrine of the Faith, *Letter to the Bishops of the Catholic Church on the Collaboration of Man and Woman in the Church and in the World*, 2004, 6). Therefore, "Every outlook which presents itself as a conflict between the sexes is only an illusion and a danger: it would end in segregation and competition between men and women, and would promote a solipsism nourished by a false conception of freedom" (*Letter to the Bishops of the Catholic Church on the Collaboration of Men and Women in the Church*, 2004, 14).

Gender ideology, on the other hand, by ignoring sexual difference and seeing it as something that can (and must) be overcome, loses the *original* character of femininity and masculinity. "Womanhood expresses the 'human' as much as manhood does, but in a different and complementary way" (St. John Paul II, *Letter to Women*, 1995, 7). A person's sex is not simply a matter of biology. "Sexuality characterizes man and woman not only on the physical level, but also on the psychological and spiritual, making its mark on each of their expressions. Such diversity, linked to the complementarity of the two sexes, allows thorough response to the design of God according to the vocation to which each one is called" (Congregation for Catholic Education, *Educational Guidelines on Human Love. Guidelines for Sex Education*, 1983, 5). Human sexuality is, therefore, a gift from God, which is received through parents and through which we can give ourselves to each other in marriage or to God in celibacy and, in him, to all people.

Where does the denial of the difference between men and women come from?

Pope Francis explains, "I wonder, if the so-called *gender* theory is not also an expression of frustration and resignation, which aims to erase sexual difference because it can no longer confront it. Eh, we are in danger of taking a step backward. Indeed, the removal of difference is the problem, not the solution. Instead, to solve their relationship problems, man and woman must talk to each other more, listen to each other more, know each other more, love each other more. They must treat each other with respect and cooperate with friendship" (Pope Francis, *General Audience,* April 15, 2015). In essence, "valuing one's own body in its femininity or masculinity is necessary if I am going to be able to recognize myself in an encounter with someone who is different. In this way we can joyfully accept the specific gifts of another man or woman, the work of God the Creator, and find mutual enrichment" (Francis, Encyclical *Laudato Sì,* 2015, 155).

Gender ideology also contradicts sexual morality. First, by radically separating sex from gender, it rejects both the procreative and unitive meanings of human sexuality, as can be seen in its promotion of same-sex relationships in which there is no true marital communion because of the lack of sexual difference. Second, based on the separation of sex and gender, this ideology seeks to make any kind of emotional relationship acceptable as marriage and family. However, despite the depth of feelings and existential commitment that may exist in such relationships, they will never be marriage due to the lack of sexual difference and therefore they cannot be the origin of a family (cf. Francis, *Lumen Fidei,* 2013, 52; *Evangelii Gaudium,* 2013, 66).

The Christians' mission

Christians are called to "drown evil in an abundance of good" (St. Josemaría Escrivá, *Christ is Passing By,* no. 72), starting from their own home. Parents should participate actively in the education of their children, because it is through this task of theirs that Christian culture is transmitted from generation to generation and it develops further. The family environment must also be such that children learn to love freely as they are loved freely, to respect others as they are respected, and to recognize the face of God as revealed to them first of all through a father and mother full of love and tenderness for them. In this way, the son or daughter discovers the beauty of motherhood and fatherhood and, consequently, of the femininity and masculinity that their parents respectively embody. When, on the other hand, the son or daughter lacks these fundamental experiences, there is a loss of humanity in society, which becomes a begetter of suffering and violence (cf. Congregation for Catholic Education, *Educational Guidelines for Human Love,* 1983).

On the other hand, Christians must of course combat all unjust discrimination, recognizing and promoting the equal dignity of all men and all women, which "must be harmonized with attentive recognition of the difference and reciprocity between the sexes where this is relevant to the realization of one's humanity, whether male or female" (*Letter to the Bishops of the Catholic Church on the Collaboration of Men and Women in the Church,* 14). Only if we are able to rediscover the beauty of the man-woman difference, of marriage and the family, can we continue to write a new page in the wonderful history of human love, with its lights and shadows.

Can we always go to Communion? Must we always go when we go to Mass? How can we know if we are in a "state of grace" (CCC, no. 1415) in order to receive the Eucharist fruitfully and with due respect?

(João Paulo de Mendonça Dantas)

Jesus Christ accomplished the work of redemption by his death and Resurrection, and in that way saved mankind, offering every man and woman the opportunity to enter into a relationship of communion with him.

Every sin is a turning away from the one who created and redeemed us. There are evidently different degrees of turning away, up to and including the separation and self-exclusion from communion with God which we call "mortal sin" or "grave sin." Man commits such a sin if three conditions are fulfilled: if it has a grave matter as its object, if it is committed with full knowledge, and with deliberate consent (cf. CCC 1857). Venial sin is a turning away from God that does not cause us to lose habitual grace by which we remain in objective communion with Christ.

St. Paul, in his Letter to the Romans (cf. Rom 12:3-8) and in his First Letter to the Corinthians (cf. 1 Cor 12:4-31), teaches us that communion with Christ also means communion with his entire Church, which is presented as the Body of Christ, and Christians are seen as living members of this Mystical Body.

When sin weakens us or makes us lose sanctifying grace, it not only alienates us from communion with Christ, but also wounds our communion with the Church. Baptism, which is *ianua sacramentorum*, the gateway to the other sacraments, offers us forgiveness of sins and supernatural life. The Eucharist is the sacrament of Christ's quintessential presence, for he is truly present there, as is said, in body, blood, soul and divinity. On the one hand, the Eucharist is the sacrament of Christian unity, because it is the sign of our communion with Christ; on the other hand, as true food and true drink, the Eucharist fortifies this communion with Christ and causes sanctifying grace to grow in those who receive it, as the Council of Trent reminds us (*Decree on the Sacraments*, Canons 6-8 on the Sacraments in General, in: DH 1606-1608).

A Catholic who is aware of having committed a mortal sin, and therefore, having lost sanctifying grace, the objective guarantee of our communion with Christ, must seek in Christ's mercy the medicine he needs, the forgiveness of his sins. On Holy Thursday, before his Passion, Jesus Christ instituted the sacrament of the Eucharist (cf. Mk 14:22-24; Mt 26:26-28; Lk 22:19-20; 1 Cor 11:23-25) in order to be able to offer all Christians the possibility of living and growing in communion with their Redeemer. John's Gospel tells us that when Jesus appeared to his apostles after his Resurrection, he breathed his Spirit upon them and said, "Receive the Holy Spirit. If you forgive the sins of any, they are forgiven; if you retain the sins of any, they are retained" (John 20:22-23). This narrative helps us to understand that the power to forgive sins belongs to Jesus himself; the breath of his Spirit indicates that his apostles are in communion of life and mission with the Lord and in his name can bestow his forgiveness on men.

When we meet someone asking us whether they can always go to Communion, we can answer that Communion makes us participate fully in Holy Mass, but that we are not always objectively in a state of grace and, therefore, in communion with Christ. It should be noted that Eucharistic Communion ought also to be a sacramental sign of our communion with the Lord, and that with mortal sin we objectively lose sanctifying grace and separate ourselves from that communion (with Christ), which is necessary to receive the Eucharist fruitfully. Therefore, the Church teaches, "Anyone conscious of a grave sin must receive the sacrament of Reconciliation before coming to communion" (CCC, no. 1385).

It is worthwhile here to recall the Apostle Paul's famous admonition to the Christians in Corinth: "For as often as you eat this bread and drink the cup, you proclaim the Lord's death until he comes. Whoever, therefore, eats the bread or drinks the cup of the Lord in an unworthy manner will be guilty of profaning the body and blood of the Lord. Let a man examine himself, and so eat of the bread and drink of the cup. For any one who eats and drinks without discerning the body eats and drinks judgment upon himself" (1 Cor 11:26-29).

As we can see, Paul urges Christians participating in the Eucharist to examine themselves before approaching sacramental Communion, having due respect for the holiness of the Lord's body and blood (cf. 1 Cor 11:24-25). Shortly before, the Apostle to the Gentiles had written, "The cup of blessing which we bless, is it not a participation in the blood of Christ? The bread which we break, is it not a participation in the body of Christ?" (1 Cor 10:16). In this way St. Paul emphasizes the reality of Eucharistic Communion. Eucharistic Communion is reserved for those who recognize that they have no mortal sins on their conscience, thus objectively preserving communion of life with Christ because they are in habitual grace.

In the same vein as Paul of Tarsus, St. John Chrysostom eloquently exhorted the faithful of his time, "I, too, raise my voice, plead, beg and beseech that we do not approach this sacred Table with a stained and corrupt conscience. For such an approach can never be called communion, even if we touch the Lord's body a thousand times, but condemnation, torment and increase of chastisements." St. John Paul II, in his encyclical on the Eucharist, after recalling the Council of Trent, taught us that "If a Christian's conscience is burdened by serious sin, then the path of penance through the sacrament of Reconciliation becomes necessary for full participation in the Eucharistic Sacrifice" (*Ecclesia de Eucharistia* no. 37).

Later in his encyclical, the Pope adds that "The Eucharist *creates communion* and *fosters communion*" (*Ecclesia de Eucharistia* no. 40). These words also help us to understand why all Catholics are called to fulfill with faith and love the commandment to keep the Lord's Day, Sunday, holy by participating in Holy Mass, even if, for whatever reason, they are aware that they cannot go to sacramental Communion. It should always be remembered that every Holy Mass allows us to hear the saving Word of God, and invites us to unite our lives to Christ's paschal and redemptive sacrifice. This experience offers us graces that enlighten our intelligence with faith and fill our hearts with charity, so that, recognizing the greatness of divine mercy and our need for conversion, we feel invited and, in some way, impelled, to confidently walk the path that Christ shows us, the path of conversion and salvation.

In church life, we not infrequently hear the question, "Can we always go to Communion?" After what we have read above, I think the reader will have realized that the answer to this question is, "No." Only the faithful who have examined themselves, and recognize that they are in a state of grace, may approach Communion. Those who humbly acknowledge that they are not in communion with the Lord because of the gravity of their sins, should not, however, turn away from participating in Holy Mass, as mentioned above, but while they are properly preparing themselves to receive divine forgiveness through the Sacrament of Reconciliation (of Confession), at the time of the distribution of the Eucharist, they can have the valid and fruitful experience of spiritual communion, that is, of a simple prayer, even with their own words, manifesting to Jesus their great desire to be able to receive him with a pure heart. As St. John Paul II recalls, it is "recommended by saints who were masters of the spiritual life. Saint Teresa of Jesus wrote: 'When you do not receive communion and you do not attend Mass, you can make a spiritual communion, which is a most beneficial practice; by it the love of God will be greatly impressed on you'" (*Ecclesia de Eucharistia*, no. 34).

I would not want to end without trying to answer another very important question, "How can one know whether one is in a state of grace in order to have respectful and fruitful access to the Eucharist?" To answer this question we can recall the Church's recommendation to conduct a brief "examination of conscience" every evening.

Pope Francis recommended this practice on more than one occasion. He spoke of it, in particular, in his homily on September 4, 2018 at Santa Marta. L'Osservatore Romano echoed this, writing, "To make every evening an examination of conscience as a prayer, to identify whether it was 'the spirit of God or the spirit of the world' that moved us during the day, is a decisive exercise in our 'spiritual combat that leads us to understand the heart and meaning of Christ.'"This is the suggestion Pope Francis offered at Mass, recalling that "the human heart is like a battlefield" where "the spirit of God, which leads us to good works, to charity, to fraternity, and the spirit of the world, which instead leads us toward vanity, pride, sufficiency, chatter," are constantly confronted (Osservatore Romano, 5.IX.2018).

Another practice that helps us avoid serious sins and develop a life of deeper communion with the Lord is frequent Confession, for instance monthly (or fortnightly), depending on each person's sensitivity. In this way we will have a greater ability to avoid mortal sins.

With daily examination of conscience and frequent Confession, the faithful will be able to develop an ever deeper and more fruitful life of communion with God the Father, through Christ and in the Holy Spirit, which will grow especially through Communion received at each Holy Mass. "By the same charity that it enkindles in us, the Eucharist *preserves us from future mortal sins.* The more we share the life of Christ and progress in his friendship, the more difficult it is to break away from him by mortal sin" (CCC, no. 1395).

But in the event that – in spite of everything – he experiences his weakness and falls into a grave sin, the believer will discover in this an opportunity to be more humble and to offer to Christ his sorrow at not being able to receive the gift of the Eucharist and, in the light of divine love, will be able to turn to Jesus with a spiritual communion.

The Church (and the Pope) insist on the need to go to confession personally to a priest. But why do we have to tell him things that do not concern him, instead of asking God directly for forgiveness?

(Vittoradolfo Tambone)

When he forgives and heals the paralytic, Jesus reveals himself to be a physician of both souls and bodies (cf. Mk 2:1-12 // Mt 9:1-8; Lk 5:17-26). For several years Pope Francis has been encouraging us to go to confession, to receive forgiveness of sins and to be reconciled with God. Pope St. John Paul II had also often encouraged the faithful to go to confession, and he himself – as later Pope Francis – made himself available to hear confessions.

Those fists on the table...

It is 1994, I have been a priest for a few months and Advent has just begun. Around 10 a.m. the phone rings and someone from the Vatican tells me that I am invited to lunch with the Holy Father along with two other university chaplains in preparation for the Holy Mass that, also that year, the Pope was to celebrate for the University students of Rome in preparation for Christmas. "What should I do?" I ask in amazement, "but go to lunch of course!"

Of course, I accept the invitation and with trepidation and a little anxiety I go to the appointment, praying not to make a fool of myself, since I have never been to lunch with a Pope! The other guests are the chaplain of the Sapienza and the chaplain of Tor Vergata together with the Cardinal Vicar Camillo Ruini and the person in charge of University Pastoral work, dear Monsignor Lorenzo Leuzzi. Everyone is very nice and affectionate which calms me down a bit... At a certain point a door opens in the hall where we were waiting and I get to my feet... false alarm: it's a Swiss guard.

I sit down again and suddenly everyone stands up. It's right this time, as St. John Paul II enters. I watch the others introduce themselves: chaplain of the Sapienza University, 150,000 students, chaplain of Tor Vergata, 80,000 students (the numbers are from memory) and then me, chaplain of the Campus Bio-Medico, 70 students. Pope's doubtful face, "70,000?", "No, just 70". Few, but good, I would have liked to add, but we are immediately escorted to the dining room, and as he sits down the Holy Father asks with real interest, "So what have you done to prepare for tomorrow's Mass?" A cold sweat, for I had done nothing. I had just been ordained, there were very few of us, I had no experience, I could have tried to justify myself with many other reasons, but they would not have changed the reality: I had done nothing! And that was a very bad thing, almost offensive. The chaplain at the Sapienza tells about the Theology Courses, organized for faculty, retreats for students and other wonderful things. The colleague from Tor Vergata is not to be outdone and speaks of absolutely brilliant chaplaincy activities.

"What about you? – St. John Paul II looks at me sympathetically – what about you?" I have to choose between lying – but lying to the Pope was a bit too much – and telling the truth. I choose truth. "Sincerely Holy Father?" laughing he replies, "Well, certainly." "Honestly, we haven't done anything."

Although I do not look at them I sense the bewilderment and embarrassment of those present, but the Pope amusedly asks, "Nothing at all?" Consistent with the choice of truth, I continue, "I mean, no we didn't organize anything special, we just tried to prepare everyone who wanted to with Confession..." The dots stay there, because the Holy Father before the word "Confession" is out of my mouth bangs his fist on the table. A painful sense of guilt assails me, thinking I have angered the Pope! Then I hear him say forcefully, giving a second and third punch on the table, "That's it! That's it! That's the best way to prepare for Holy Mass, with a good Confession! That's it, that's the way to do it." I was surprised, relieved, but above all glad to see him happy. Since then that fist on the table and the conviction that one of the best ways to encounter God is through Confession has remained in my heart. So many times over the years, I have been able to see (it is a privilege that leaves me astonished) that the question that is at the heart of so many boys and girls is precisely "How to find the peace of God's mercy," how to, even if...

But who invented the Confession?

To decide to go to confession, we need to understand the motivation behind the decision. Why should I go to a priest and say the worst things I have done and that I am sorry?

It is I who have sinned, I who must ask forgiveness, I who have offended God, it is I whom God must forgive, it is I who talk to God and ask forgiveness from him, so the priest has nothing to do with it. How many times will we have gone through this perfect syllogism that is really convincing. An unassailable syllogism (even if it is not a true and real syllogism) which, for that matter, does not in any way mean to say that I forgive myself. To receive forgiveness I must receive it from the one I have offended, and I have offended God and it is to him that I ask forgiveness.

Yet the Catholic Church continues to teach that "individual and complete Confession, with the corresponding absolution, remains the only ordinary way by which the faithful are reconciled with God and the Church, unless a physical or moral impossibility dispenses them from such a Confession" (*Catechism of the Catholic Church*, 1484).

"But who said that? Come on. It's you priests who want to control everything and everybody. Sorry I'm not mad at you who are... in short who aren't... Yeah, I mean, you can tell..."

In these situations, I have to ask, "In your opinion, who invented Confession?" For some it is a trivial question, almost a rhetorical question. But it isn't so for many others in an age in which astonishing religious ignorance is rife. Indeed, when asked "who invented Confession?" one of the most popular answers is "the Church in the Middle Ages." Finding out that it was Jesus himself is usually a welcome surprise that predisposes them to read the passage that describes the crucial moment, the moment when Jesus invented Confession and entrusted it to priests, namely Chapter 20 of St. John's Gospel:

"On the evening of that same day, the first of the week, while for fear of the Jews the doors of the place where the disciples were standing were closed, Jesus came and stood among them and said, 'Peace be with you'" (Jn 20:19). Jesus died on the cross, rose again, and appeared to the apostles and immediately set the record straight: "I haven't come to tell you off for your unfaithfulness, I haven't come to give anyone the sack, I haven't come to take revenge...I have come to say, 'Peace be with you.'"

"So saying, he showed them his hands and his side. Seeing the Lord, the disciples were filled with joy. Jesus said again, 'Peace be with you. As the Father has sent me, I also send you'" (Jn 20:20-21). And now Jesus does an amazing thing: "He breathed on them and said, 'Receive the Holy Spirit'" (Jn 20:22) and immediately afterwards he utters the key message of that evening: "If you forgive the sins of any, they are forgiven; if you retain the sins of any, they are retained" (Jn 20:23). Simple, loud and clear.

Understanding that Confession is a sacrament instituted by Jesus seems like a trivial discovery; instead, it is an essential discovery, which sometimes requires some time to discover (re-discover) what a sacrament is, what sins are, what happens to Jesus when I commit a sin, what happens to me when I commit a sin. This journey will obviously be made in many ways and along different paths. It seems to me that the Gospel is the best shortcut. In the face of this Gospel passage, I don't remember anyone being convinced that we confess alone and directly to God.

If Confession is a time of conversion, we need God to make it happen. Benedict XVI said: "To repent and believe in the Gospel are not two different things or in some way only juxtaposed, but express the same reality. Repentance is the total "yes" of those who consign their whole life to the Gospel responding freely to Christ who first offers himself to humankind as the Way, the Truth and the Life, as the only One who sets us free and saves us. This is the precise meaning of the first words with which, according to the Evangelist Mark, Jesus begins preaching the "Gospel of God": "The time is fulfilled, and the Kingdom of God is at hand; repent, and believe in the Gospel" (Mk 1:15)" (Pope Benedict XVI, *General Audience*, 17.II.2010).

The Samaritan woman is converted because Jesus shows her that he knows her, Matthew because Jesus calls him, the Centurion because he sees Jesus die, St. Paul because Jesus dazzles him and speaks to him. It is always Jesus who takes the first step and wins souls, draws them to something as profound as conversion. To understand and choose Confession, one must understand and choose Jesus.

I believe in Jesus, but in the Church?...

He was a first-year student and came into my room without knocking, even without greeting, introduced himself saying, "I am an atheist," I answered politely, "How do you do, I am Don Victor." He didn't even smile. Patience. He continued very firmly, "I am an atheist and you don't have to convince me of anything." I approved. "If you agree I will come every so often, ask you a question and you, without wanting to convince me, will tell me what Catholic theology says about it." I agreed. He pressed me, asking, "When do we start?" I made myself available and he chose to start right away with the first question, "What is the Holy Trinity?" I thanked Heaven that I had been rereading for a week the part of the Catechism of the Catholic Church on the Holy Trinity and, trying not to make a mistake, I answered, "The mystery of the Holy Trinity is the central mystery of Christian faith and life. It is the mystery of God Himself...." As soon as we finished repeating point 234 of the Catechism, without any comment he said, "That's okay," and left.

He came back two more times asking who Jesus Christ was, I knew and told him. The fourth time he had changed, knocked on the door and asked permission (surprise!). He smiled at me (surprise!) and sat down, he had always stayed standing... He looked at me and exclaimed, "But if I don't believe what can I do about it?" I, I remind you, was not there to convince him (that was the deal!) and I remained silent. But he looked at me and pressed me, "So? What can I do about it?" It was a real question. It was also a good question that required a good answer. So I told him about that sheep that got lost – St. Matthew talks about it in chapter 18 of his Gospel – maybe it had fallen into a ravine. Maybe, if we want to put it dramatically, it had broken its leg. After all, what could it do? It could only do one thing to get its Shepherd back: bleat. And by dint of bleating, the Shepherd found it and rescued it... I did not add anything more, he said nothing, and left. That evening I left the University later than usual, it was dark, I went to the Chapel to greet the Lord and, in the last pew in the shadows, I saw him. "And what are you doing here?" I asked. "I'm bleating," he replied. I greeted him with a nod and let him bleat in peace. A couple of days later he came back with a very serious question, even his face was very serious: "If I believe in Jesus but only and only in Jesus, can I say I believe?" This was not in the Catechism. I thought about it, because it was important: only in

Jesus... but in the sacraments? And in the Church, Holy and Catholic? And in the Communion of Saints?... The answer was simple though: if you believe in Jesus you believe in everything Jesus said and instituted, so – I told him, "Yes, if you believe in Jesus, believe!" Wow. Remember that line by Nietzsche where he more or less says to Christians, "If you had resurrected faces, I would believe!!!" Well at that moment, faced with that answer that student's face changed, it became so full of joy that it looked like a resurrected face to me. With tears in his eyes he said, "Then I believe and I want to confess." He was truly happy that he could re-become a Christian, because he believed in Jesus, "in Jesus alone and only in Jesus."

But what if one has committed an unforgivable sin?

Knowing Jesus and understanding Confession can at some point come up against the tragedy of our personal misery, which, at times, can seem really too much, even for God. Yet, it is precisely inner situations such as these that can help us discover even more who God really is, contemplating him as a merciful God.

It had been a few days that a student had been trying to open up, but she could not. This time, however, she succeeded and, without batting about the bush, asked me, "Excuse me, but if one has done an unforgivable sin what does one do?" "One confesses of course," I answered naively. She looked at me with a hint of pity… "Yes of course. But if the sin is unforgivable, one cannot." "You have had an abortion, haven't you?" Predictable answer. And it was an unforgivable sin, she explained, because nothing more could be done, because the baby had died and there was no going back, apologizing, doing anything to make it right. She was feeling bad, but really really bad, thinking that nothing could be done: her action was unforgivable. It is really horrible to feel bad, to be convinced not that we have done a bad thing, but that we "are bad," to think that the evil done has changed who we are, to find out upon awakening from a nightmare that the nightmare is reality: I really am a cockroach. That was pretty much that girl's situation.

She needed to look to Heaven to find the way out of her torment. She needed to think about where her child was. I told her, "He is safely in Heaven He is in Heaven, you can't have any doubt, not even think about it for a moment. He is in Heaven happy and content with God, Our Lady and with many Angels and he has a mother." "Of course, Our Lady," replied the student. "Wrong answer. It's you. You are her mother. This child-saint is happy because he's with God, but he's waiting to be able to do what he's never been able to do and that like every good child-saint wants to do at all costs. Embrace Mommy, which is you. So you know what you have to do to make everything right? Get ready to go to heaven and love your child. The first step, if you want, is to go to confession then, calmly, many other good things."

Why do we cry when we are happy? Why do you cry a lot when you are very happy? She was very happy and I keep asking the Lord that with her child-saint, one day, they will live happily ever after. Just like in fairy tales.

Act of contrition

Confession does not end with making the act of contrition, it ends with a greeting of peace, but the act of contrition is important because it leads us towards real contrition, love sorrow. It is a gift for ourselves and it is a joy for all of Heaven since, as Jesus assures us, "there will be more joy in Heaven for one converted sinner than for ninety-nine righteous ones who do not need conversion" (Luke 15:7). I imagine an explosion of shouts and exultation from all the Saints and Angels of Heaven (and they are truly many) like the fans who shout together with the goal that wins the World Cup, and this is because love sorrow attracts that Love – in Dante's words – "which moves the Sun and the other Stars." So, every Confession ends in a great celebration!

Why does the Church still maintain the rule of celibacy for priests? Isn't the lack of priestly vocations in so many parts of the world and the sexual abuse perpetrated by priests good reasons to open the doors for the ordination of married people?

(Carlos Villar)

The issues raised here seem to require an urgent response. A positive response that, moreover, seems obvious to anyone. However, such an answer moves in a *business*, functional and efficiency *logic*, which makes it impossible to understand the Christian phenomenon in depth, since such an approach includes only visible results. This happens even with questions that have to do with other strong options such as the indissolubility of marriage, the sanctity of the life of the unborn child or the family as the appropriate place for childbearing.

However, this functional and worldly logic forgets the ultimate truth about the Church, namely that she is not a merely human organization with good ends, but a divine and human institution that has its origin in Christ, not in itself. Consequently, a functional view is incapable of understanding the Church. In fact, the Church does not create, but *guards* a precious treasure that has been entrusted to her. Beyond the fashions and crises that may arise over time, she is called to *protect* and *manifest* the gifts God has bestowed upon her.

Thus, the ultimate reason for maintaining or changing an element that is part of the Church is not so much whether it is more or less effective, but whether it is something God wants for the Church.

In fact, ever since the dawn of Christianity, the criterion of the Gospel has clashed with the mentality of the world. The beatitudes that Jesus proclaims from the very beginning of his preaching are the antithesis of a *business logic*: blessed are the poor, the meek, those who mourn, the persecuted... From a human point of view, the beatitudes are a doomed proposition. Who would follow someone who promises tears, who talks about turning the other cheek and being poor? Likewise, an entrepreneurial mindset would not have left the institution in the hands of a bunch of fishermen, nor would it have kept a three times denier like Peter as its first president. Nor would it have let so many *human resources,* such as people living in convents and monasteries, waste so much time and energy in prayer, when there is a lack of arms to meet the countless needs of a suffering world. From a functional point of view, one could say that the life of an enclosed nun is unproductive; from the point of view of Christ, however, it is a powerful force that sustains and gives light to the whole Church.

Celibacy and Abuse

The recent abuse crisis has brought into focus a dark and devastating reality. The cases that have come to light within the Church are particularly important because they involve people called to make God's free and eternal love present in the world. And these very people have betrayed their sublime calling and inflicted terrible harm on innocent beings. At the same time, this crisis has highlighted a problem that is deeply rooted in other institutions, starting with the family and continuing in many other educational institutions. Therefore, calling for the cancellation of celibacy because of the terrible sexual abuse by priests would have the same meaning as wanting to erase the family as a community of love, or to eliminate all educational relationships. Rather than eradicating this, perhaps the solution lies in becoming aware of the risks involved and finding ways to heal these realities and prevent such pernicious drifts from occurring.

An Objection

It could be argued that, unlike the indissolubility of marriage (which is an essential element of marriage), celibacy does not belong to the essence of the priesthood. That is, a priesthood without celibacy in the Church is possible within Catholic dogma, as is seen in the Eastern Catholic Churches, in which most of the priests are married. In this sense, it would be possible for a pope to modify the rule of mandatory celibacy for priests in the Latin Church.

At the same time, it is important not to forget that rather than a canonical provision imposed by the Church on its ministers, celibacy – unlike other prescriptions – is a gift rooted in the newness that Christ brought into this world by becoming truly human. A newness that gives rise to a new way of loving on earth, which is the one he chose for himself and which is at the heart of the Gospel. This is not the case with other canonical requirements that have been stipulated in the course of history, such as the precepts of fasting for one hour before communion or going to confession at least once a year.

Christ not only lived celibacy, but he called and continues to call some to follow him as virgins for the Kingdom of heaven. In this sense, being something that comes from the Gospel, the Church is aware of the spiritual richness of this gift, so dear to the early community. After the rich young man's rejection of the proposal to leave everything to follow the Master, Peter gives voice to the feelings of all the apostles, "We have left our possessions and followed you." And Jesus replied, "Truly I tell you, there is no one who has left house or wife or brothers or children for the Kingdom of God, who does not receive much more in the present time and eternal life in the time to come" (Luke 18:28-30).

The Beauty of Celibacy

Sometimes there are things that have their meaning not so much in necessity as in beauty. A flower or a poem is not necessary for survival, but it is important for life, as so many saints throughout history have shown us, being fascinated by such a gift.

Something of the sort happened to John, the beloved disciple. Jesus enters into his life and that encounter opens John's heart. From that evening, the heart of this fisherman from Galilee is already all for Christ. All other loves fade, vanish; not because they are bad or unattractive, but because now John has no other interest than following Jesus, knowing him more and loving him more. He has been wounded by the beauty of Christ and nothing is the same as before. Jesus is the Love of loves, and from that moment on – remember it was four o'clock in the afternoon – nothing distracts John from following Jesus.

Therefore, celibacy is a way of loving that Jesus Christ inaugurated with his life on earth. He is true God and, at the same time, true man, with a heart of flesh and a human sensibility. In his time on earth he experienced the cold of winter, the heat of summer and the weariness of the burden of the day, like other men. Actually – ontologically – that the Word entered time and became flesh is not a representation or external covering. We have here a key point for our reflection: this man – Jesus Christ – unfolded his humanity and mission with a virgin heart. Our eyes are thus opened to a clear truth: Jesus' life is the life of the man who lived his humanity (his being a man) in the fullest and deepest way. An existence that spreads throughout history through a celibate life, full of a virginal love for the Father and for all mankind. It is a fact offered to us by Revelation and a reality into which we can enter to discover the path of apostolic virginity as a source of fullness, not only supernatural but also human. Jesus' love for the Father and for all mankind stems from a virgin heart, large, passionate, totally open to his received mission of being spouse of the Church with a full donation to all.

The priest is called to live – as a first fruit – this same mystery of Christ the celibate. By divine gift he is inserted in the way of loving that Christ inaugurates on earth (with an undivided heart) and that every man is called to live in fullness in the hereafter. Thus, celibacy consists in a call – by divine mercy – to live a very deep human and supernatural fullness, a capacity to love so great that it is not limited to the love of a human creature. Therefore, it would be a pity to miss the beauty of this gift because of a merely functional view of celibacy, as if its motive were to guarantee the availability of time for certain pastoral activities.

Beyond this consideration, it must be said that a person called to celibacy, by God's mercy, begins on earth the way of loving that will come to fulfillment in eternity. In a sense, he is indeed called to prefigure – to anticipate – the communion we shall enjoy in Heaven, where there will be no possession, no separation, but the living in one another in Christ, the Son, in an eternal, not temporary, communion. This reality is highlighted by St. Paul when, in the First Letter to the Corinthians (1 Cor 7:32-34), he defines the unmarried person as one who "is anxious about the affairs of the Lord," which are none other than human beings: the unrepeatable and unique faces of each and every man, with their joys and tears (cf. Ps 56:8).

The sacred minister is called to fill his heart with faces, above any pastoral structure, institution or method. A heart called to expand like Jesus', to reach his measure, which is that which is without measure, embracing the whole world and, at the same time, every individual. The priest is called to welcome the whole Church into his heart. Called to be shepherd, physician, guide, teacher. A ministry in which virginity springs forth with the passion of one who knows that he is full of Christ's love and, out of this love, earnestly desires to love all the souls entrusted to him.

Biographical Notes on the Authors

Arasa, Daniel

Born in Barcelona (Spain), he holds degrees in Journalism and Theology. Since 2001 he has taught at the Pontifical University of the Holy Cross (Rome), where he is Dean of the Faculty of Communication. He also works with the news agency *Rome Reports TV*, specializing in coverage of the Pope, the Vatican and the Catholic Church, and is a Consultor of the Dicastery of Communications.

Ascheri, Valeria

Born in Genoa in 1976. MA in Philosophy (1999), PhD in Philosophy of Science (2004) at the University of Genoa and Licentiate in Institutional Communication (2013) at the University of the Holy Cross. Since 2011 she has been Extraordinary Professor and tenured lecturer for the area of Philosophy at the Higher Institute of Religious Sciences (University of the Holy Cross) and Guest Lecturer in the faculties of Philosophy of the Angelicum, Urbaniana and Regina Apostolorum Pontifical Universities, where she teaches courses in Metaphysics, Epistemology and Science and Faith. She has also worked in the past with the Pontifical Council for Culture (STOQ Project) and the Pontifical Academy for Life. She is currently a pastoral worker and catechist at St. Pius X Parish in Rome. Email: ascheri@pusc.it

Borgonovo, Graziano

Born in Monza in 1960, priest for the Diocese of Lugano in 1991. Degree in Philosophy at the Università Cattolica del Sacro Cuore in Milan and Doctorate in Theology at Fribourg University in Switzerland. Professor at the Faculty of Theology in Lugano (1994-2001). Rector of the John Paul II International Philosophical Theological Seminary in Rome (2003-2009). Official of the Dicastery for the Doctrine of the Faith (2010-2024). Currently teaches at the Pontifical University of the Holy Cross and the aforementioned Università Cattolica. On Feb. 5, 2024, the Pope appointed him Undersecretary of the Dicastery for Evangelization, Section for Fundamental Questions of Evangelization in the World.

Calabrese, Gianfranco

Lecturer in Dogmatics-Ecclesiology and General Catechetics at the Theological Faculty of Northern Italy - Affiliated Theological Institute of Genoa. At the Higher Institute of Religious Sciences in Genoa, he teaches General Catechetics and Introduction to Theology. At the Higher Institute of Religious Sciences of the University of the Holy Cross in Rome he teaches Catechetics and Introduction of Psychology and Pedagogy. His numerous publications include *Ecclesiologia Sinodale. Punti fermi e questioni aperte* (2021).

Cano, Luis

Born in 1963, graduated in Law and Doctor of Theology. Member of the Saint Josemaría Escrivá Historical Institute. His field of research, in addition to Opus Dei and its founder – particularly his preaching and writings – is the history of devotion to the Sacred Heart and Christ the King. He is professor of Church History in the Second Millennium at the University of the Holy Cross and at the Higher Institute of Religious Sciences at the Apollinare (Rome). He is involved in evangelization and family promotion activities in Rome. Email: lucano@pusc.it

Cattaneo, Arturo

Born in Lugano in 1948, architect and priest of the Prelature of Opus Dei since 1979. Doctor of Canon Law and Doctor of Theology. Lecturer in both disciplines, at the University of Navarre (Spain), the Faculty of Theology in Lugano (Switzerland), the University of the Holy Cross (Rome), the Faculty of Canon Law San Pio X (Venice) and, since 2010, again at the Faculty of Theology in Lugano. Since 2012 he has been a member of the Theological Commission of the Swiss Bishops' Conference and from 2014 to 2020 he was Consultor of the Pontifical Council for the Laity. Author of numerous publications in the fields of canon law, ecclesiology and marriage. Email: arturocatt@gmail.com

Cencini, Amedeo

Lecturer in various Pontifical Universities in psychology subjects in the area of formation. He was for several years a formator in his institute (Canossian Fathers). Since 1995 he has been a Consultor of the Dicastery for Institutes of Consecrated Life and Societies of Apostolic Life; since 2023 he has also been a Consultor of the Dicastery for the Laity, Family and Life. He has been a member of the Italian Episcopal Conference National Service for the Protection of Minors and Vulnerable Persons. For several years he has been a Pontifical Delegate to religious institutes in difficulty. He has published numerous essays on spirituality.

de la Morena, Gonzalo

Degree in Industrial Engineering from the Universidad Politécnica of Madrid in 2011. Priest in 2016. Doctorate in Dogmatic Theology at the University of the Holy Cross (2019), where he currently teaches in the area of Christology. Among his writings is *Genesi dello scandalo cristiano. Origine storica della fede nella divinità di Gesù*, soon to be published by Città Nuova, Rome.

de Mendonça Dantas, João Paulo

Doctorate in 2009 and Habilitation in Theology in 2014 at the Faculty of Theology in Lugano (Switzerland). From 2011 to 2013 he taught Systematic Theology in the Catholic Faculty of Fortaleza

(Brazil). In 2015 he participated in the founding of the Catholic Faculty of Belém (Brazil), where he teaches Systematic Theology. From 2019 to 2021 he was an assessor of the Commission for the Doctrine of the Faith of the Brazilian Bishops' Conference (CNBB). Since 2015, he has also taught Theology Courses at the Faculty of Theology in Lugano. He has published several books and articles in Portuguese, Italian, English and French. He is currently Rector of the Church of Our Lady of Mercy, in Belém.

di Marco, Emanuele

Born in Lugano in 1982, he is a educationalist and theologian. Ordained a priest in 2011. 2014 Doctorate in Pastoral Theology at the Pontifical Lateran University. In the same year he graduated as a formator from the Saint Peter Favre Institute of the Pontifical Gregorian University. Lecturer in Pastoral Theology at the Faculty of Theology in Lugano. Director of the Office of Religious Teaching in Schools and the Catechetical Office of the Diocese of Lugano.

Ducay, Antonio

Priest and Ordinary Professor of Christology at the University of the Holy Cross. A graduate in civil engineering, after obtaining his doctorate in theology, he has specialized in Christological and Mariological issues. Since 2020, he has been director of the Department of Dogmatics at the Faculty of Theology of the above mentioned University.

Forte, Bruno

Archbishop of Chieti-Vasto, member of the Pontifical Council for Christian Unity and of the Joint Commissions for Dialogue with the Chief Rabbinate of Israel and for Dialogue with the Orthodox Churches. Doctor of Theology and Philosophy, he was Professor of Dogmatic Theology at the Pontifical Theological Faculty of Southern Italy in Naples He has received honorary degrees from several universities: Lublin, Princeton, Melbourne, Chieti-Pescara. In Salzburg he was awarded the Theologischer Preis for Lifetime Achievement by the Catholic Academies of the German Language in 2011. Some of his major works are *Simbolica Ecclesiale* (Edizioni San Paolo, Milan) in eight volumes and *Dialogica* (Morcelliana, Brescia), likewise in eight volumes.

Goyret, Philip

Born 1956. Industrial engineer, priest, doctor of theology, and professor of ecclesiology at the Faculty of Theology of the Pont. University of the Holy Cross. His teaching, research and publications focus on ecclesiology, ecumenism, sacramental theology and priesthood. From 2016 to 2024 he was the Dean of the Faculty of Theology and from 2010 to 2023 the Rector of the Church of San Girolamo della Carità (Rome). He is currently Chaplain of the University of the Holy Cross and a member of the Governing Committee of the Italian Society for Theological Research.

Hauke, Manfred

Born 1956, priest of the Archdiocese of Paderborn (Germany). Since 1993 professor of Dogmatics at the Theological Faculty of Lugano (Switzerland). Within Dogmatics, his publications have specialized in Mariology. He is an ordinary member of the "Pontificia Academia Mariana Internationalis" and president of the German Society of Mariology. Among other things, he directs the scientific series "Mariologische Studien" (Regensburg) and "Collana di Mariologia" (Lugano). For more detailed Curriculum Vitae and scientific publications see https://manfred-hauke.ch

Jerumanis, André-Marie

Born 1956 in Leuven (Belgium). Priest of the diocese of Liege (Belgium) (1985), *Fidei donum* in Lugano since 1995. Doctorate in medicine at UCL (Louvain) (1981). Doctorate in theology at the Alphonsianum (Rome) (1998). Ordinary Professor of moral theology at the Faculty of Theology in Lugano where he teaches Fundamental Moral Theology, and Bioethics (2009). Director of the Hans Urs von Balthasar Study Center at the Faculty of Theology in Lugano. Member of the Bioethics Commission of the Swiss Bishops' Conference (2009). Member of the Pontifical Academy of Theology (2021). Among his publications: *L'uomo splendore della Gloria di Dio. La sfida estetica della cultura postmoderna per la morale cristiana*, EDB, Bologna 2005; *In Cristo, con Cristo, per Cristo. Manuale di teologia morale fondamentale*, Camilliane, Torino 2013.

Malo, Antonio

Born in 1957 in Zaragoza, Spain. Priest of the Prelature of Opus Dei. Graduate in Philology and Philosophy in the University of Navarre (Spain) and Doctor of Philosophy in the University of the Holy Cross, where he has been Professor of Anthropology since 2006. Director of the Doctor of Philosophy program at the Faculty of Philosophy of the same university where he is also Assessor of the Family and Media Project. Visiting professor at various American universities. His writings and research interests are in the anthropology of affectivity, action theory, human relationships and gift. Among his most recent publications: *Uomo o donna: Una differenza che conta* (Milano 2017; in German: Berlin 2018), *Antropologia del perdono* (Roma 2018), *Transcending Gender Ideology* (Washington 2020), *Svelare il mistero. Filosofia e narrativa a confronto* (Roma 2021) e *Invito alla lettura del De Anima. Un commento antropologico* (Roma 2022). Email: antoniomalope@gmail.com

Maspero, Giulio

Born in 1970, a priest of the Prelature of Opus Dei, he is a physicist and theologian, Professor of Dogmatic Theology at the University of the Holy Cross. He is currently Dean of the same faculty. Has a special interest in patristics and the relations of theology with philosophy and literature.

Massmann, Nicolas

Priest, doctor of dogmatic theology at the University of the Holy Cross. He is currently chaplain at the *International College Müngersdorf* (Cologne) and is mainly involved in youth and family ministry. He specializes in contemporary theology, particularly in the thought of Joseph Ratzinger and Romano Guardini.
Email: nmassmann@campus-muengersdorf.de

Pațulea, Călin-Daniel

Studied at the Major Seminary of Blaj (Romania), and at the Faculty of Theology in Lugano (Switzerland). Since 2000 he has been professor of Sacred Scripture: Old and New Testament in the Major Seminary of Blaj and in the Department of Pastoral Theology, Faculty of Greek-Catholic Theology, University "Babeș-Bolyai" Cluj-Napoca. Guest lecturer at the Faculty of Theology in Lugano. E-mail: calin.daniel.patulea@usi.ch; danielpatulea@yahoo.it

Paximadi, Giorgio

Ordinary Professor of Old Testament Exegesis at the Faculty of Theology in Lugano and priest of the same diocese. Graduated in Classical Literature at the Catholic University of the Sacred Heart in Milan. Licentiate in Theology at the University of Fribourg (Switzerland) with a thesis directed by Fr. J.D. Barthélemy O.P. Licentiate in Sacred Scripture at the Pontifical Biblical Institute in Rome, under the direction of Fr. Luis Alonso Schökel S.J., and Doctorate in Biblical Sciences, under the direction of Fr. Pietro Bovati S.J. Author of articles and monographs on linguistic and exegetical subjects and specializing particularly in priestly texts.

Pérez-Soba Diez del Corral, Juan José

Born in Madrid in 1964. Ordained priest for the diocese of Madrid in1991. Ordinary Professor of family pastoral care in the Pontifical Theological Institute John Paul II for Marriage and the Family the Sciences (Rome). Guest professor in the Faculty of Theology at the San Dámaso Ecclesiastical University in Madrid.
Email: perezsoba@istitutogp2.it

Petagine, Antonio

Born 1974. After several years of research at the Catholic University of Milan, he taught History of Medieval Philosophy from 2011 to 2013 at the University of Urbino and was a researcher from 2014 to 2016 at the University of Fribourg in Switzerland. At the University of the Holy Cross, he was lecturer, from 2016 to 2018, then extraordinary professor of History of Medieval Philosophy. Since 2019, he has been teaching History of Philosophy at Roma Tre University. His publications specialize in metaphysics and anthropology, with a focus on the great authors of the history of medieval philosophy.

Río, Pilar

Lecturer at the Institute of Liturgy of the University of the Holy Cross, where she teaches Liturgical-Sacramental Theology of Baptism and Confirmation, Liturgical Ecclesiology and Christian Initiation. Among her latest publications: *Chiesa e liturgia, Apporti del rinnovamento liturgico all'ecclesiologia del XX secolo* (Roma, 2020) e *La liturgia, epifania della Chiesa. Teologia e Magistero da san Pio X al Concilio Vaticano II* (Roma, 2021).

Rossi, Espagnet Carla

Professor of Spiritual Theology at the University of the Holy Cross and Mariology at the Istituto Superiore di Scienze Religiose all'Apollinare of the same University. In 2024 she was appointed Director of the Institute. She has published several articles on the themes of the family and the presence of women in the Church, as well as on Marian themes, and some monographs. The latest is *Missione Famiglia*, Rome 2024.

Staglianò, Antonio

Born 1959, PhD in fundamental theology at the Gregorian University. From 2009 to 2022 Bishop of Noto. In 2022 he was appointed president of the Pontifical Academy of Theology. Since 2024 he has also been a consultor for the Dicastery for the Doctrine of the Faith.

Tambone, Vittoradolfo

M.D. degree. PhD in Systematic Moral Theology. PhD in Bioethics. Ordinary Professor of Forensic Medicine at the Campus Biomedico University in Rome. Director of the Bioethics & Humanities Research Unit at the same University. Coordinator of the Healthcare Bioethics Center of the Fondazione Policlinico Campus Biomedico in Rome. Member of the National College of Forensic Medicine. Visiting professor in some Universities and Lecturer at the Lateran University. Member of the Italian Society of Legal Medicine. Member of the Board of the National Federation of the Orders of Surgeons and Dentists for the renewal of the Code of Medical Ethics.

Troconis, Isabel

PhD in theology, professor of dogmatic theology at the University of the Holy Cross. She has also collaborated with the master's program "Filosofía y Religión según el pensamiento de Joseph Ratzinger" at the *Universidad Internacional de la Rioja* (Spain) and with the "Acreditación en Pedagogía de la Fe" program at the *Universidad Panamericana* (Mexico). Most of her publications focus on Joseph Ratzinger's theology (relationship between ontology and history, anthropology, Christology, reason and freedom).

Vanzini, Marco

Priest of Opus Dei and Associate Professor of Fundamental Theology at the University of the Holy Cross. His research focuses on issues of the religious phenomenon, theological method and the relationship between science and theology, as well as the theme of Christ's Resurrection. For years in his pastoral work, he has been especially dedicated to university students.

Villafiorita, Andrea

Ph.D. in physics in the University of Modena and in theology in the University of the Holy Cross. Tenured lecturer in dogmatic theology area at the ISSR Ligure and ITA in Genoa. He has a special interest in theological anthropology and Christian ecology. He is a priest of the Diocese of Genoa, where he is involved in youth ministry and is chaplain of a care home.

Villar López, Carlos

Born in Barcelona, Spain, in 1975. Graduated in History in 1998 in the University of Barcelona. Doctorate in Theology in the University of the Holy Cross in 2007. For years he has worked in youth ministry, formation of seminarians, accompaniment of engaged couples and young married couples. In 2022 he was appointed spiritual director of the Roman College of the Holy Cross (Rome) and since 2024 he has been a professor in the Department of Spiritual

Theology at the University of the Holy Cross where he gives lectures on anthropology and spirituality. His latest publication: *La verdadera noche es luz* (ed. Cobel), an essay on spiritual life in light of the mystery of the Cross.

Zaccaria, Giovanni

Born 1979, priest of the Prelature of Opus Dei (2012). Degree in Medicine and Surgery at the University of Verona (2003). Doctorate in Liturgical Theology in the University of the Holy Cross (2013). Teaching at the Institute of Liturgy at the same University, where he is extraordinary professor of Liturgy of the Sacraments. Author of several articles and books, including: *Liturgy. An Introduction*, with Prof. J.L. Gutiérrez Martín (Rome 2016); *La Messa spiegata ai ragazzi (e non solo a loro)* (Milano 2018); *Immitte Spiritum Paraclitum. Teologia liturgica della confermazione* (MSIL 80 - Città del Vaticano 2019); *Sacerdoti, re profeti e martiri. Teologia liturgica della Messa crismale* (BELS 203, CLV – Roma, 2022).

Abbreviations

CCC *Catechism of the Catholic Church.*

DH H. Denzinger - P. Hünermann, *Enchiridion symbolorum,*
definitionum et declarationum de rebus fidei et morum.

GS Second Vatican Council, Pastoral Constitution *Gaudium et*
spes.

LG Second Vatican Council, Dogmatic Constitution *Lumen*
Gentium